# War with the R.F.C.

# War with the R.F.C.
## Two Personal Accounts of Airmen During the First World War, 1914-18

A Soldier of the Sky

George F. Campbell

Outwitting the Hun

Pat O'Brien

*War with the R.F.C.*
*Two Personal Accounts of Airmen During the First World War, 1914-18*
*A Soldier of the Sky*
by George F. Campbell
*Outwitting the Hun*
by Pat O'Brien

FIRST EDITION

First published under the titles
*A Soldier of the Sky*
and
*Outwitting the Hun*

Leonaur is an imprint
of Oakpast Ltd

Copyright in this form © 2016 Oakpast Ltd

ISBN: 978-1-78282-511-1 (hardcover)
ISBN: 978-1-78282-512-8 (softcover)

http://www.leonaur.com

Publisher's Notes

The views expressed in this book are not necessarily those of the publisher.

# Contents

A Soldier of the Sky 7
Outwitting the Hun 135

# A Soldier of the Sky

Captain George F. Campbell R.F.C.
"Fighting Scout of the air"

# Contents

| | |
|---|---|
| Introduction | 13 |
| Why I Joined the Flying Corps | 15 |
| At the "Ground School" | 18 |
| The Flying School on Salisbury Plain | 20 |
| My First Solo Flight | 27 |
| Flying Across to France | 33 |
| My First Flight to the Line | 39 |
| Lost in the Clouds | 50 |
| The Squadron Combat in the Sky | 62 |
| Brought Down by "Archie" | 72 |
| "F. P. Number One" | 82 |
| Strafing a Hun "Sausage" | 88 |
| An Air Duel on the Somme | 98 |
| The Battle that Blinded the Boche | 103 |
| The Major's "Field Day" | 110 |
| Wounded Again—"Napoo!" | 115 |
| The Song from a Stretcher | 121 |
| Back Home in Blighty | 126 |
| Glossary | 131 |

Dedicated
To
All Who Have Answered the Call
Of Patriotic Duty
In
The War of the Allies
For Humanity

# Introduction

This is the authentic story of a British airman and his remarkable experiences as a "fighting scout" in the war. But it is more than a mere recital of personal experiences in the Flying Corps, The circumstances under which the author served his country in the air make it a document of thrilling human interest.

Captain George Frederick Campbell became "a soldier of the sky" to avenge the loss of his entire family in the war. Already a soldier of the king before the war broke out in August, 1914, he was serving in India as a lieutenant of the Highland Light Infantry when his regiment was ordered to the European front, immediately after war was declared by Great Britain against Germany. In a few weeks he was fighting to stem the Hun advance on Paris, His father, Col. Colin Campbell, of the Scots Guards, and his three brothers were already with their regiments at the front.

Then, first, his father fell, killed in the memorable retreat from Mons. At the battle of Loos, his brothers, Bruce and Jamie Campbell, both lieutenants, fell with their faces to the foe; and in a trench raid not long after his remaining brother, Capt. Blaikie Campbell, was killed. The menfolk of his family were gone, but an invalid mother and a loving sister remained to mourn in the old ancestral home in the Mull of Kintyre, back in bonnie Scotland. Then his sister, bent on an errand of mercy, embarked on the ill-fated *Arabic*, and was counted among the lost when the vessel was sunk by a German torpedo. This final crushing blow killed the mother. The author, then a lieutenant of the Highlanders, was left alone.

At the Battle of Neuve Chapelle in 1915, Capt. Campbell was severely wounded, having his hipbone shattered by a bayonet thrust through the abdomen. Several months in hospital followed, during which he brooded over his losses and meditated revenge. On his recovery, he was declared unfit for further duty in the trenches with his regiment. He then sought and found his opportunity for further service, in the Royal Flying Corps.

For two years, until again severely wounded, he fought the Hun in the air. Only a part of what he did is modestly, though thrillingly, recounted in these pages. And in justice to the gallant author it must be said that it was only after repeated urgings that he consented to tell the tale.

Many German aeroplanes have fallen before this intrepid "fighting scout." Just how many, no man can tell. But he has officially participated in bringing down eighteen, and several more are unofficially credited to him or to his assistance. Few men have passed through such an experience as his and live to tell the tale.

Capt. Campbell probably owes his life, as well as much of his military success, to the fact that he comes of hardy, fighting stock. His grandfather served gallantly as a British officer in the Indian Mutiny of 1857 and the Crimean War of 1859, and bore honourable scars to the day of his death.

Educated in England, Capt. Campbell left Marlborough College, Gloucester, at the age of 19, and entered Sandhurst Military Academy, where he received a thorough military training. His service in the British Army prior to 1914 included two years in India, where he was engaged in frontier patrol work and became a thorough soldier.

In the early days of the great war he participated in the battles of Mons, the Marne, and Neuve Chapelle, besides numerous minor engagements and trench raids. Probably no man alive has seen more actual fighting on the ground and in the air.

Today, (1918), Capt. Campbell shows few outward traces of his wounds and his sorrows, though the effects remain. And while he is incapacitated for active service in the air,-the doctors having forbidden him to fly at any high altitudes, he would gladly return and "do it all over again," if he could, for his heart and soul are in the war that has cost him all his loved ones. Now in the United States, he is doing what he can to aid the British-Canadian recruiting missions, urging all his compatriots domiciled here to do their patriotic duty. For, as he says, no man with red blood in his veins should fail to heed his country's call, and this war is for humanity.

May this book stir the sluggish soul to action, where such a stimulus is needed! To the patriotic American it will come as a revelation of what it means to gain the supremacy of the air, which is needed to win the war. And every' word of it is true!

The (Original) Publisher.

## Chapter 1

# Why I Joined the Flying Corps

"Petrol on!—Switch off!—Suck in, sir!" The snappy cry of the air mechanic to the army flyer, as the soldier of the sky prepares for flight, still rings out clearly in my memory. I heard it first on Salisbury Plain; then at the starting-point in Hampshire from which I made my first flight to France; and then as a fighting scout I heard it, many a time after, at the dawn of day on the Western front of the world's greatest war.

I hear it now, with the pilot's answering cry, "Petrol on! Switch off!" as I begin to set down, while recollection remains vivid, some of the events and experiences of my two years in the air service. Two wonderful years! Two terrible years! Two years of unutterable sadness! Two years of revenge!

Of course you have heard of a Scotch mist. Perhaps you have met the real thing in its native haunts, and know just how it feels. Well, the day which I have in mind was a day in August, 1915, somewhere in Fifeshire, Scotland, when the heavy mist and the cold ate into the very marrowbones of a wounded man, and sent my spirits down to zero.

There I was, troubled very badly both in mind and body. The physical bother of sciatica, aggravated by the mist, was bad enough in my convalescent condition, but that was nothing compared with the mental anguish of a discovery I had made that day.

I had learned at the battalion depot that I should be of no further material use to my regiment, the Highland Light Infantry, on account of my last wound, received in the Battle of Neuve Chapelle on March 10, five months before. This hip wound had been patched-up very nicely, but left me slightly lame, and so far as further infantry service in the trenches was concerned I was declared out of it.

This was a nice predicament to be in, when I had counted on getting back to the front with the regiment. I simply had to get back, just to ease my feelings. Probably there was an underlying desire for the satisfaction of some sort of personal revenge upon the Hun. In a way I wanted to get my own back, for in the war I had lost my father and three brothers, killed in action; my sister, torpedoed on the *Arabic*, and my mother, who died from the shock. That was indeed a score to be evened up. No man can deny me the right to harbour thoughts of vengeance, though God knows I tried hard enough to keep the thought of duty uppermost. But the blood of my kin cried aloud to me from the battlefields of France and Flanders, and the white faces of my mother and sister haunted my dreams. I simply must get back to the fighting line. But how?—that was the question: How was I to get back when the doctors had ruled against me? "Fit for home service only!"

Then, in that chill and penetrating mist on a bleak hillside of bonnie Scotland, tortured in body and torn with unspeakable emotion, but fired with keen desire for another and a harder go at the enemy who had given me such a bitter personal grudge to wipe out, I cast about in my mind for some way to return to the front.

"By Jove," I said to myself after taking stock of the possibilities. "I have it! The Flying Corps! There will surely be a chance for me in the aviation branch of the service. I know I can be of some use there, even if I am slightly lame." And then and there I determined to make application to take the examination for entrance to the Royal Flying Corps, that gallant body of men which had already gained imperishable fame for itself and had nobly earned the nation's gratitude.

That evening my application was duly posted.

I had never flown in any kind of a machine, nor had I ever been near an aeroplane up to that time, but as I recall my feelings on that day, I had a peculiar sort of intuition—call it a hunch, if you will—that I could fly. There is an indescribable something (at least I cannot describe it) which leads you to believe, almost to know, that you can do a thing, whether you have ever tried it before or not. That is the kind of feeling I had when I applied for a chance at flying service, and it was a sure-enough hunch.

It was only a few days until I was ordered to take the physical examination for the Flying Corps. A sound constitution and perfect eyesight helped me with the doctors, and, in spite of the handicaps of my partially-healed wound and lameness, I was finally accepted by the War Office after about fifteen days' waiting in grave suspense.

When the good news arrived, on September 1, 1915, I was ordered to report for training at once. Accordingly I started to pack my kit in feverish haste, eager to be off. But the news was too good to keep to myself. So hurrying up to the mess I had to tell everybody, my brother officers and all the boys I found at headquarters. The "lame duck" had a new lease of military life—a splendid prospect of getting back to active service at the front!

The boys all congratulated me and said I was very lucky to be able to pass the examinations. As I was the first officer of the regiment to be posted to the Flying Corps, they all expressed a hope that I would make a good showing in the air, if only for the sake of the regiment. This I promised them I would try to do, and I can sincerely say that I never forgot that promise, made in the hour of my most regretful farewells to the regiment.

Next day saw me *en route* to Reading, in the south of England, where one of the "ground schools" for the preliminary training of flying men was located.

The ground-school work, by the way, is an all-important part of an air pilot's training, as I was soon to discover. It is there that you learn all the airman must know about engines, the theory of flight, aids to flight, wireless telegraphy, aerial navigation by night and by day, bomb dropping, observer's duties, and a whole lot of other things that may not strike a novice as necessary, but are absolutely essential nevertheless to the making of a soldier of the sky. The equipment of a flying man, physical, mental, and technical, must be complete and first-class in every respect, or he will be handicapped from the take-off and his life is the stake.

CHAPTER 2

# At the "Ground School"

Arriving at Reading, I found that the ground school was quite a large one and known as the best of its kind in the country. There must have been from six to eight hundred fellows there, training for the R. F. C. Most of them, like myself, were army men and had been transferred at their own request from regiments of the line and other branches of the service. Nearly all had been "across" at the front and had seen active service. In fact, the material for pilots at that time was exceptionally good, because having had experience in trench warfare the men were accustomed to gunfire and it was a matter of small consequence to them. Nonchalance in this respect is a great advantage to a pilot in his early flights on the fighting front or in enemy terrain, where he is liable at any moment to receive a warm greeting from "Archie." That is the name given by British airmen to the anti-aircraft artillery of either side.

When I reported at Reading, however, I was unacquainted with "Archie" and had yet to learn his name. I presented myself at the orderly room, handed in my name, and was allotted quarters in a fine large room facing on the court of an ancient college, in which many of my fellow-novices were billeted.

A "batman," or soldier servant, met me in the corridor and informed me that my luggage had arrived and that I was just in time for dinner. Oh, joy! This was welcome news after my journey down from the north, and I promptly made my way to the large refectory or mess hall where dinner was being served. This mess, I may remark, was a bit different from most regimental messes, because you had to do all your own waiting, and nobody made a fuss over you, even though you were an officer. It was a good, as well as a democratic, arrangement, for it was much quicker to serve oneself in cafeteria style and the plan allowed us all more time to ourselves for study or—otherwise.

A due regard for candour, and the traditional truthfulness of a Scot, compel me to state that it was mostly "otherwise" with a good many of us novices at Reading, at the time of which I write. However, I did manage to find a wee bit of time occasionally for study of matters that I thought I needed most to know.

Saturday was always a half-holiday at the ground school, and gave an opportunity for a weekly trip to London—about an hour's ride— which most of the boys embraced. Some spent the weekend at Henley or Windsor, both of these favourite resorts being only a few miles from Reading and also on the River Thames, with splendid facilities for boating. On Saturday afternoons and all day on Sundays the embryo flyers dotted the famous old river, usually lazing about in punts and canoes with lady loves from London or the upriver towns. A few men would remain each week in their quarters at Reading for alleged purposes of study.

My course at the ground school lasted for five weeks, when there were examinations and my wee bits of study counted well, for I came out with very good results. The following Monday morning I received orders to report forthwith at the Central Flying School on Salisbury Plain. There, I learned, it was quite possible that I myself, a soldier of the king, might be called a "Hun." In fact the young flyers on the ancient plain are quite frequently called Huns by their instructors and elders, the "Hun" in this case being a recent corruption of the old army pet name "young 'un," applied to a youngster in the service. There were several other things that I was to learn at the Flying School.

CHAPTER 3

# The Flying School on Salisbury Plain

As I approached the stage of actual flight in my training, I was filled with curiosity about my probable sensations and behaviour when I found myself at last "up in the air." My first aerial joyride came sooner than I had expected.

The Central Flying School of the R. F. C, at Upavon, Wiltshire, turned out to be an enormously long and exceptionally good aerodrome, with L-shaped hangars which allowed a great many machines to be stored away at night. Situated in the midst of the great Salisbury Plain, with its wide stretches of level ground, and famed for its Druidic remains like those at Stonehenge, it was an ideal spot for the first flights of those who, like myself, had everything to learn about "taking off" and landing in a "plane" or "bus," *alias* an aeroplane. The word "airplane," by the way, had no standing with us.

After reporting to the camp commander I was put under canvas, or in a tent, but the weather being fairly good for October, tenting was not half as bad as might have been expected. The next morning I was allotted to a flying party or squadron, and then it was that I took my first ride in a plane.

I happened to be standing around, awaiting my turn and gazing about in wonder at the evolutions of some of the more advanced pupils, who were fighting sham battles over the drome.

"How soon shall I be able to do such things and meet the Hun in the air on even terms?"

I was just asking myself the question and resolving to do my best to speed the day, when suddenly I was roused to sharp attention by the clear and distinct drawl of one of the officer instructors, who wore a monocle in his right eye and stuttered very badly:

"All right, you—wh-what's his name? Guggug-get your bally hel-helmet on and cuc-cuc-come up with me. I'm gug-gug-going to give you a joyride."

And he meant me! You may be able to imagine my feelings at that moment—about to go up for the first time! I had a strange sort of sensation—felt rather queer in fact—and thought it must be a ease of the malady commonly called "cold feet." But I did my best to fight it down, so as not to betray my state of mind to the rest of the boys standing around the hangar door, for I observed that they were grinning and nudging one another. To me they seemed to be anticipating some sort of excitement or amusement—at my expense, I supposed—and this added greatly to the discomfort which I confess I felt.

Afterwards I found out why the boys were grinning. The instructor who had addressed me was no other than the most reckless pilot—at least for "stunting"—that was attached to the drome at that time. I was an absolute novice and it was generally known that he "put the wind up" everybody he took up, by his crazy, harebrained stunts. "Stunts" have a decided tendency to make a young flyer a bit dizzy, especially when performed close to the ground, which was his favourite arena for hair-raising performances with new pupils as passengers. Reckless though my stuttering instructor may have been, he looked a very innocent sort of chap for the kind of reputation he carried. But flyers cannot be judged by their looks, I found that out more than once later on. So did the Huns!

But on with my first joyride! With many misgivings, which I tried hard to disguise, I proceeded into the hangar and got a flying helmet, as directed. These helmets are so constructed that if you fall and land on your "napper," or if any kind of missile resulting from an accident should hit you, the helmet will protect your head somewhat.

Putting on the massive thing (commonly called a "Hun helmet"), I was then handed a pair of army goggles. These are of rubber, with two Triplex lenses inset to prevent splintering of the glass should the wearer be hit in the eye. I was well wrapped up in heavy clothing, for I had heard it was very cold "up there"—an idea common to new aviation pupils, who are often seen going up wrapped like an Eskimo with an instructor lightly clad. Then I followed my instructor out to the machine, which was standing ready several yards from the hangar, on the edge of the "tarmac." This, by the way, is the portion of an aerodrome immediately outside the hangar doors—B, stretch of smooth ground, asphalted or oil-surfaced to prevent dust from being blown into the shed or the picking up of earth and stones by the engine propeller when it revolves on starting.

The machine was set "facing into" the wind, a slight breeze having sprung up. I looked at the big "bird" for a minute, trying to puzzle out how I was going to climb into it, when I was struck by a bright idea—"Do as the instructor does!" So I watched him closely, as I disliked to appear foolish in front of all the other boys, standing around with their eyes riveted on me.

But in spite of my best efforts I did not get into the machine without getting tangled up in some wires which I had learned about at the ground school, but had forgotten for the moment—the "drift wires." Once seated, however, in the rear seat of the cockpit, I began to feel more comfortable.

"Put on your belt—strap it around your waist!" ejaculated the "O. C. plane," with the slightest symptoms of a stutter.

I complied to the best of my ability—everything seems so different in an aeroplane; at least I thought so at the time.

Then I looked around, but could see very little of the mechanism, except a queer crosspiece in the centre of the nacelle, with grips on it to take hold of. I grasped these and found that they moved backward and forward, as well as with a seesaw movement, or up and down like a rocker-arm. These I soon found to be the controls of the "ailerons," or little wings on the trailing edge of each plane, like little flaps.

I was just wondering where to put my feet, when I looked forward and spotted the rudder bar, which bore traces of feet having been placed there before. All of these things were connected up "in dual"; that is, they were connected up to the front seat in which the instructor sat, directly before me.

Once more I glanced about me and marvelled at the numerous wires on the machine, which was a Maurice Farman Shorthorn, Then I recalled hearing that someone once asked during an examination how to rig an aeroplane of this model, and the reply of a Cockney rigger was somewhat sarcastic:

"You puts a canary in between the wings of this 'ere blinkin' machine, and keeps on a-stickin' in wires till 'e just cawnt get hout."

Just then I noticed that two mechanics who had been standing near the machine had suddenly got busy. One of them was kicking the chocks under the wheels of the undercarriage. The other man, getting in between the tail booms, called out distinctly:

"Petrol on! Switch off! Suck in, sir!"

The instructor immediately complied with this request by moving the throttle forward, and glancing at his control switch he repeated, "Petrol on! Switch off!" This done, the mechanic started turning the propeller around to "suck in" the fuel mixture, then stopped suddenly and called out, "Contact, sir!"

This call was repeated by the pilot in front of me and immediately complied with, whereupon I heard the roar of the 8-cylinder, 80-horsepower Renault engine, which soon dropped into an idle, rhythmic mutter lasting about a minute, to get the engine warmed up.

My instructor being satisfied with this, proceeded to open up his throttle gradually, until there was a steady roar; upon which he immediately throttled it down again, being satisfied with the "revs" indicated on the revolution counter (about 1450 revolutions per minute).

Then, with a quick wave of his arm from right to left (meaning "Cast off the chocks"), the plane was free to move.

All the while I sat intensely interested in the proceedings. I kept my eye glued on "the man in front" of me. It was fascinating! He seemed so nonchalant about everything he did that I began to admire his work, every bit of it.

While I was cogitating in this fashion I was surprised to find that we were moving ahead slowly, the chocks having been removed from under the wheels. With the nose of the plane pointed "into the wind," the pilot now looked around to see that all was clear, then opened up the throttle—and we were off!

Suddenly, like some strange live thing, with the engine now working "all out," the machine "got its tail up" and we sped away up the aerodrome. I felt a bit bewildered at first and the whole affair was full of mystery to me, never having seen an aeroplane "take off" before.

Soon the machine gathered speed and began to run much easier than at first. The sensation of the ground gradually receding from me was simply grand! I seemed to be sitting still, with the earth slipping past me very quickly. Then the wonder of it dawned upon me. I realised that I was in the air! How buoyant it felt—and what a marvellous sensation it was to be able to look all about one, on all sides, above and below, and at the same time to feel something solid beneath one's feet.

I can never forget that early-morning scene on Salisbury Plain, spread out like a map below. How beautiful and peaceful the countryside looked! How far removed it seemed from scenes of bloody strife! Who would have thought, gazing from that smoothly soaring plane, that war, with all its horrors, was being waged less than two hundred miles away,—that in a couple of hours we could have flown to the bloodstained trenches of the western front, to find ourselves saluted by showers of shrapnel!

Little did I realise then how different would be the scene soon to be unfolded to my view from the air in shell-torn France. Here all was peace and beauty in the landscape. There I was to find the air filled with the smoke of battle, the roar of big guns, the noise and concussion of high explosives, and the black cloudbursts of enemy shells.

I experienced no dizziness on my first joyride until my instructor started some of his customary antics with the plane. Then I realised how much I loved the ground. After awhile, though, my uneasiness wore off considerably and I even began to think I felt at home, when suddenly the motor stopped! I had been so busy gazing about me that I had not noticed the pilot shutting it off. Naturally the machine would have lost its speed if he had not put it into a gliding position, and I soon saw—and felt—that we were dipping rather suddenly toward the earth. The feeling was anything but pleasant at first, but when I saw the ground rapidly coming up to me I felt relieved at the prospect of being once more on *terra firma*.

Once landed, the pilot "taxied" the machine up to the tarmac, got down, and called up to me: "That's all this morning! Better run down and get a bite to eat and come back at nine."

I found my way out of the machine after the same puzzling movements I had gone through at the outset. Then I went up to the timekeeper. I asked him, "How long was I up?" He replied, "Twenty minutes, sir."

"What do I have to do now?"

"Nothing, sir. I have entered it on the flying time sheet,—except that you might have to put it into your logbook."

This book, by the way, is an exact account of what you do in the air, the type of machine, the date, hour, whether solo or dual flight, time, height, and course that you flew, etc. In the remarks column you tell what you did.

I accordingly entered up all that I had done in this book and kept a record from then on of every flight. The book is signed at the end of every week by the commanding officer.

Then I went down to the mess and there I found the other "Huns," who were all trying to talk at once, giving their version of what they had done in the air that morning; also making little remarks about

STARTING UP THE PROPELLER ON A PLANE

how good or how bad their instructor was. This mess was very similar to the one at Reading, but the food was much better.

The general routine of the school after early-morning flying was so arranged that all advanced pupils, that is, those who were "on their solo" or "on their own solo" went back to the hangars and continued flying to 11:30 a. m. The new pupils, or Huns, from 9 o'clock until 11:30, usually had to practise buzzing, wireless, and attend a lecture on theory of flight, or engines. These lectures were delivered in the instructional sheds by one of the instructors, generally a different instructor every day specializing in some particular branch or subject.

I was among the Huns at first. However, after the first few days I had managed to get in a few hours' dual flight, so that at the end of five days, after doing about two hours and fifty-five minutes in the air, I was ready for my first solo.

Chapter 4

# My First Solo Flight

The following morning I appeared at early-morning flying, feeling very "windy," for I had a hunch that I was going to be sent off alone this morning. I had a feeling of uneasiness all the time I was kept in suspense, waiting for a machine to become vacant. Nevertheless I did feel confident that I could fly all right, even though the instructor had bawled me out a little bit now and then.

I was waiting around when presently a machine came gliding in, landed on the big circle in the centre of the aerodrome, taxied up to the shed, and as it came near, the engine still running, I heard a voice call:

"Get your grummet on, Scotty. I'm going to take you around once." (The old flyer usually calls the flying helmet a grummet.)

At last I was "for it," so I jumped up quickly and ran out, putting on my helmet as I ran. By this time I had mastered the difficulty of climbing in and out of the bus, and when I found myself in the front seat I really began to think I was getting to be quite a "bird man,"

Above the roar of the motor I heard the instructor yelling to me:

"All right now, Jock. Taxi her out and take her off. Be sure to keep her into the wind, and mind—watch yourself. Think what you are doing, for it's up to you now. I am not going to touch it. You're flying this bus, so bear that in mind!"

This put me on my mettle and I determined to do my best. Then, with all the precautions I had been taught about taking a machine out—that is, making sure by looking around that I was not going to bump into anybody—I opened up my throttle and the machine started moving across the aerodrome. Facing it into the wind, I opened my throttle a bit more and began to "take off."

Fortunately I did everything correctly,—taking off, flying around the aerodrome, turning and banking, shutting off my engine, and landing. As I landed, my instructor said:

"That's very good! Take her off solo now. I am going in. Make one circuit and land, and if it's all right I'll wave to you to go up again."

"Very good, sir," I replied.

Then I looked around me, saw all was clear, put my hand on my throttle, and started to open it up very gradually.

You can just put yourself in my position and imagine what it would be like to fly around for several hours with a competent flyer, then have him suddenly leave you, and find yourself alone for the first time in an aeroplane. To say the least, it's uncomfortable.

As the machine bounded forward I felt,—I didn't imagine,—that it was much lighter. The consequence was that in the usual manner I poked her nose forward, to get the tail up. You must get the tail up to get it into flying position, with the tail skid off the ground, allowing the plane to roll easily.

Once in flying position, the plane seemed to rise very rapidly. I sat rigid in the seat, very much against instructions, because you are told to fly in "an easy or restful position." Mine was anything but easy. My eye was glued straight ahead of me, on the air speed indicator, or Pitot tube, instead of watching where I was going, at least I imagined it was glued there. Nevertheless I was lucky, because the field was a good one and no obstructions in the way.

Up, up, up I seemed to soar, feeling unusually light and I must say bewildered. I had never prayed very much in my life and the boys that have been "over there" usually have seen some awful sights—sickening ones, and sometimes they question, "Is there a God, to allow such things to occur—people killing each other and massacring each other, grappling at each other's throats?" But I did not stop to question the existence of God when I was up in that machine. As I say, I had never prayed very much and I had been out at the front, mind you, and in a tight corner now and then; but this was one time that I breathed a prayer. I knew no regular prayer, but kept saying over and over a little sentence I heard some time or other that just eased my feelings a little bit. You know, it sort of reconciled you somewhat; made you feel as if you were not alone after all, but had someone to fall back upon.

When I found I was going along very nicely, felt the weight of the machine on the controls, and realised that they were sturdy and not the flimsy little things you might imagine, I felt more at home; at least I gradually began to feel more at home. On, on, straight ahead I went!

I looked below me and spotted a tiny little river. Then I spotted a little village, which I knew to be Pewsey. How easy it was to see things up there! No wonder, the unlimited value of an aeroplane in war!

Then I began to debate in my mind just when I was going to make my little turn. Which should it be, left or right? There are rules for traffic in the air, you know, as well as on the ground.

I had forgotten what circuit I was doing, and instead of my really flying the machine, the machine was flying me; because it seemed to go where it wanted to, not where I wanted it to. I decided to take it in hand at once; so being determined to make a successful solo, I gripped the controls a little bit harder. Then remembering my instructions about "banking," I proceeded to do a left-hand turn, running over the instructor's words in my mind.

A little bit of left rudder,—just a tiny little bit; now a tiny little bit of aileron,—(that is, you pull down the control stick to the left)—not too much. And now keep her nose up just a little bit. Steady! Down a little bit. Then gradually round we go!

I kept glancing now and then at my Pitot tube. "Don't let it get below 45 and not above 70 m.p.h." (miles per hour), I remembered the instructor telling me, "when on a turn." This I bore in mind very vividly.

Having mastered the turn quite successfully, as I thought, I really did feel more at home, so proceeded to fly straight down the aerodrome. I was passing the hangars flying south, the hangars being sharply below me on my right, and felt so confident about the whole thing now that I thought it would be a good idea to let them see how well I was flying on my first solo. As I passed the hangar,—my hangar,—I noticed my instructor and some of the boys standing there very interested in my flight, because first soloists have a delightful habit of creating a little bit of excitement one way or another; some by crazy, unforgivable antics in the air and others by coming down and trying to make a hole in the ground. The motto of this particular procedure, adopted by the school, is *"Ascende,—descende,—crashe!"*

When I got opposite the boys I very flippantly waved my hand, two fingers up, which is a sign of greeting used quite frequently by flyers when passing another plane, and usually implies familiarity. As I did this I noticed that the instructor turned to some of the boys, evidently telling them something. But I turned my attention to other things of more importance just then, I began to think I would like to get on the ground and wondered how I was going to do it.

Of course, I had been instructed in the art of landing, but I just could not make up my mind to pull that throttle back, thereby losing the power of my engine, and as for sticking my nose toward the earth, that didn't appeal to me at all. But the same old feeling soon came over me,—"I'll not be beaten, so it's got to be done!"

This thought had no sooner flashed through my mind than I had acted; but mind you, I looked for what seemed a long time at that throttle before I plucked up courage to shut the engine off. The engine was now turning over quite slowly; to keep up my speed I had to put my nose down; therefore I was gliding and very nicely too, for it is always smooth running all the way down. I had been up to 2,500 feet when I shut off. As the earth came rushing up to me I felt my controls, to see that all was in order. I wasn't going to break my neck if I could help it.

Down, down I went,—nearer and nearer swept the earth,—until very, very gradually I started flattening out a few feet off the ground. As I flattened out, the machine lost some of its speed, then it settled, but was rolling fairly rapidly. I had breathed a sigh of relief as I felt the earth once more, but imagined I had seen some sort of a ditch straight in front of me that I was going to hit. So acting on the fleeting thought I yanked back my controls, the result being that the machine, having a certain amount of speed, started to soar once more. Failing in the attempt though, it stood on its tail for about half a second, then—crash! I had hit the ground a good wallop,—I had "pancaked" and smashed my undercarriage.

Can you imagine my disgust, after flying around in the manner in which I did, and landing,—mind you, I had landed, but had not lost my speed;—then doing the trick that I had done! Wouldn't it make you feel rather sheepish or even foolish? I know it did me.

Well, there I sat in that machine. Of course, I wasn't hurt by a ten-foot bump like that, but I was sort of dazed by the result and kept thinking and thinking. I was roused from my reverie by my instructor (wonderful fellow, he covered ground when he wanted to!) tearing out across the aerodrome and yelling at the top of his voice: "You silly ass, what the hell do you think you are up to? That was absolutely uncalled for! Good God, man, you're one of these chaps that is really a waste of good time. Really, you know, I can't quite make it out!"

He kept this up for about a minute longer, then strolled off to the hangars. I kept my tongue in my cheek and said nothing; the less you say to people in authority, especially some people, the better for you in the long run. I was just going off after him when he suddenly turned and said:

"I say! You had better stay where you are. If you don't know what you are obliged to do in a case of this kind, you had better learn now. Huns, you know, are obliged to stay by their crash till it's brought in! I suppose you did not know that."

"Well-er—that is to say, sir, I—I believe I read something about it, sir," I answered.

"Well, you know now anyway," he said. "Perhaps you will profit by the experience of helping the 'Ac Emmas' take it in."

"Very well, sir," I said, and sat down rather dejected. The "Ac Emmas," by the way, are the "air mechanics"—A. M.—so called from the system of pronunciation adopted by signallers to make each letter sound distinctly different from every other. Thus A is called "Ac" and M is pronounced "Emma."

Sitting there waiting for the mechanics, I felt particularly sore to think that I had tried so hard, only to get snubbed like this. Once again my spirits dropped down to zero. I began to think, "Was I going to be released for that crash? Think of it—to be released from the corps so soon!" I determined I would watch the ground more closely in the future. "An imaginary ditch—that was all, but it was enough to get me in 'Dutch.' It was no ditch at all, but a thick grass line,—so arranged that it *looked* like a ditch to me at first. Of course, one has to get accustomed to using one's eyes in the air, not now and then, but all the time."

The mechanics were just pulling up in front of the machine as I came to the conclusion of this mental debate, so I took a hand and helped load the machine on to the trailer they had brought out with them.

About an hour later we had completed our task, and I repaired to my quarters, thoroughly disgusted with myself and things in general. The remainder of the day I spent in the workshops and attended a lecture, and was so busy taking down notes that I had no time to think of my episode of the morning.

Every day after that saw me improving in my duties, especially in my flying, for at the termination of about a week or ten days I was transferred to another squadron, using service-type machines, then what was known as the Vickers Chaser, a two-seated affair with a 100 H. P. rotary engine in the rear.

Now came the real interesting part of flying. I used to fly at all times of the day and sometimes at dusk, and got used to the general experiences of "bumpy" days, clouds, ground mists, cross-country flying, landing at will, and forced landings. In fact, I became a very proficient pilot in all these lines and only with a limited amount of time in the air at my command. Little did I think that within a few short days I would be on my way to France in a new type of machine of the single-seater class, or what is known as "the fighting-scout machine."

Everything was running smoothly now, the days flew by very quickly, and I began to look around and saw signs that portended my moving very, very shortly. In fact, the pupils that were a little more advanced than myself were being called to the orderly-room every day, I presumed for orders. The next thing you would see was Mr. Pupil a full-fledged pilot, with his bright yellow coat (on which he immediately poured oil, as a rule, to colour it down, and make him look as if he had seen service), his heavy flying boots, and last, but not least, you would notice that he had invested in one of the latest model flying helmets and Triplex goggles, which was a very wise idea, for you will see the reason later.

Presently the new pilot would strut down to the mess with his kit; get his personal things in order; go around and have a wee "deoch-an-doris" with a few of his pals, winding up with "Goodbye, old man, I'll see you later or else be pushing daisies." Back would come the answer, "Best of luck, old man! Cheero, old thing! Don't forget to write!"—and away he would go in a Flying Corps tender to the railway station at Pewsey.

All these boys were made of the right stuff, and treated the war as a big game of cricket; all willing to take a chance, and nine times out of ten to give one—the long chance, the chance of a man's life, or "the sporting chance." This was the spirit that had made the flying service in France what it was, all the boys being sportsmen at heart.

Do you wonder that the Flying Corps is called "the corps *élite*"?

Chapter 5

# Flying Across to France

One fine morning in December, 1915, I woke up and found a surprise in store for me. It was my turn for France!

Think of it! My second time over! At last I was going to have a crack at the blighter from the air!

I was very much excited about it this time. Before, in the early days of the war, I was excited at the prospect of active service as I was now, but in a different manner. This time I was anxious for revenge, and revenge I was going to have if I could get it.

At 9 o'clock I proceeded to the orderly-room and got my certificate, graduating me as a full-fledged pilot; in other words, a fighting scout or a "stunt merchant." From my certificate I discovered that my total flying time solo in the air, all things completed, as well as every subject, was 16 hours; which was not bad for a man who had never seen an aeroplane less than two miles away before.

My pilot certificate entitled me to wear "wings." This is an embroidered emblem of outstretched wings, four inches long and one and one-half inches wide, worn on the left breast of the tunic above the pocket. The wearing of these wings for the first week or so made one feel very self-conscious, and it was often amusing to see how promptly newly-made pilots would flaunt their wings among their fellows and go swanking about for the benefit of comrades not yet so fortunate as to be entitled to wear them.

At the quartermaster's stores I then drew my flying kit, which was issued by the government *gratis*. It consisted of articles described officially as follows:

Coat, flying, officer's, for the use of one.
Boots, leather, suede, sheepskin lined, one pair.

TRENCHES ON THE WESTERN FRONT

Photo taken from a plane showing a ruined village: the German front line trenches are in the foreground.

Gauntlets, fur, trigger finger, one pair.
Helmet, flying, leather, service, one.
Goggles, Triplex lens, rubber, one.

This was your complete outfit for the air; if you wanted to use it. The only thing that I found of any use at the front was the coat. The boots were very useful, except that, if you had a forced landing near the lines, and got into a sea of mud, they proved to have the same constitution as a piece of blotting-paper. The gloves were all right if you wore silk ones underneath them, silk and wool being a very warm combination. As far as the helmet and the goggles were concerned, I think it's a wise plan to get a pair to suit you, especially goggles. A lot depends on those.

Having received all my kit, I suppose I did the same as nearly all the other boys before me; I applied for leave and as usual didn't get it, so had to be content with taking my orders, proceeding to Farnborough, receiving my machine, and from there crossing over to France. However, I did have a little consolation in the fact that there were four others going with me. We got a very good send-off, going in a little batch like that, and the night before our leaving the mess was a place of disorder,—at least I have recollections of its being so.

"To report forthwith" was the wording of our order, and "forthwith" meant immediately upon receipt of the same. However, I didn't lose a night's sleep over it, nor did the other boys.

The next day found us in Farnborough. This was the place where you got your machine. I went up to the hangars, received my logbooks,—both machine and engine logbooks,—inspected the plane to the best of my ability, put on my flying coat, and jumped into the machine.

The mechanic thrust a huge lifebelt in on top of me.

"What's this thing for?" I asked.

That's in case your engine fails while crossing the Channel, zur," said he, with a broad Somersetshire accent that I recall to this day.

"How pleasant," I thought, "to land in the sea in an aeroplane, in cold weather like this!" But even so, I figured that it was better to take a chance without the lifebelt than with it, bundled up as I was, even then. Consequently I threw it out. The mechanic looked at me, but didn't express any surprise. I myself thought it was an act of bravado, which was lost on him.

I then gazed about me on my machine. It was a single-seater of a type which I had flown only once before. The one I flew before had a dummy machine gun on it. This machine had the real thing. The machine gun stuck up directly in front of my face and had everything from drums of ammunition to Verey's lights. This plane also had a full complement of instruments, some of which I had learned about in ground school but had never used in actual practice.

Finally I got everything all settled and fixed, signed the receipt for the machine, ran my engine up and noted the time it took me to get started, taxied out to the aerodrome, and took off due east toward France!

I tell you it was a grand sensation, leaving for the front by air for the first time. I looked around me and saw the peaceful country below. Then to think that within two hours' time I would be somewhere in France; not only "somewhere," but pretty close to the fighting line, almost in the shell area.

As I flew on at about four thousand feet altitude, it being a very "dud" day, the clouds being low, with slight rain, I automatically kept a course which led me straight over Kent County, the garden spot of England. I was following a railway line, a very prominent one, and had no difficulty in seeing the ground, so observed the quiet and peacefulness of everything below me.

I passed over Folkestone, then flew out over the sea and followed the line of cliffs a short way from Dover. These cliffs are very prominent and can easily be distinguished. Then I turned directly east by south, in a straight line for the nearest point of land in France.

As I was pulling out of sight of land in England, the last thing in my vision of that country was the Dover cliffs, and I felt a sort of little lump in my throat. Old England seemed to be bidding farewell to me. Little did I expect I would see it again!

Four thousand feet is a very ordinary height at which to travel cross-country, but ten thousand feet is a little bit more to my liking when crossing the Channel. Then if your engine pegs out, you have a better chance for safety. It didn't strike me that I was unlucky that day—flying so low—for as you know you like to see things yourself, and I could not at that time rely very much on my ability to steer a straight navigation course up above the clouds. Besides, the clouds being only 4,600 feet up, I had to travel below them to see, otherwise I would never have been able to do much or able to tell when I reached France.

As it was, I relied on my being able to see a stray trawler or boat that happened to be in my line of flight; so that if I did "conk out," or my engine give out, I might be able to glide to within a short distance of the boat. Not much to rely on, to say the least. Sometimes in these days, boats don't travel as often as they used to. On this particular day I was lucky in this respect. Several boats were going over. I caught up with two of them, and the third one being within sight of France I felt pretty perky, so decided I would fly low over the boat, which I did. The boat was full of troops, who were very enthusiastic and cheered and waved most gleefully to me. Presently, I rose up again and made for the distant shore, which I reached in the course of about 15 minutes.

Crossing the town of Calais I kept on my course a little bit northeast, passing over several canals and following a main thoroughfare which brought me to No. 1 Aircraft Depot, where I had to report my arrival and leave the aeroplane. This place was easy to distinguish, being a huge rendezvous for all machines, either going or coming across the Channel.

I did the whole trip in an hour and forty minutes from England. I didn't seem to hurry at all either, because I fooled around a little bit on my way over. I have since made that trip in exactly 45 minutes, from an inland station to an inland station.

Getting out of my machine at the depot, I reported at the headquarters office, deposited my logbooks, and received instructions to "stand by" and await orders from brigade headquarters, farther up the line.

While I was waiting around this station, I observed a great many things that were new to me. Among other things there were many different types of machines which I had never even seen before. I ran into several of the boys who were in "the pool," which is the place where all new officers have to report and await their turn to be allotted to a squadron. Conversation was very brisk and boys who had only been over there a matter of a week or so asked you enough questions about "home" to give you the impression that they had been out there several months instead of being newcomers like yourself.

It getting dusk, I started to look about for some place to sleep, one of the boys said that there were no billets in the place, but that if I went down to the town with him and had dinner, I could get fixed up at the hotel where he was staying. We talked a good while about things in general and then departed for the hotel. The town was quite a good size and the hotel was of the average French type. Hotel du

Commerce. The food in this place was famous . I had been there before. It was a place where all the French gourmands have been known to go. I got fixed up with a room and went down and had a very wonderful dinner, which cost me twelve *francs* ($2.40). It was getting pretty late and being tired I went to bed, thinking, as I was dozing off to sleep, that for one thing at least I had no cause for regrets,—I wasn't leaving anybody behind *this* time, to worry about my welfare. So finally I fell asleep—once more in France!

CHAPTER 6

# My First Flight to the Line

Two days later I was ordered to report to No. — Squadron, —th Wing, R. F. C, in the —st Army Corps.

This was a fighting scout squadron, stationed about 15 kilometres, or 9 miles, from the line. I was driven up to the place in a Flying Corps tender. These tenders are Crossley touring cars, with special bodies on them to accommodate about six people each side, on benches.

Arrived at the squadron late in the afternoon, I reported at the headquarters office to the commanding officer, who was Major L——.

"Sir," and I saluted sharply, "I wish to report having been posted to your squadron."

"Ah, that's good," he replied. "We need a couple of pilots just now. Come inside. What's your name, by the way?"

"Campbell, sir."

"Come inside, Campbell. Take a seat. How many types of machines have you flown, Campbell?"

"Well, sir," I answered, "I have flown about six different types of machines before I came to France."

"How many hours' flying have you got?"

"About twenty, sir?" I replied.

"Um-m! Kind of rushed you over, I should say."

I agreed that they did, and dropped him a hint that I had not got any leave recently. Leave, you know, is a very essential part—I might say the most enjoyable part—of a soldier's life. He always looks forward to it, and when he loses it or it is cut off, he naturally, if he is an old soldier at all, will start "grousing." This I did, I believe, for the first day or two I was in France, as I naturally felt I was entitled to a little bit of leave.

"Well, it is getting kind of late," said Major L——. "Have you had anything to eat?"

"My last meal, sir, was my lunch."

"Well, fill in that next-of-kin book and sign your name to it, and the orderly officer will fix you up with a billet. Then you can come down and I will introduce you to the boys, and we'll have tea."

I complied with the order, and we left the office and walked down several hundred yards to an old *château*, which was once a very beautiful place. On the way down I had a chance to observe my commanding officer. He was a well set-up chap and had a very dignified bearing. He had blue eyes, iron-gray hair, and a small iron-gray moustache. In short, he looked a regular soldier, but his temper, I was soon to find out, was anything but a soldier's.

As we walked down to the mess the thought flashed into my mind, "Would I 'pull' with this officer or not?"—and the answer, or rather the feeling I got, came back in the negative. Little did I know that within a few weeks I would be glad, more than glad, to leave this squadron—all on account of my C. O.

We had a short conversation on the way to the mess, in which I was very eager to ask him all sorts of foolish questions. He seemed to pass them over very nicely, thinking me only a "kid," I presume. However, I didn't realise this at the time.

Arrived at the *château*, I got a glimpse of the building. It had been a fine large white structure, like a castle, of a type common in France. A fine driveway, entered through a large gate, led to the house. The grounds were filled with large shrubs, but everything had deteriorated through lack of care.

Through a side door we entered a long corridor, all the ornaments of which had been taken down. Here I left my wraps and we passed into a fine large dining-room, all inlaid in cypress, with a huge chandelier over a table in the centre of the room. I noticed that the table was set for tea.

"Have a chair, Campbell," said the C. O. "Orderly! Or—oh, there you are! Bring some tea at once, and be quick!"

While we were waiting for tea to be served other officers came in. I noticed that one of them had several decorations on his breast. It was he that spoke up:

"Well, sir, I think we finished a couple on that last patrol all right, for a battery phoned up to say that they got the report from one of their forward observers that he had noticed the fight and was sending in a report."

"Ah, congratulations, C——! That's good work,—good work, I call it! Hope we get more than that tomorrow. By the way, this is Lieutenant Campbell, who has come to our squadron."

I got up and shook hands with each one in turn. The last one I rather liked. It was he I made a pal out of later on. Just then another officer came in. I noticed he was a captain.

"Ah, Burns, just in, eh? This is Lieutenant Campbell. I think he will be in your flight."

"Oh, by Jove, I was wondering when we were going to get that other pilot," said the captain, turning to me with, "How do you do, Campbell?"

I replied by shaking hands with him and saying I was very glad to meet my future flight commander.

"How long since you left home?"—meaning England.

"Oh, about five days now," I replied.

"I suppose you were out here before. Oh, of course you were! I see now you have been wounded," he said, looking at the gold wound stripe on my left arm.

"How silly of me to ask that question, to be sure."

I rather liked this man, so I mentally said I could follow him anywhere he went,—and later on I did, until I got the bug in my head that induced me to stray away "on my own" occasionally, looking for trouble, and incidentally getting into hot ashes about it afterwards. Just at this minute, though, the orderly officer came in and I immediately got busy with him about fixing me up for a billet. So I hurried up my tea and took my departure with him to the top part of the building, and found a small cubbyhole of my own to sleep in. Feeling dog-tired, I made up a sort of bed in the room and presently was fast asleep.

The next thing I remembered was waking up with a start, for I heard a sound uncommon at that hour of the night. It was 10 o'clock when I awoke, looked at my watch automatically, and observed the hour on the luminous dial. Then I noticed that the sound came through a window high up in the wall of my room. Jumping up to this, I made out that it faced on the main road and that a large body of troops was passing. There seemed to be at least a brigade of them, and the men were making all sorts of sounds that seemed queer to me,—very different from those that come from English battalions on the march. In the morning I found out that they were French troops, coming up to our section of the line.

Once more I lay down on my makeshift bed, after taking off some of my clothes. My kit had been sent across ahead—or behind—me, and I did not expect to see it for a week. I knew what the luggage service was like, from my former experiences at the front.

Next morning I woke up rather early and the first thing I heard was the roar of many engines, all of them in flight. I walked out and was just in time to see a formation patrol, going out to the line. It was all so wonderful and I was so anxious to do something that I hastily dressed and swallowed some breakfast, practically on the run. Then I hurried up to the drome, but disappointment awaited my arrival there.

I discovered that no machine had been allotted to me as yet, though the arrival of one was expected almost immediately. However it did not turn up for two days and I was near saying something to the C. O. in regard to the matter, and asking him if I could not use someone else's machine. Had I known how difficult that was just then, I would have spurned even the thought of getting another fellow's machine.

Then my "bus" arrived, on the third morning of my wait. I was just crazy to try it at once, but had another wait ahead of me. This was because they had to overhaul the engine, for usually the arrival of a new machine necessitates, as an added precaution, the instalment of a new engine. The old one, having as a rule flown its required 80 hours, then needs an overhaul itself.

Having nothing better to do, while waiting, I put in my time by taking a closer look at the drome itself, that is, its landing area and nearby surroundings, to see what difficulties would arise in my landing and taking off. A new or strange aerodrome often presents a lot of peculiarities different from those we are familiar with. I discovered that this drome was considerably smaller than most of those in England, but that all the pilots managed to get into it without much difficulty. What they could do, I figured that I would be able to do in time, so I did not worry much on that score.

Conspicuous by their absence from the drome, however, were certain things that I was accustomed to at home. These included the large "landing circles," "pylons," circuit flags, and "smudge fires." All were missing here, being found only on instructional aerodromes. I discovered later that there was another reason for their absence. Such marks being very conspicuous from a height, would more easily betray the aerodrome to hostile aircraft flying near.

At the far end of the aerodrome was a huge ditch, in process of being filled in. *That*, at least, I bore in mind. I made a mental note that I would steer clear of that ditch, and particularly noted its location. If

The "Spad" Machine

A Type of fighting scout machine used on the Western Front by the Allies

the wind should happen to be blowing from that direction, I would be careful not to overshoot the mark and run into it.

The next day I was told that my machine was ready, so after breakfast I went up to the aerodrome. I was looking over my new bus when the flight commander came up. Incidentally, I was attached to Capt. Burns' flight, known as "C" Flight. He said:

"Campbell, I think you can take a flip around this morning and get a look at the country. Pick out all the prominent landmarks and then, once you have got these in your head, I would advise you to take a look at the line. But mind, you'd better keep this side of it!"

"Righto!" I replied. "I don't think I will lose myself. It's quite clear 'up top' today and I will be able to see a good way off. I will be quite all right, sir." I saluted and withdrew to the sheds, donned my flying kit, and wrapped myself up well.

Then I made for the "office lorry" to get a map. All Flying Corps units in France are on wheels, so that they can be moved about rapidly. Hence the service motor-trucks become "office lorries," "workshop lorries," "stores lorries," and so on.

In the office lorry, I asked for a map of "this particular sector," pointing out the place on the huge map on the wall.

"Very good, sir," the orderly replied.

I received the map and was going out of the door when the C. O. met me on the threshold.

"Ah, Campbell, I believe you're going up, aren't you?"

I saluted. "Good morning, sir. Yes, sir, I am going up to look around and get my bearings."

"Ah, that's good," he said, "Be careful and don't crash that bus. God knows we have only got just enough now to 'carry on' with."

I nodded, agreeing with what he said and implying that I would not crash the bus, saluted, and withdrew.

The machine was a devilish thing to look at. It had somewhat the appearance of a pugilist, with a lower jaw which seemed to stick out. A wicked-looking affair, I thought. Beside the machine were two mechanics. One of them was puttering around the engine. As I drew up, the other saluted. I returned the compliment, at the same time asking him, "Is she ready?"

"Yes, sir."

"All filled up?"

"Yes, sir."

I glanced quickly around the machine, then climbed into it, noticing as I did so that it was a far superior machine to most I had flown before.

Just then, as I happened to glance that way, I saw the C. O. watching me intently from the office lorry. So I made up my mind that I must be careful not to do anything to make a bad impression. He might get one, I thought, just by watching my procedure in starting up the machine, taxiing out, and taking off. I certainly did not want to make a "bloomer" of it.

In a clear voice the mechanic called out: "Petrol on!—Switch off! Suck in, sir!" I complied with this and repeated at the same time, "Petrol on! switch off!"

The petrol in these machines is pressure fed, so there was a slight pause till the petrol was forced into the cylinders. Then the usual revolving motion is given to the propeller by the mechanic turning it round, one blade after the other, to churn up, or vaporize, the mixture.

"Contact, sir!" called the mechanic.

I answered, "Contact!"

The great motor at once roared up and I knew by the feel and sound that I had a good one. I buzzed it for half a minute on the thumb switch, then I ran my engine up "all out" and looked at my revolution indicator. It registered 1050 r. p. m.

"That's O. K.," I thought, and throttled it down; then gave a wave of my arm, meaning to cast off the chocks, which hold the machine stationary when you run the motor "up." This done I buzzed my engine and taxied out, facing into the wind on the drome. I looked about. "All clear," came the salute from the first mechanic, so I opened my throttle.

Rapidly I sped up the aerodrome, straight up into the wind. Gradually the movement of taxiing became very smooth. I was rising! Up! Up! Up! I soared higher and higher, rising very swiftly. I hardly seemed to be moving now, although I was really travelling quite 90 miles an hour. I got well above the ground and could see fields now a thousand feet below. Still higher! Three thousand feet!

Then I cast my eyes about. Looking to my left, facing north, the large town of Armentieres could be seen. The canal running by it looked like a little strip of mirror. Away off to my right I noticed a pall of smoke that hung heavily in the sky and saw that it came from a huge foundry or munition factory, I knew not which, at T———. This was a very valuable landmark to me, for it was only a quarter of a mile from my own 'drome on the north side of it. Six thousand feet!

Still higher I soared. The steady hum of the motor seemed to lull me into a state of rest. I began to imagine I was the only human being in the universe, and that I was looking down now on what was a tiny map. Eight thousand feet! Higher still I climbed. Now I had a feeling of exhilaration, for the cold air started to bite into me by this time and I felt like living—living! Ten thousand feet!

I was satisfied now to turn my attention to the earth once more, as it stretched below me. I could see very easily all around, and looking off into the distance could see at least twenty miles on every side of me. The feeling at that height is wonderful! The sight is wonderful! Grand, that's all you can say. You begin to think you are lord of all you survey.

Throttling my engine down now to an easy drone, I started off, took a last look at the tiny aerodrome, which I could just make out, and turned northeast. I intended to turn east when I got to A——, then to turn and follow the line south till I came to L——, and from there fly home.

At length I passed over the Bois de Nieppe, which was a huge forest, and a very good landmark, in that particular sector. One might get this forest confused, though, with an exact reproduction of it on the Him side of the line, not very far from Lille. A slight mistake of this kind has caused many a pilot from both sides, that is, from the German side as well as our own, to make the fatal mistake of thinking that he was on his own side.

There is an aerodrome at the end of the wood near Lille, and I have in mind the case of a whole flight (five machines) that landed there by mistake, and only discovered their fatal error when it was too late to get away. Three of these pilots I knew personally.

The pilot cannot always be blamed for such a mistake. Owing to the fact that very "dud" weather often crops up suddenly, he may be unable to get his bearings or to distinguish landmarks through the heavy ground mist. Sometimes he gets caught in a storm or fog. Then he is unlucky indeed if he gets lost.

Thirty minutes after starting off northeast, I looked down and discovered I was over Ypres (pronounced somewhat as if spelled Eeper", though the Tommies usually call it Wipers"). This is a large town and the war has made its name familiar to all who read. I had spent many an hour there when I was in the "Mud Crushers'" battalion, early in the war. I just recognised the town, but that was all.

Jove! how Ypres had changed since I left it! Shelled to atoms! That is how I found it—one of the most beautiful of historic towns in the north of France. This was what war could do to a city in a few months under shell-fire! I now had an opportunity to observe what shell-fire looked like from the air. Away below me on my left (for I had now turned southeast and away from Ypres) I noticed an engagement going on; that is, an artillery bombardment or duel. I could see now and then a flash from a battery, although the battery itself was cleverly concealed and fairly well behind our own lines. I looked and could almost see the shot. At least, so I imagined. Of course it wasn't the shot, for that would be impossible to see; but I mean that I could almost follow the shell, for I could see it explode 20 or 80 seconds after seeing the flash of the gun.

Later, on the Hun side, I glanced around me on my own level after a time and noted some of our boys flying in formations up and down the line; one formation being higher than I was, one on my own level, and several other formations at different altitudes right down to within 100 feet of the ground. It was certainly a thrilling sight from the air. Some were flying in twos and threes. Smaller batches—these were the rovers, usually fighting scouts—were mooching about, looking for trouble.

I was just wondering when I was going to be one of these rovers, and thinking how wonderful it would be, when I suddenly saw a huge burst of "Archie" almost directly in front of me, about half a mile or so away. I noticed that it was white, fleecy Archie, and knew that it must be ours; for I had often heard that the difference between the Hun Archie and ours was that theirs was H. E. (high explosive) or a sort of coal-box, emitting a dense black smoke, and ours was shrapnel and fleecy white. So I knew right away that it must be our Archie that was breaking right ahead of me. This excited me considerably, for I surmised that there must have been a Hun across our lines some place where it was bursting. I looked—yes!—by Jove, there he was—about 3,000 feet higher than I, and directly in front of me. Jove! what a chance to do something! If only I had a bit of height! Nevertheless I went on and on after him, and opening my throttle as wide as I could to get the full power of my motor, I started climbing.

But it was of no avail as far as I was concerned. The Hun had all the advantage, especially height. Still I did manage to keep up with him a bit and at the same time managed to climb until my altimeter registered 12,000 feet. I had gained some! Still I was away below him and I felt chagrined not to be able to do something, even if only to get close enough to him to "stand on my tail" underneath him and shoot up at him. I followed on and on, not noticing where I was going at all. I had my eyes glued on that Hun and would have given anything to get him. Think of getting one on my first trip out to the lines!

Just then one of the boys dived out of the sky, presumably from nowhere, for I had not seen another machine following the Hun besides myself, and I was away below him—no use whatever, I thought—and thought right. I then noticed our machine keep on and on, dodging like the old mischief—then down, straight as a die—straight at the Hun, who seemed perfectly oblivious of the coming attack and the fate in store for him. When suddenly the attack came, he made a frantic effort to dodge and escape it.

As our machine dived I could see the pilot was firing at very close range, not more than 50 yards, I should think, for the tracer bullets used give a streak of smoke and fire as they pass through the air, and you can see if you are hitting the mark or not.

*Zip-zip-zip-zzzzzzin!* What's that? Fire, Gad, he's on fire.

My God, what a sight! To be hurled to destruction from a height is bad enough, but to catch fire is infinitely worse. Heavens! Down, down, he goes, thick black smoke leaving a trail like a death pall. This Hun was certainly doing what is known as "hanging his own crape up."

I followed the blazing machine down with my eyes until it seemed to disappear to nothing, the flame having died out. Presently I was certain I saw it crash.

So closely had I been watching the whole proceeding that now, when I looked about me, I found that I did not recognise the country below. I looked a little bit harder. No, I was right—where could I be? I gazed at my map, then I gazed at the ground. They did not coincide at all. Then, looking around me in the air, for the first time I noticed very heavy clouds coming up. This was a nice predicament to be in, the first time out to the line. Lost! Away, evidently, away south of my position and a storm coming up!

I decided to return by what I imagined was the way I had come. I judged I had then been out an hour and a half. Then I faced around the other way and looked. Yes, I was in for a storm all right, and a beauty too. Thick, dirty black clouds seemed to extend for miles. I had to go right towards these. I knew that as long as the fair weather kept up and I could see I would find my way home all right. But I ran slam-bang into the storm before I could realise its proximity.

Now my experience of flying in the clouds in thick weather was very slight, so I may add that this was particularly unpleasant to me. In the first place, I knew that if I turned back to get out of what I had run into I would probably have questions asked me on my arrival at the Squadron, as to what I was doing away south, where I had no business. This thought spurred me on my way a bit and kept me on what I thought was a due-north course, which would bring me, so I imagined, somewhere over La Bassee. From there I would turn west by south, following the canal, and thereby hitting my own aerodrome. This was how I planned it in the storm. How it came out you shall presently see.

CHAPTER 7

# Lost in the Clouds

If you have never been up in the clouds, I'll try and give you an impression of what good heavy weather in the air means to a new pilot. To an old pilot weather is of little consequence.

Clouds are of varying densities, and as you pass from one density to another the effect is rather peculiar. Hot or warm air rises, as you know, and cold air falls. So if a cloud or a series of clouds happen to come in your line of flight, you experience what is known as a "bump" of warm air as you leave a cloud and strike the open, or pass from one cloud to another in a series. Bumps may affect a pilot at any height from the ground up to 2,500 feet. The result of a bump is that you rise very rapidly a few feet or so, then drop bodily and suddenly as you pass into a heavier cloud or colder stratum. Travelling low in the air, one may also experience bumps, according to the nature or undulations of the ground. Thus a warm-air bump may come when passing over ploughed ground or over a wood.

When travelling at the rate of 90 to 100 miles per hour, bumps do not as a rule affect a pilot very much. But they buffet you about quite a bit, and if you are not used to them you are apt to get somewhat bewildered.

After the experiences noted in the last chapter, I was flying along at a height of about 12,000 feet in a heavy storm cloud or rather a huge bank of clouds. I was lost in the clouds! It felt very lonely and dreary up there, and also cold and clammy. My goggles got all fogged up. My windshield started dripping dew. And—ugh!—the rotten feeling when you realise that you are lost in such miserable conditions as these. I was disconcerted to a degree that I hated to admit.

I was now flying entirely by instrument—and this kind of flight was new to me. Still I had the theory and principles of it in my head

THE AUTHOR IN SOME CHARACTERISTIC POSES ON THE AERODROME

Note what a hangar looks like. These are all camouflaged by large daubs of varied colours of paints. They are made of canvas.

(learned at the ground school), so I kept on in a northwest-by-west course, as I imagined, steering by my compass. I kept glancing at my other instruments now and then, and noted that I had developed an extraordinary lot of speed. From this I judged that I had my nose down a bit.

When in fog or clouds, you understand, you can see nothing, and it is often the case that flyers don't know when they are "on a bank," climbing, or diving. Such positions may be maintained unconsciously for several minutes, and then they suddenly come out of the cloud and are surprised to find they are almost on their ears. Old pilots, of course, can tell in an instant what is taking place, but I am speaking now of new flyers.

On one occasion, I remember, a pupil came out of a cloud upside down, landed after a fashion, and when he was told he came out "on a loop," he could hardly believe it.

In my case I had pulled back on my "joystick" to ease the speed of the machine, then I had to stick it forward, for it was too much. Well, I kept this up, in the awful fog and mist, for about fifteen minutes.

I now glanced at my watch and noted the time. I had been out almost two hours and had only petrol for about three-quarters of an hour more to spend. "I must see where I am," I thought, so dived down to try and penetrate the clouds. Down, down, to 10,000 feet. Still clouds!

Eight thousand feet—and still the clouds about me maintained their density. Farther down—to 6,000, and then to 5,000 feet. Now I imagined I could see them thinning out. Four thousand feet! Ah, at last I could see—when "*crump-p-pr!*" God! What was that? I heard "*crump—crump—crump*"—three times in succession. I looked around wildly, and saw black "Archie." German Archie!

"What is this?" I thought. "Have I really flown over the German side of the line, in weather like this? With only three-quarters of an hour's petrol, and my compass all wrong!" For now I judged my compass had led me astray.

What a situation to be in! Lost in such a manner that I did not know how far I was over the line, and had no way of finding out, only having a small map of my own sector. Can you imagine anything worse than that?

Now what was I to do? Which way was I to go? Which way was I flying? My plight was certainly a puzzler. Here I was, my first time over the lines in the air, and I did not know one spot from another in the sector I was flying in—and had no means of finding out. Just then, to make matters worse, a thick drizzle began. Then—*"plop-plop"*—somewhere on my right two more bursts of Archie tended to rouse me to action. What could I do? Happy thought! I remembered that I had "taken off" into the wind on the aerodrome, and as the wind was due north at that time, I judged that it was probably still north. So taking a good look around, though the ground was fast disappearing from my view once more, I caught a glimpse of some smoke coming from a farmhouse.

I figured that I must be at least 20 kilometres on the enemy side of the line, judging by the quiet aspect of the surrounding country and the absence of shell-holes. Turning therefore in the opposite direction to that in which I had been going, and thinking I must have been blown south quite a bit, I faced straight up wind and a little to the westward. Then I checked my compass—yes, it was all wrong, now I could see, at least judging from the way the smoke was blowing. But I was taking an awful chance! What if the wind had changed from north to east, and I was flying into Germany still and didn't know it? What if I descended only to find myself a prisoner of war?

Now, finding my compass steady, I checked it carefully with the wind, and found that if I flew due west by the compass, I should be flying in reality about north by west. So, taking the only chance I seemed to have to avoid coming down in Hunland, I flew back out of sight of black Archie, into the clouds. Keeping on for about fifteen minutes, I then decided to come down, look around, and see if I could recognize any landmarks. But hardly had I put my nose down out of the mist when—*"cr-rump!"*—again I was startled, and looked to see how near the shot was. Seeing it was black, I returned to my old friends, the clouds and mist, for they were friends indeed now.

How far over the line could I be? How far into the Hun territory? That was the vital question, now that my freedom depended upon a few gallons of petrol. Oh, if only I had not paid so much attention to that combat in the air! True, I had gained some valuable experience, I thought, but what good was it going to do me now, if I came down on the Hun side? A prisoner—ugh—how I hated the very idea. Think of it! Only about two and a half hours of flying on the front, then to be taken without even a single scrap with the enemy. It would be humiliating, to say the least.

On, on I went, now getting desperate. Oh, to be able to land *just* clear of the enemy! I could not see the ground at all now, and to add to my misery I was getting soaked to the skin and frightfully cold. Visibility was a thing of the past to me now, for I could hardly see the outside spar or strut on the end of the wings of my machine.

"*It never rains but it pours,*" I thought, and the adage came true as I soliloquized about it. How it did pour! This time I gave myself up—doomed! Then—"*cough-cou-cough!*" came from the engine. Great Caesar! Petrol all gone! That was it, for the engine started backfiring several times—then stopped altogether. Frantically I worked my "fine adjustment," or throttle, but to no avail. I looked at my altimeter. Eight thousand feet! Fog below—fog all around.

How was I to land? What *could* I do? Putting my nose down to a gliding position, I reached for a Verey's light, found one loaded with red, put it up over my shoulder, pointing out, and waited to give a signal of distress.

Down, down, now rapidly, now a bit more slowly. Seven thousand feet! Still fog. Five thousand! Still not a sign of lifting. Three thousand! No sign of the ground. There must be a fog right down to the ground, I thought. What was I to do?

Down to 2,500 feet! "Steady, old man! Steady! Slow up a bit!" I looked at my Pitot tube—my air-speed indicator. Seventy miles per hour! "Too fast," I thought, so pulled up a little. Fifty-five m. p. h. "Ah, that's a bit better."

It takes much longer to tell this than the actual time that elapsed. It was not more than three or four minutes from the time my engine stopped till I got down to about 2,500 feet of the ground, where a peculiar feeling came over me. Nothing but an intuitive sense that I was near the ground saved my life that day. Mind you, I could see nothing of the ground, and knew nothing of my whereabouts. How was I to know that I was nearing a plateau a couple of thousand feet higher than the surrounding territory, which I had been flying over. But such was indeed the case—and something which I do not understand seemed to tell me that the ground was near, even though the altimeter had registered 2,500 feet a moment before. This caused me to fire the Verey's light to attract attention in case I "crashed" and at the same instant I yanked back my joystick. No sooner had I acted than the end camel "*Cr-cr-a-ash!*"—and temporary oblivion for me!

When presently I opened my eyes, I felt them swollen and sore. I looked around as well as I was able, and could see nothing but sky—sky everywhere—or rather what seemed to be sky, but was in reality fog and mist. Then, for the first time, I realised that I was lying on my back, but still in the machine. I undid the strap around my waist and cocked myself up on the edge of what was left of the plane. In a sort of dazed way I surveyed this mess, at the same time rubbing the back of my head. Then I noticed that my machine gun, instruments, and other paraphernalia, which should have been in front of me, had disappeared in the most mysterious way. At first I thought I was "seeing things," but no!—a closer look showed me that the whole nose of the nacelle had been wiped away completely. It had been broken or snapped off directly in front of where my feet would be, if on the rudder bar.

Gazing about me at the debris, I tried to figure out just what had happened, and decided that when my "sixth sense" induced me to pull up the machine suddenly as I did, I had given the joystick such a yank that the plane, in "zooming up" so quickly near the ground, had caught the apex of its tail booms on to a big sheaf of dried beanstalks, many of which I saw in the field nearby. This had evidently resulted in pulling down the nose forward and stopping its forward movement. Then, the nose having dropped, the forward impulse remaining in the tail of the plane had tipped the tail clean over the head part, and the booms hitting the ground again, it had to stop. But the main body of the machine, still moving, had rolled itself up in the tail booms, with the result that I found myself in the position described.

As I sat in the midst of the wreck, gazing contemplatively around, I heard voices and saw several men dashing towards me. I could make out their forms, but not their nationality, "Well, come, let's get over to the mess," said the major most hospitably, "and we'll get you fixed up. Hungry?"

"No." I replied, "but if you've got a cigarette I'd be much obliged."

"Certainly, certainly. Perhaps you could stand a nip of something too, eh?"

"Jove, you're right in that. It would steady me a bit, sir. I admit I feel a trifle wobbly."

I noticed he was a jovial, red-faced chap, and I took an immense liking to him at once.

"By the way," I said, "do you mind helping me a bit? I think I've hurt my ankle. At least it feels a bit painful."

"Oh, I'm sorry. I did not notice you were hurt in the foot. Just sit down here and I'll have a stretcher sent over. Here, Strange," he called to one of his men, "run over—"

"Oh, no, no, sir," I protested. "I don't want to be carried. I'm not as bad as all that, you know. I can hobble over all right, if you'll let me lean on you. It's only very slight."

Gad, though, it did pain now! But I kept it to myself, not wishing to appear on the sick list so soon as all that. I knew that would be my lot if I gave in to the pain and the doc got wind of it. Then it would be back to "the pool" for me again, and I had business over the lines.

"I say, Major, what corps do you belong to?" I asked then. "I've been trying to make out for the last few minutes."

"Oh, we're only greenhorns as yet. We've only just arrived. We're of the Second Contingent Canadians—the 4th Division Ammunition Column, on our way up to the Salient (Ypres). I hear it's pretty hot up in that part. Is that right?"

"Well, sir, I cannot say, so far as the ground is concerned or the air either, for I'm like yourself, only just arrived at the front—about a fortnight ago."

During this confab, the major was helping me toward a small estaminet, converted for the time being into an officers' mess. There I received a most hearty welcome from all hands.

"Can you wait for lunch till your foot is fixed up?" asked my good Samaritan as soon as we arrived indoors.

"Oh yes," I said. "As long as I don't have to stand."

An orderly produced a bowl of hot water. I bathed my bloody face and sprinkled some boric powder over it. I got one glimpse of myself in a glass. White as a sheet! "Gad, I do look scared," was my mental reflection as I caught sight of the ghastly facial reflection in the cracked mirror that certainly did not flatter.

"Take off your boot, laddie," said the major, as he came along with all sorts of paraphernalia to fix me up comfortably. My foot had swollen a good deal and was badly wrenched, but fortunately had not been crushed in the crash. The major bandaged it with his own hands, and I hobbled on an old broomstick into the mess-room.

All the boys of the mess were sitting down to lunch, full of curiosity to see me and hear my story. A flyer was a novelty to all of them. The lunch was a good one, and conversation was very brisk. At their urgent request I explained to them the mysteries of flying, although myself a novice at the art. It was indeed a case of ignorance being bliss, as some chap said long before flyers began to crash.

Presently the M. O. came in, looked at my foot, then at my head, and pronounced me all O.K., but said I must lie up for a day or two. Slapping me on the back, after his examination, he cheered me with his verdict, "You're all right, captain," promoting me very kindly.

"There's nothing at all for you to worry about." You see he didn't know my C. O. back at the aerodrome.

"Thanks very much, doctor," I said. "Glad I don't have to take one of your Number 9's, anyway." (A "No. 9," I may remark for the benefit of the uninitiated, is the mammoth cathartic pill of the army, a favourite prescription for all ordinary ailments and a sure cure for imaginary ones.)

"Perhaps you can tell me," I continued, "how to get a report through to my squadron. I've got to break the news to mother"—meaning my motherly C. O. Shall I say "motherly" or "step-motherly"?

"Certainly," replied the doctor to my anxious query. "There are two R. E.s (Royal Engineers) here on the canal, who are stringing a telephone line, and they may be able to cut in and get you through." You wait here. We'll attend to all that. No need to bother. You can't walk. Take it easy."

I remonstrated at first, but as he was my superior officer (the Doc was a major) and the job suggested being congenial to me, I made very little fuss about it. Prospects of a good dinner and a comfortable bed appealed to me just then.

"By Jove," I thought, "sometimes it's worthwhile to crash, for the fuss they make of you—some people, that is,"—thinking once more of the reception awaiting me when I returned to the squadron.

Half an hour later one of the engineer officers appeared. He was an Englishman, and looked at me very curiously.

"I say," he began, "are you the chap that wants to telephone? If so, I think I can take you down in my dory. The canal is only a few yards away. I'll tap a line and then you can telephone from the boat."

This looked like a trip on the canal to me and the plan was a good one, so I hobbled out of the house on my old broomstick. Many of the Canadians were standing near the *estaminet*, and as I appeared outside, I heard their voices, saying "There he goes!" "That's him!" All seemed curious to have a good look at a flying man—a sort of new species of human being to nearly all of them at that time.

Crossing a small bridge over the canal nearby, the "R. E." and I came to a small boat, in which sat a "sapper" at the oars. We got in and rowed along the canal for about ten minutes, the R. E. plying me with questions, which I answered noncommittally.

Then we came to a bend in the canal and I saw a line of field telegraph poles and engineers working on them, stringing wires. Turning the boat in to the bank, the sapper jumped out, trailing a length of wire behind him from the boat, where the R. E. sat beside me, with a field telephone in his hand. The sapper climbed one of the poles and attached his wire at the top, connecting the field phone with a trunk line, I presumed. Then the officer, after a few preliminaries, got in touch with the G. H. Q. (General Headquarters) and I was soon speaking to one of the staff there. I reported what had happened to me and asked him to relay my message to my Squadron, giving my position and that of the wrecked plane. I had previously learned that I came down near Watten, a few miles west of St. Omer.

We then started back to the Canadian mess. On the way the R. E. said, "Would you like to drop in at my houseboat? It is on the canal here, and may remind you of the Thames. Not bad for France, eh?"

I admitted his claim and remarked, "Pretty soft for you, old chap."

He said: "Somebody had to do this work here, so why not I? I'm no chicken! Had a pretty rough time of it in the early days over here."

Then I found that he had been in the old 27th Division on the front, and must therefore have fought in the Second Battle of Ypres.

Arrived at his "houseboat," it turned out to be a barge with a shack built on the deck. I found a very comfortable room inside, decorated with souvenirs and with a real carpet on the floor. The R. E. evidently liked his little comforts, and I don't blame him. From some secure hiding place he pulled out a bottle of "Johnny," and also produced some biscuits, so we had an enjoyable time. This, I thought, would certainly be an oasis for rest and refreshment while I was waiting for a Flying Corps tender to arrive from my squadron at A———, which I had learned was about 100 kilometres away. It would take a full day at least for the tender to reach me.

That night I spent in the quarters of my friend, the Canadian major, who gave me his bed. I don't know where the major slept. He certainly was a good fellow.

Next day the tender arrived and I rode back to the squadron, after taking a hearty farewell of my Canadian hosts. Before leaving I acquired a souvenir, in the shape of the first steel helmet I had seen worn on our side, for they were new then. The boys in the Canadian mess wrote their names on the helmet for me, in memory of my sudden descent from the clouds among them. My smashed machine was disassembled by the mechanics from the aerodrome, and we took it back with us on a trailer behind the lorry.

I arrived at the squadron about 4 p. m. and immediately hied me to my bunk, with as much secrecy and as little limp as possible. I did not

SUNSET FAR ABOVE THE CLOUDS

Photo showing what it looks like to an aviator flying above the clouds at a height of 12,000 feet: also peculiar reflection of the setting sun.

report officially that day, but sat down to think over my report and the explanation I had to give to my martinet. Dinnertime came and in the mess there were many curious questions by some of the other pilots. I was led into a lengthy, discussion of my experiences, and in the midst of it Major L—— came in. He looked hard at me and said:

"I see you're back, Campbell."

"Yes, sir," I replied.

"How did you come to get lost?"

I explained about the bad weather coming on suddenly, causing me to lose my bearings. Then he said:

"We heard you going over the drome and could almost see you. We sent up rockets for your benefit. Why some of you people can't use your heads is a mystery to me!"

The thought came to me, "Had I fooled myself into believing that what I had seen in the air was the result of enemy gunfire? Was it, after all, nothing but rockets? No, it was black Archie and made a loud crash. Rockets don't do that!"

But I said to the C. O.: "Well, sir, I'd have been glad to see a rocket, and should certainly have landed had I seen one, even in a strange aerodrome. I wasn't at all anxious to stay up in that weather, sir."

"Um-m-m!" was all he responded, and he turned away.

My reflections were anything but nice, but I had to grin and bear it. This was a fine reception to get after what I had been through. And to think how easily it might have been worse—and I had got safely out of it! So I threw back at him rather defiantly:

"Well, sir, it might have been much worse. I might have been captured—or dead. I consider I have done very well, sir."

"What you consider is of no consequence," retorted the major, turning to the buffet and pouring out a glass of port.

I said no more, but thought a whole lot. "Well, I suppose he'll try to get rid of me now," I reflected. "Dud pilots are not of much consequence to anybody."

But I made up my mind then and there to carry on and show them I was all right, and that I still had my nerves with me, for I felt confident my experience of being lost in the clouds, followed by a crash, would not hurt my flying, but would prove valuable to me in the long run. So I finished my dinner in silence, feeling very much disgusted and dejected by my reception.

After dinner I went up to Capt. Burns, my flight commander, and asked: "Any orders for me, sir, in the morning?"

"No, Campbell," he said. "I think you can lie up for a bit, till that foot of yours is strong. How is the foot, by the way?"

"Not bad, sir; I can fly if you want me to." I was very anxious now to hide my injury, in my strong desire to do *something* right away, to atone for my "bloomer."

The next day I took it easy and my second machine arrived at the drome. I determined to make this one last longer than the first. It was overhauled immediately and late that night I was told by Capt. Burns that I was for early morning patrol next day. He allotted me my position on the flight and gave me instructions what I was to do on the patrol.

"You being top man, Campbell," he concluded, "all you have to do is to 'sit on top,' and when we dive follow us down and keep a sharp lookout to prevent them from slipping in behind us."

This, I thought, would be a position of some importance. Anyhow, it was something useful, and I went to bed early, satisfied to know that I was to engage in my first "formation flight" next morning.

## Chapter 8

# The Squadron Combat in the Sky

"Four-thirty, sir." (*Knock—knock—knock.*) "Get up, sir! Early morning flying!"

Gad, that sounded familiar! It put me in mind of the aerodrome on Salisbury Plain, not so very long before. I poked my head out from my blankets. By Jove, it was cold, and the bed felt, oh, so comfortable. I started to rise. With the first movement came a sharp twinge in my injured foot. "Afraid I can't make it! Gad, but I must, though. I've got to 'sit on top' of the patrol this morning! Buck up, old boy!"

With that I jumped out of my bunk, donned my clothes in a hurry, and rushed down to the mess-room on the ground floor of the old *château*. I was feeling more at home now, so yelling out "Orderly, bring me some breakfast!" I scooted for the washroom, dashed cold water over my face, and felt better.

Returning to the mess-room, I found Capt. Burns busily digging into a rasher of bacon and some fried bread—a favourite article of food with all soldiers at the front, when they can get it.

"Good morning, Campbell," greeted my flight commander. "Well, I suppose this will be your first real trip over the lines, eh?"

"Yes, sir," I replied, "and I am mighty glad to be going up with you."

"Well, all I want you to do this morning is to sit on top and stick close to the patrol. Never leave it for an instant. A great deal depends on that, so you must stick to the formation."

"Aye, aye, sir. Very glad to do it."

He then gave me a few hints about dodging anti-aircraft gunfire, or "Archie," as we invariably called it. "Don't let it put the wind up you," he said. "It's only important for the moral effect. You may think you will get it all, being the last man in the patrol, but you won't."

I nodded, saying I understood and had seen a gun or two fired before. But I had got his meaning, and knew what to expect. Then an orderly brought my breakfast, which I gobbled up, all the while feeling rather restless in my chair. It's a sort of feeling that all flyers know; a feeling hard to explain, but it's there! You feel you are going to do something exciting. It's very like the sensation that comes over one unused to travelling, when about to take an important or unusual trip, only more so! The tension is at its highest and the mental strain the greatest just previous to moving off. That's about how I felt just then.

Two of the other boys of the flight came in presently, and another captain—Capt. Roberts.

Good morning, boys," said Capt. Burns. A little O. P. this morning," meaning that we were to go on "offensive patrol." I had learned already what that meant.

Gazing out of a window, I saw that the dawn was just breaking and that the day promised to be dear.

"I say, Drake," ordered the flight commander, "you might go and rush up Lewis. He's going to be late. That blighter sleeps his head off." Exit Drake in a hurry.

Still munching some food, I swallowed my coffee in haste, not wishing to cause any delay, but having a keen appetite, Capt. Burns rose from the table.

"Come on, you chaps, let's get up," meaning to the aerodrome. "We've got to run our engines up yet and we don't want any dud ones this morning."

Just then Lewis came rushing down, with only half of his clothes on. Standing at the table, he hurriedly grabbed mouthful after mouthful of food. He wasn't going to miss his breakfast, even if he was late. Turning with his mouth full, he called out: "I'll be right up behind you, boys."

We went on to the aerodrome. There I got my flying kit on, glanced over my new machine, got into it, saw everything was in order, and the usual procedure for starting up followed. I ran my engine up and it sounded O. K. Then I let it "idle," throttling down very slowly. I was waiting for the others. Then I heard the captain's voice in final warning:

> Don't forget, Campbell, you're top right-hand man; and stick to the patrol. Rendezvous at 6,000 feet over the drome. When I fire a red light, follow me to the lines!

I had already learned the signals (Verey's lights) which were then in use by the patrols. They were, by the way, something like this:

1. A red light fired on leaving the drome implied that the formation was in order, O. K., and that we were taking off to the line.

2. The same light, fired over the line, was a signal for attack, or a signal of distress. That is, if a red light was fired by the leader while on a formation patrol, the machines being more or less spread out, the signal meant that he was going to dive for an attack. Fired from a solitary plane, the light meant distress as a rule, and was usually answered by fighting scouts diving to his assistance, if the pilot in distress was within an area or zone where help could be rendered by others.

3. A green light, fired over the line, usually meant that the pilot had a gun jam or a dud engine and was "going home," or some similar mishap. This signal was to notify the rest of the patrol that they were a man short and could not rely on the former number of machines being on hand. This was important information, especially for the flight commander.

4. A white light, fired from a plane, was a signal which might mean anything, according to previous arrangement among the members of the patrol.

All or any of these vari-coloured lights might also be fired from an aerodrome in thick weather when a friendly machine was seen to be passing over it, in case the pilot did not recognize the drome and wished to land. At other times, usually at dusk, these lights might be fired from a plane, on coming close to the ground. They lit up the surrounding country and enabled the pilot to see his position more distinctly.

It may not be amiss for me also to say here that the British flyer never refuses a fight, but will always attack when an opportunity presents itself, even if the odds are against him. That is an unwritten rule of the service, always lived up to with most scrupulous care. I am speaking now more particularly of the pilots of the fighting scout plane, which is a single-seated machine, built for speed and effective offense. But the airmen of the reconnaissance and the bombing machines, and of the "contact patrol" planes too, live up to this rule or motto whenever they are molested or interfered with by the enemy, never running away from an encounter.

Now to return to my first flight with the patrol. After waiting a bit I saw Captain Burns turning his machine around and the three other boys of the formation following suit. I promptly awoke to action, ready to start after them. With a last glance around, I noticed it was getting lighter. Fifteen minutes more and I should be over the line! Now we're off!

Away we go, like a flock of ducks. One, two, three, four, start. Now myself!

Up we go, spiralling round, close on each other's tails by this time, and getting each other's "backwash." This sensation, by the way, I had already become used to.

Four thousand feet up! I looked around. Everything seemed so calm and still in the early morning light. I had a mental picture of the surroundings, from my first flight from this drome, and noted with some satisfaction how easily I recognised the landmarks. I looked at my altimeter. It registered 5,500 feet. Soon a signal would come from our leader.

Away in front of me, still climbing, I saw him, with his streamers trailing out behind. At that moment I seemed to hear the "*plop*" of his Verey's light, and spied a long white column of smoke and a red ball of fire dropping down from his plane.

The signal!

But still we climbed—up, up—straight out toward the line, flying northeast from the drome. I had now gained my allotted position as right-hand top man. We flew in V formation, looking more than ever like a flock of ducks. On, on! Gradually, in the distance I saw the faint outlines of shell-torn ground. It was of a dull brown colour, spattered with myriads of little mirrors, where water had collected in the shell-holes and was reflected up to me. Ten thousand feet high!

Directly below me, extending right and left, lay the trenches. From that height they looked like a jagged rent in the earth, zigzagging several miles wide in spots, and gave one the impression of having been torn there by the wrath of God!

At this point I fired three or four shots from my machine-gun, as is customary among our fighting scouts, who test their guns in this way as they cross the trenches into "Germany."

Now I paid most of my attention to the ground below, though at the same time keeping a weather eye around and upward in the sky. Still up we went. On and up! How strange! Surely we must be over the German lines by now. Yes, there lay the line! Evidently "Archie" was still sleeping, I thought.

This idea had only just entered my mind when—"*Cr-crump—cr-crump—cr-crump!*" Up came black Archie, straight in the centre of our patrol. Gad, it did put the wind up me. But it didn't seem to faze the boys in front of me, for straight on they flew, with only an imperceptible side-slipping motion to show that they noticed it. Their sideslip could not be seen from the ground, but covered several yards at each operation, to fool the gunners' aim.

Now the shells came up thick and fast. They were on my right, on my left, all around, and below me. "*Cr-ump!*" Gad, that was a close one. Another! I tried to force myself to keep cool, remembering how my captain had belittled "Archie" to me only that morning.

Automatically,—as I had been taught to do when shell-fire came too close for comfort,—I "crabbed" or side-slipped, like the others. This is a necessary precaution, for when the enemy gunners get that close to you, they usually put "the bracket" up; this being a salvo of guns, so directed as to make it pretty hot for you if you once get caught in it. When "the bracket" is put up by Archie, the fighting scout immediately dives, in order to get out of range. The dive compels the Archie batteries to change fuses in their shells, which gives the flyer a chance to take up a new position.

On, on, went the patrol! Now we must be at least fifteen kilometres on the other side, for the trenches were getting dimmer and dimmer as we flew into the enemy territory.

Getting pretty well used to Archie by this time, I kept looking around me. Suddenly I noticed several other machines in patrol formation in front of us, but slightly higher. We were now at an altitude of 13,000 to 15,000 feet. Gad, it was cold!

But who were these chaps ahead of us? What were they? Were they Huns? The thought thrilled me. Why couldn't I tell a Hun machine at a glance? But I couldn't then. That's what bothered me. I must follow my leader.

On we went, flying straight at them and gradually climbing higher. Suppose it was an enemy patrol up there! Immediately on the thought I cleared for action; that is, I loosened from its container on the side of the machine a spare drum of ammunition for my Lewis gun. One drum of forty-seven cartridges was already in place on the gun.

I then cocked my machine-gun, stiffening in my seat as I did so, ready and eager for action. If an opportunity presented itself, I was determined to do something. I had a triple purpose: To retrieve myself in the eyes of the squadron after the mishap with my first machine; to settle my private score with the Hun; and, as I said to myself, "show them what a Scot is made of."

Now I noticed my commander turning up straight into the sun. All of us trailed after him. Yes, that must be a Hun patrol, for they turned straight on a course to cut in ahead of us. My heart was now pounding rapidly. God! We were going to fight!

The enemy was trying to put himself between us and the sun. This I knew would be a decided disadvantage to us. Sixteen thousand feet! We were almost on a level now with the hostile patrol and saw that they numbered eight machines in all, against our five, "So much the better," thought I. "More targets for us, old chap," and I fondly patted my machine-gun.

Now a great struggle for the advantage of height took place. First this way, then that, we turned, keeping our formation as closely as we could. The Hun seemed to be counteracting every move we made.

Presently I noticed that two of his machines were not moving quite so fast as the others. They were gradually falling behind and below the rest. This, I thought, was our opportunity, our opening for a move. Then I saw the two Hun machines put their noses down, trying to get in front of and below their comrades, where they would be in a safer position. This move would also enable them to act as a decoy for us, by drawing our fire should we, too, dive.

At last! There it was! The red ball of fire! Our signal to attack! I gulped and wondered what my action should be, not having decided on whom or on what I was going to dive. Then remembering my instructions to "stay on top and follow down," I pulled myself together to obey, though itching all the while to dive at the low man of the hostile bunch, whose position seemed to present a wonderful opportunity to me.

The Huns, realising that we were now in the advantageous position they had been trying to get, did a sharp turn and started dashing off inland—farther into "Germany."

All this time, while we were manoeuvring for the advantage of position, Hun Archie had been firing a regular barrage directly in front of us and between the opposing forces. This was decidedly disconcerting, to say the least, but failed to stop us.

Captain Burns led off the attack, by turning sharp left, away from the sun, thus getting it behind him, and diving straight at four of the

A Nieuport Scout Machine

Doing sentinel duty in the sky at a height of 10,000 feet above the trenches.

hostile machines, now below him and scarcely two hundred yards away. One Hun had gained height and remained on top.

Down and forward—straight at them—went three more of the boys of my own flight. What was I to do? Follow them? No! What about that Hun on top? I was now being menaced by him.

Remaining above, I first made a feint, as if turning away from my own patrol. Then I did exactly what the Hun least expected me to do, I should judge. Putting my nose down suddenly, and thus getting up an enormous speed, I "zoomed" up straight at him. This threw him off a bit, I think, for he turned and putting his nose down, started going like blazes from me, leaving me on a higher level.

Looking away down below, there was the scrap being carried on. One of the Hun machines was evidently disabled, for it was going down in a spin. All I had was a fleeting glance at him, but that was enough, and it certainly bucked me up. I had at any rate driven away my particular opponent, for the man I had "zoomed" at had "beat it" for home. Rapidly debating whether I should follow him or follow my patrol, I decided to do the latter, as my Hun raced away from me farther into his own territory.

I waited no longer. Orders were orders. "Stick to the patrol!" Then I "stall-dived," that is, I shut my engine off and pulled my nose up into the air until the engine stopped dead; then, suddenly whipping over sidewise to the left, I dropped like a plummet. Down, down, down—faster, faster, faster! The wind whistled past me. I heard it in the flying wires—first humming, then singing.

The patrol once more assembled itself. I flattened out about 500 feet over my comrades and descended slowly and gradually, taking up my original position in the flight.

Not a shot had I fired, but the patrol had evidently accounted for at least one of the enemy machines. Looking far down, I could just see it. Yes, there he was, still dropping! Following the falling plane with my eyes, it presently told its own tragic tale, bursting into flames on hitting the ground.

Now a quick glance around gave us the satisfaction of seeing that we had cleared the air. Away below us on our left (we were now travelling south and east) was Fritz, driven out of the sky, of no use whatever in his present position. Our combat was won!

But a surprise was still in store for me. We had cleared away that little lot, but Archie meant to take it out of our skins now, and this he proceeded to do. Great showers of black Archie came piling up—

around us, below, on every side—a regular barrage. Gad, but it was hot!

One shell burst right under my left wing, rocked the plane, and sent my heart up into my mouth. Let me tell you this: They can say as much as they please about Archie being only good for morale, but I give you my word that if I hadn't had a good leader that day, I should have felt pretty "jumpy," and most likely would have pegged out. As it was, our superb leadership and the cool manner in which the other boys acted (at least, from a green flyer's point of view) in response to his manoeuvres, tended to keep me steady on the job.

We were now nearing the southern limits of our sector, so turning north and west again, constantly being banged at by Archie, we flew for the remainder of our allotted time, but no more Fritzes appeared. I was getting pretty dog-goned cold, wishing I could get down to the ground, and gazing longingly away off into the distance, where I imagined I could see my little roost—when suddenly the welcome signal of a green light, fired by our leader, told me we were proceeding home.

Once across the line, on the way back to the aerodrome, the fighting patrol almost invariably indulges in a series of antics and evolutions that delight the boys in the trenches and behind the lines below. A favourite stunt of some of the most daring pilots is to "stall-dive" from a great height to within a few yards of the German trenches, and fire what remains of their ammunition at the Huns. Then swooping across No-Man's Land, clearing their own trenches by fifty feet or so, they often career madly around back of the lines, "contour-chasing." This stunt consists of slipping along very close to the ground, following its undulations, then suddenly zooming up over some house, or wood, or encampment—and incidentally "putting the wind up" everybody within sight of their mad antics.

When first indulged in over the front, these stunts were the cause of great anxiety for the safety of the exuberant pilots; but when it was seen how much they enjoyed such venturesome proceedings, the daily antics of the airmen became a source of amusement to all who witnessed them. This style of flying particularly appealed to me for a while, and I gradually became quite a "stunt merchant."

Arrived at the aerodrome, after being out for two hours and a half on the early morning flight, I received orders to "stand by" for offensive patrol at 2:30 in the afternoon. The intervening hours were my own. I did my second patrol that day (we usually did two patrols daily), but nothing eventful happened.

In mess that night we talked over our experiences of the day. I discovered that it was Captain Roberts who had brought down the Hun that morning. Usually the bringing down of an enemy flyer was celebrated as an event in those days. But such events grew common in the life of the fighting scouts after a while.

CHAPTER 9

# Brought Down by "Archie"

One morning in April when I was seated at breakfast in the old French *château*, chatting with a few other members of the pilots' mess, an orderly came in, saluted, and handed me a slip of paper which read:

Stand by for bomb raid—10:30.

This was something new. It was the first time I had been assigned to accompany a bombing expedition. Being a flying scout, I knew that I was not going to drop any bombs on enemy positions, but that my function in the coming raid would be to protect the bombers. In such a case the flying scouts "sit on top" of the bombing machines, either in front of or behind them, and act as escort. You see the same kind of thing in football, where the man with the ball, running down the field, is protected from opponents by the interference of his teammates.

When I got into my machine that morning and ran the engine up, ready to start, I found there were ten of us going on the raid as escorts. Captain Burns had allotted my position as left-hand forward top man, next to the leader. The man on my right was deputy leader. Captain Burns was to be the "rover," that is, he was to tool back and forth ahead of and over the bombing machines, keeping his eye peeled for hostile aircraft. We flew in an inverted V, or wedge-shaped formation, well above the bombers, and were there to intercept any attack that might be made upon them.

The formation patrol is an excellent method of beating off attack, for if an attack is made by a single enemy or a number of enemy machines, the particular pilots attacked do not swerve from their course to any degree. Some friendly machine is covering them with its fire. If a hostile patrol were to dive on the rear of our protective patrol to surprise us, the gunners in the bombing -machines could fire backward with their rear guns while travelling forward. Thus they would be putting up a form of defence while the rear scout machines would fly to attack the enemy in their turn, and put them to flight. Such an encounter is unusual, however, on bomb raids like ours that morning, for Fritz likes to have the advantage of superior numbers, and we were flying in force.

Before we left the aerodrome, orders were given for the escort to rendezvous overhead at 4,000 feet, then take off behind the leader, and again rendezvous over the Bois de Nieppe, a few kilometres behind the line, as high as we could get in a short time. There we were to wait for the bombing patrol to come and meet us at a certain hour.

When everybody had got these orders definitely fixed in his mind, "after orders" were impressed upon us. When the bombing planes had dropped their "pills" on the objective, we of the escort were to "stall-dive" on to the position bombed, and strafe it with machinegun fire. This sounded good as well as risky to me, for we were going to bomb Seclin, about 50 kilometres behind the Hun line. This town was in a particularly uncomfortable area, with several barriers of "Archie" for us to pass. Our objective was a great railway junction, and therefore well protected. Probably forming part of the so-called "Hindenburg line," it was one of the main junctions for the transportation of German troops.

To show how well this particular raid had been planned, the bombing squadron had information as to the exact time certain troop trains would arrive there, and had timed their flight so as to arrive on the scene at the precise moment the three tracks would be filled with troops. You can imagine that this would necessitate pretty fine work on our part, and it did.

Taking off from the drome and rendezvousing above, as per orders, we flew from the first to the second rendezvous, and there waited about five minutes, when the bombing squadron put in an appearance. While waiting we flew around in a circle, or back and forth, always keeping our formation.

We were now at a height of 12,000 feet. The bombers arriving somewhat below us, came up. Then we manoeuvred for position, while the bombing machines kept straight on. When we got into alignment, a Verey's light was fired, and we were off on the raid into the enemy's territory.

Reaching the line, travelling straight southeast, going into the wind, which came from that direction, we crossed the line a little south of La Bassee. Then we got it! There are certain places, you know, where you can cross without seeing Archie, as a rule, but when he catches sight of a formation patrol, he does his darnedest to break it up. Breaking up the formation gives hostile patrols a chance to attack.

But Archie was not very successful this trip, at least as we went over the line, for we kept straight on and he did not faze us. By this time I had got used to Archie and was a bit inclined to be contemptuous.

"Dirty blighters!" I reflected. "You can fire at us and if you hit us you do us in. And our only possible comeback is to fire a few drums of ammunition in your direction—which cannot hurt you and only seem to make you fire all the more furiously."

After flying about 30 kilometres we turned slightly west and crossed Turcoing, which was almost on the border of Belgium. Again we turned into the wind.

If the wind at and near the ground level is blowing, say, from the north, its course is found to be changed about 15 degrees clockwise, that is, from west to east, when one reaches a height of 3,000 feet or over. This is due to the revolving motion of the earth. As the earth revolves from west to east, its action or motion causes the air near the ground to move with it. Above 3,000 feet, however, the wind becomes "constant" in its direction, and a northerly wind is found to be coming from a point about 15 degrees northeast. This fact in meteorology must be taken into consideration by the bombers of the air service. In dropping a bomb they must travel "down wind," for the current of the air will drive it off its mark, if not allowed for.

Accordingly our direction was changed after leaving Turcoing. Now, travelling in a southwesterly course, we presently arrived at our destination. Seclin! This I immediately spotted. Here the escort planes dropped back slightly to the rear, while the bombing machines rushed by in V formation.

"Archie" came up now in clouds. It looked as if our formation was likely to be broken, and I began to be pretty "windy." A certain sense of uneasiness came over me. I dreaded the idea of landing in Hunland a prisoner. Then I saw that all the bombing machines, instead of side-slipping in and out—as we usually did when shelled by Archie—were travelling straight down wind, keeping a steady course toward Seclin, now in front of us below.

Watching the bombers, I also kept an eye out for the approach of hostile machines. I noticed there were several about, but they were not in the mood for attack.

Ah! What's that little speck down there, travelling so rapidly? There's another! And another! I counted at least a dozen, dropping forward and downward, directly under each of our bombing machines. Bombs, of course! I had never actually seen a bomb dropping before. Fascinated, I riveted my gaze on the unusual sight, to watch for results, even though Archie was pestering us every moment.

Down, down, dropped the little specks. Smaller and smaller they grew to my sight. Each machine, as it dropped its "pills," changed its direction to the south, I saw, to baffle Archie and make the formation complete once more.

Then, all at once, I saw huge columns of smoke arise from the ground. Our bombs had found their mark!

Archie now came up in dense bunches. He was going to get his own back if he could. For a while I could not see the effect of the bombs, and following my leader paid no attention to what was happening below. I knew that very soon I should be near enough to see the ground quite distinctly.

Now the Verey's light! My signal! I shut off my engine, pulled my nose up into the air, and "stalled." Hovering only a moment, then— *s-swish!*—the snapping movement of my nose dipping forward, at the same time tipping over on my wing-tip to the left—I dropped straight down in a vertical dive.

Down, down, I followed the rest of the patrol, who had anticipated the move and started quicker than I. A drop from a height of 16,000 feet to within a few hundred feet of the ground in about half a minute, say 25 to 30 seconds, seems to the lay mind to be quite a feat. It is! The downward speed is enormous. You see the ground come rushing up to you with a rapidity that can hardly be comprehended. But the army flyer learns to do this as part of his day's work, and gets used to it.

"Emma Gee" (M. G.)—my little machine gun, being now trained for my objective, all cocked and ready, I waited, tense in my seat, wanting to get down even quicker. I passed through the heavy smoke of the bomb explosions on the ground—now rising like a huge white column, but becoming a dense black column as I got nearer. Then, as I shot out on the other side of the smoke, I beheld a sight that burns in my mind to this day. (*Machine Gunners on the Western Front, The Emma Gees* by Herbert W. McBride & *The Canadian "Emma Gees"* by C. S. Grafton is also published by Leonaur.)

Several tons of bombs, dropped in one position, create awful havoc. Add to this the terror of a big fire and the general chaos of masses of people dashing hither and thither, not knowing where to go to escape they know not what, raining upon them from the sky! That is what I saw. Our bombers had attained their objective at the busy junction, had trapped the enemy troops, and I felt exultant at such a successful outcome of our raid and the accuracy with which our bombs had fallen. This certainly was something worthwhile.

Looking closer, I saw three trains—or what was left of three trains—piled in debris around the obliterated junction station, which was now blazing merrily. On my left a large factory on a siding was also ablaze. There was not much time for looking around, but I took all this in; then turned my attention to a sight of more importance to me just then. This was no less than a horde of Hun troops, frantically firing their rifles up at us. I could almost hear the shots.

Then ensued a mad minute of "strafing!" My comrades of the patrol, I could see, had opened fire straight into the mass, and the Huns were dropping like flies. Training my gun, while my plane was still diving, on a group of the Boches, I observed a machinegun on the ground, spattering away at us. Then, pulling my Bowden-wire control on the joystick (which operates the trigger of the gun out in front of you), I opened fire. At last! One full drum of ammunition I fired, then feverishly reached for another, at the same time letting the empty drum drop into the nose of the nacelle, instead of replacing it in its container. Clapping the fresh drum on to the spindle of the Lewis, I saw I was now travelling at a gliding angle, at diminished speed. Again I fired into the group of Boches, and noted with satisfaction that my shots took effect. All that remained of the group were running like mad and ducking beneath the debris of the railway trains.

All this occurred in a remarkably short space of time, and quicker even than one can read about it , the Boches that could move had disappeared into every discoverable nook and cranny.

On flew the patrol, over the blazing buildings of the Seclin junction, flying so low that we could feel the heat arising from them as they burned. Now being below Archie, he could not depress his guns sufficiently to injure us, though a few machine-guns were returning our fire from places of vantage. These did not bother us much.

I was a bit disappointed that I could not get in more shots at the enemy, but I had at least done something. Then spying what looked like some new stacks of grain in a field, I released at them the remainder of the cartridges in my gun, the same being of the incendiary type. Being only a few hundred feet up and dipping my nose as I fired,

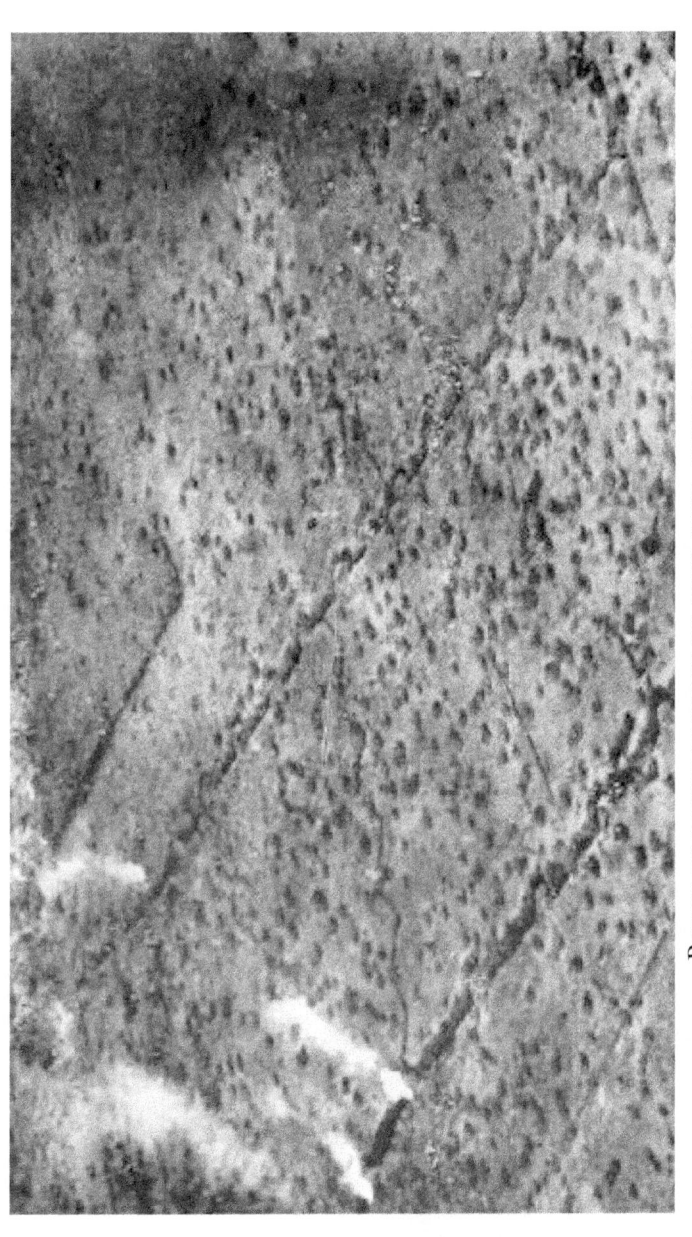

PHOTO OF BATTLE IN PROGRESS OVER SHELL-RIDDEN AREA

The white smoke shows shells exploding. Note the white dots they are troops going "over the top." The trenches are very plainly to be seen from the air.

my aim was good and I saw a spiral of smoke arising from my target, which meant a little more damage to the enemy. Again I put a fresh drum of ammunition on the Lewis.

We now started climbing back to our old position, our bombers being well on their way home by this time. Glancing up, I soon saw our top patrol sitting on the bombers' tails, protecting them as before. Everything had worked out fine for us.

Up, up, up, straight up! Now we began to get some Archie again. Then, gad, how it did come up! So far we had not lost any of our machines, by accident or otherwise. I was exulting over this fact and my own small share in the success of the raid; was yelling and hollering to myself, although I couldn't hear my own voice, owing to the roar of my engine; and altogether I felt supremely happy over our wonderful feat. I knew that we should be commended and that a good deal of credit would be given us on our return. This thought was particularly pleasing, after some of my former experiences.

Now we were approaching the line on our return trip, being within a few kilometres of it and flying at an altitude of about 8,000 feet. Then, as luck would have it, we had to pass over our pet Archie, situated in the Bois de Biez. This fellow was remarkably accurate in his fire, as I knew from one or two previous trips into his zone. In my exultant state, however, a little thing like a sharpshooting Archie did not strike me as serious, and I did not pay him the respect of turning out from him.

Just then one of my cylinders started "cutting out," being sooted up. Immediately my high spirits fell. It's a nasty feeling to have—finding yourself on the "other side," gradually dropping behind the main body of the patrol and wondering when the next cylinder is going to cut out; because when one goes another usually follows. Almost as soon as I thought of it, the thing happened. I now began to wonder how I could reach that line, and cross it a bit—just a little bit!

Disheartened, I saw the boys away ahead of me, streaming on. Then I noticed a Verey's light, the signal to beat it for home, and saw them all dive like mad and start their funny home-going capers, like a lot of colts let out to pasture. Zooming and diving and spiralling on their way, they plainly showed their delight at the outcome of the raid.

I struggled on and on. It seemed as if I never would cross that line. Now I couldn't avoid that Archie in the Bois, even if I would. I simply had to cross him—and he was determined to get at least one of us, if he could. Was I to be his victim? Egad, how his shots came up at me!

I was decidedly "windy" now.

Glancing at my instruments, I noted that I had been out 2¼ hours and also saw my altitude was over 8,000 feet. "It's quite a nice shot for Archie at that height," I assured myself, when—"*Cr-rump—ah—shee!*" Lord, that was a close one! Again it came—"Crump—*crump—cr—*" Then something happened! *Zowie!* Down went my nose, my tail going over my head. Right straight under my tail—a regular beauty!

Just as I was looking to see whether my planes were hit, the most awful vibrating began, shaking me up so that I could not see a thing. My head seemed to be shaking off my shoulders. With an effort I flattened out the machine a bit, trying to make it glide easily, and at the same time frantically grabbed at my throttle, shutting the engine off.

Subconsciously I knew what had happened. The sudden dipping motion of my nose going down and my tail going up, from the concussion of the high-explosive shell underneath me, had thrown my drum of machine-gun ammunition out. The plane being of the pusher type—that is, with the engine and propeller behind the pilot—the ammunition tray had hit the propeller, snapping off one of the blades. The other three blades of the propeller revolving, gave the machine a very wobbly motion, and caused the intense vibration. My speed through the air by gliding—even after the engine was shut off—caused the propeller to revolve just the same, so the faster I glided the greater shaking I got.

Well, thought I, it was a pretty long way down—8,000 feet—quite a drop!—and I reckoned that if I didn't slow up the machine would very soon collapse in the air from the vibration. I made the plane glide as slowly as possible, but matters went from bad to worse, in spite of all I could do.

First, my inclinometer (the instrument for telling the angle you tip your plane to on a "bank") broke away from the dashboard. Next my watch went. Then the dial of my revolution counter. In fact, all of the instruments in the machine started jumping about. I still kept my nose straight for the line, meaning to cross it somehow if I had a chance. Archie kept pounding away at me, but now I was dropping in height all the time he could not get the range so easily, having to change his fuses so often.

And then the inevitable happened! The vibration caused my left wing, attached to the centre section of the machine, to drop so much by the loosening of the wires that I started spinning. "Ye gods," I thought, "I'm done for this time!"

Down, down, I went, everything seeming to fly around me in a whirlwind now. Faster and faster! I began to get dizzy. Then the ground loomed up to me and I thought: "The only way to save myself now is to put my engine on. The 'torque' will have a tendency to straighten the machine out for a moment or so, and give me a chance to make some sort of a landing." So I tried this and discovered that it would do the trick after a fashion. That was good to know—it would help a bit. The plane started spinning again, and I expected every moment that the wing would collapse—not paying much attention to the fact that by now I had crossed the line, and was on my own side, at any rate.

Realising that I was getting quite close to the ground, I now kept manoeuvring the machine in such fashion that it would no sooner get into a spin than I would get it out and going nearly level, until it dropped into another spin.

Engrossed in this performance, alternately spinning and straightening out, I suddenly saw right ahead and only a few yards below me, an immense slag-heap, betokening ironworks nearby. Being levelled out at the moment, with the thought, "That's an easy drop!" I yanked back my joystick—and landed like a bat on the side of the slag-pile, badly shaken but quite intact!

My throat felt dry and parched, as I realised that I had had another lucky escape from death or a prison in Hunland. But I was not yet free to gloat.

Cutting loose from my belt as soon as possible, I had only just jumped clear of the machine when it began tumbling and slithering down the steep side of the slag-heap. I looked back at the line, which I had so fortunately succeeded in crossing before I came down. I could see the trenches, and reflected:

"There's almost a direct observation on this point from the Boche trenches and gunners. They are only a few hundred yards away and can easily see me here, on the side of this hill. This is no place for yours truly!"

The thought spurred me to action. My poor machine had gained some velocity in tumbling down the hill, zigzagging in all directions. I started away at right angles from it, but had gone only a few yards when—"*Cr-rump—Cr-crash!*"—I was knocked forward on my face. Quickly picking myself up, covered with dust and debris, I ran blindly, madly, from the spot, making for the opposite side of the hill.

Looking behind me just once, before I passed out of sight of my plane, I witnessed the effects of a "direct hit." *Plunk—crash!* Right in the middle of the machine! Gad, I thought, it's easy to imagine what my finish would have been, if I had stuck in that machine, unconscious from the fall. Luck always seemed to be with me.

Knowing something of the methods and the dangers of trench warfare, I now crawled around, keeping my head down as much as possible, and soon stumbled upon an O. F. (observation post) of one of our batteries. A man in the hole yelled to me as I approached:

"Here you are, sir! This way!"

With the utmost alacrity I complied with the direction, and breathed a deep sigh of relief, once snuggled down in that pit. Pretty well shaken up, I reached for a water-bottle which I espied in a corner, but didn't have strength enough left to lift it. The last act of my flight had certainly taken the wind out of me.

Seeing I wanted a drink, one of the men in the O. P. jumped for the bottle and handed it to me. The officer of the post in the meantime was inspecting my face, for I was bleeding at the nose. I put the bottle to my lips and took three or four good swallows, discovering the contents to be rum! This changed the picture for me, and I made a rapid recovery, talking to the officer and asking him where I was and how I could report to my squadron.

I had taken off my flying-coat, and the officer, seeing I had been in a Scottish regiment, began to call me the inevitable "Jock," saying:

"That's easy, Jock. This is the Nth Battery, Nth Brigade. I'll ring up Army Corps headquarters and get through for you."

Presently I was talking with the C. O. of my squadron, notifying him of my position and the total loss of my machine. The news of the machine I held back until the last. Still, I argued to myself, being brought down was not my fault. So I worried no more about it that day. If I was going to get it from the C. O., there was no way of escape, so why worry about it at all?

I remained in the observation post—most welcome and hospitable hole in the ground!—until nightfall, when one of the trench guides came through from a post in the rear, and guided me to the village of M———. There I waited in an *estaminet*, sipping muddy water called beer and drinking *cafe-au-lait*, until a tender came for me. I was then about 15 kilometres north of my aerodrome.

It was late that evening when I arrived back at the drome. I made out my report to the night orderly, looked to see if there were any orders for me for the following day, found none, and went to bed.

CHAPTER 10

# "F. P. Number One"

On the morning after the bombing raid, not being called for early patrol, I surmised that I was "for it" in the afternoon. The surmise was correct.

A stiff west wind had sprung up. This blowing toward Hunland, limited our routine activities in the air to "line patrols." The main object of these patrols was to prevent the Hun from flying into our territory. We were satisfied if we could keep him on his own side when the direction of the wind gave him such a decided advantage.

Line patrol was very ticklish work, because of the difficulty of keeping on our side of the line in the stiff west wind. If you happened to do a left-hand turn when travelling south along the line, you suddenly found yourself on the other side—blown there by the strong wind—and had to fight your way back against the wind.

The Hun had an advantage in a west wind, because he could come up against the wind, cross our lines, and if pursued dash back home with the greatest ease, the wind at his back.

Sometimes it happened to our line patrols that the enemy drew them unthinkingly across the line, farther than they wished to go. Then, suddenly remembering that they had to fight their way back against the wind, they would have to abandon the chase. In coming back their speed would at times be so diminished by the wind that they would be practically standing still in the air, thus giving "Archie" a wonderful opportunity to wing them. And Archie was seldom slow to seize such opportunities.

A line patrol consists usually of only two machines. When I went up that afternoon I patrolled up and down the line, dodging in and out of clouds, and keeping a sharp lookout for Fritz; but nothing occurred to break the monotony of the patrol. You may find it hard to believe that flying, especially close to a battle front, could prove monotonous; but it certainly does, to an army flyer on patrol, when nothing eventful happens. I returned to the drome after my two hours' patrol, feeling miserably cold and disappointed at having had no action.

Half an hour after I landed at the drome, I was asked to go up again, to chase several Boches who had broken through the line patrol that had gone out to relieve us.

The siren alarm sounded, and the C. O. (Major L——) rushed out. Vastly excited, he yelled at us to hurry up and get in our machines. Being thus spurred to action (he was very good at cursing) we dashed for our planes. Not having my own machine now, it having been destroyed by shellfire on the previous day, I was using another man's until a fresh plane could be procured for me. Now planes, by the way, are like horses or human beings—they have their own peculiarities, and differ from each other, or from all others, in many little points. I moralize thus for a reason, as you shall presently see.

Anxious to get into the air without delay, to have a go at the Boches, I started the machine, gave the signal "All clear!" taxied round, and was taking off up the aerodrome. But I had not paid sufficient attention to the fact that I was taking off "cross wind." The result was that the machine going in one direction—forward, while the wind forced it sideways, the inevitable accident happened. I wiped off my undercarriage wheels, and went slithering along the ground on the belly of the machine; incidentally breaking the propeller and mucking things up generally. It was an uncalled-for mess, and I realised it! I felt like kicking myself.

Well, there was nothing to do but get another plane as soon as I could. So I hopped out, as two mechanics came running to meet me. As they drew up I said:

"Never mind that mess now! We've got no time. Run out 5942— and hurry! I must get up with this patrol."

We all dashed back to the hangar together, I in my heavy flying kit, and got out the machine. The C. O. was nearby, stamping and fuming around in great shape. I pretended not to hear or to see him, knowing only too well that I should hear him soon enough.

I climbed into the machine—No. 5942—got my engine started, and hurriedly "ran it up." I looked at my revolution-counter. Only 850 revolutions per minute! Something was wrong! Gad, what rotten luck! To draw a dud engine at such a time! I buzzed it and buzzed it, hoping against hope! No use! I knew exactly what it was—a sooted plug! So I shut the engine off and yelled to the "fitter"—the engine mechanic, the other man being a "rigger":

"Hurry up! Get around behind there and find out which cylinder is missing."

I felt sorry for that mechanic, knowing what he was in for, if he hadn't cleaned those spark plugs. The rules of the aerodrome were ironclad. All machines must be kept in readiness for flight at an instant's notice, when once on the "serviceable" list.

The fitter soon discovered that it was No. 9 cylinder that was missing. It was a rotary engine, having nine cylinders. This being duly fixed, I started the engine once more. Again a cylinder missed!

"Great Caesar, man, why in h— aren't these plugs clean?" The situation was serious for all hands, and language like this was forced from me. I started fuming and raging myself now.

Looking off into the dim distance, I could see our own "Archie" breaking around the Huns I should have been chasing by this time. Four small specks showed me where my luckier comrades were trailing on nearer and nearer to them, heading into the north, I knew it would be impossible for me to catch up with them, but still I would do my best.

Then the storm broke! Like a raging animal, the C. O. rushed up.

"What's the matter with this machine?" he yelled at the mechanic.

"Plugs, sir," answered the fitter, shortly.

"Are you sure?"

"Well, sir, the plugs looked clean enough. I cleaned 'em just after the last patrol, sir, this morning."

The C. O. stamped around in front of me, looking black as thunder. Then he snapped out:

"Get out of that machine! Let me see if I can run that engine up!" I presume he thought he could do it better than I. At any rate, he didn't. The engine still balked. Climbing out, he called:

"Flight Sergeant Grimes!"

"Coming, sir!" The sergeant ran up.

"Make out a crime-sheet against this man! I'll teach you fellows to be a bit more careful to maintain the running order of these machines."

"Which one, sir?" asked the flight sergeant, meaning which of the two mechanics who stood by—the rigger and the fitter.

"Bring them both in!" snapped Major L——, stamping off to the office lorry.

## A BAD CRASH

One of the machines that landed in the barb-wire entanglements just outside our trenches. This was the finish of a successful fight in the air in which two enemy planes were brought down. The pilot was saved.

After asking the engine mechanic a few questions, to which the man replied, looking very sullen as he stood by, the sergeant turned to me and asked what I had found wrong with the machine. He noted the replies on a piece of paper, and withdrew.

Turning to the fitter, I said: "Never mind! We'll try to pull you through all right." Little did I realise how hard it was to explain matters satisfactorily to a martinet.

Giving me a grateful look, the man went on cleaning the plugs on the engine. Our mechanics, I knew, had no easy job, especially in good flying weather, when they often had to work late at night to keep the machines in flying trim.

Next day I was detailed to "stand by," as what we called "waiting man." This at the best of times is a monotonous job, but it was made most unpleasant by our fussy C. O. His idea of "standing by" was to insist on your waiting around with your full flying equipment on, in a little coop next to the office lorry. This was most uncomfortable, especially in hot weather, and made the waiting pilot feel like a messenger boy or a taxi-driver.

There was a little joke among the pilots, by the way, especially in artillery squadrons. An observer would dash up to a machine and yell to the pilot as he climbed in, "Ypres, as quick as you can!"—just as he might say, "Drive to the Savoy!" to a London taxi-driver. And the pilot would meekly answer, "Taxi, sir"—if only to him or his observer and "kid him along" into thinking he was of the utmost importance, a passenger on very important duty. The Flying Corps pilot, however, as a rule, knows as much as the observer, and often more, of what is to be done in the air. Still, "*C'est la guerre!*"

At 10 o'clock next morning we had "orderly room," the court of summary justice in a military unit like a regiment or a squadron. The two miserable mechanics were pulled up on the carpet. I tried to intercede for them, but to no avail. One of the men—the fitter—was given "twenty-one days' F. P. No. 1" for "neglect of duty," with an added remark from the C. O., "and it will probably buck you up a bit!" The other man was reprimanded—for nothing! Such is life in the army—at times.

Now "F. P. No. 1" is the short army term for "Field Punishment Number 1," a method of discipline applied only when a force is in the field, or on active service, as in wartime. The sentence meant that the offender would be tied to a wheel (of a gun carriage or truck) out in the open, and there exposed, two hours each day, for a period of twenty-one days. The "stocks" of old were not a marker to this form of military punishment.

The sentence was duly carried out, and in the most dramatic manner. The whole squadron was formed up on the aerodrome in a hollow square. Even the pilots of a flight just about to go up on patrol were compelled to stay and hear the sentence read out by the C. O. in his most impressive style. The miserable culprit stood in the centre of the square, with a guard on each side, as if he had committed a murder and was going to be shot! Every man present stood stiffly at attention.

When the sentence had been duly read, the C. O. himself directed the operations of putting it into effect, instead of delegating to the sergeant-major, as was customary, the performance of this unpleasant duty, which most British commanding officers find extremely repugnant to their feelings. Turning to the guards, he gave the commands:

"Squadron! 'Shun!—Stand at—ease!"

At this point, where the sergeant-major usually took over the prisoner, the C. O. himself carried on.

"Prisoner and escort! Right—turn! Quick—march!" And marching them over to the workshop lorry, the C. O. supervised the operation of lashing the prisoner to a wheel. Loose lashings often mitigated the severity of the punishment somewhat.

This common form of army punishment in the field is known to the British "Tommy" as "crucifixion." It is more of a mental and moral punishment than a physical one, and hurts a great deal worse. Sometimes, however, it entails physical suffering as well, especially if the culprit has to stand out for two hours a day in weather that is miserably wet or cold.

"F. P. No. 1" also puts a black mark on the man's conduct-sheet. This means that promotion of any kind, which most men look for, will come very slowly, if ever, to him.

The scene that day set me to thinking. I had only been a few months with this squadron, but I wanted to get away. What a relief it would be to be transferred! I felt that my work there was handicapped by the personality and disposition of the C. O. Any change would be welcome. And, strange to say, something told me that a change was coming soon.

## Chapter 11

# Strafing a Hun "Sausage"

The gramophone in the mess was playing "Keep the Home Fires Burning." I had finished my patrol duty for the day, and was lounging around on a fine afternoon in June; smoking a cigarette and taking things easy after putting up my machine at the aerodrome, which I could see from the mess-room windows, about six hundred yards away. Then my comfort was rudely disturbed.

Rushing up the driveway to the *château* came an orderly, mounted on a motorcycle with a sidecar. This usually spelled trouble. When the sidecar came in that way, we knew that a pilot was wanted in a hurry, at the drome.

All the other boys were out on duty or sleeping in their bunks, and I was the only one in the mess. The orderly dashed up the steps, knocked at the door of the mess-room, opened it, and as he saluted said:

"Sir, the C. O. wants you on the drome at once!"

"Righto!" I responded, and emptying my glass I ran out to the sidecar. In a few minutes I was entering the C. O.'s office on the drome.

The major was seated at his desk and Lieut. H—— stood by. I saluted stiffly and stood waiting.

Turning round in his seat, the C. O. addressed us both.

"There's a Hun sausage (balloon) reported broken away from its moorings at Bapaume, and it's drifting north over our lines. It's just about to leave the sector below us, on our side. Want you to escort that, just as long as it stays on our side! If it drifts to the other side, destroy it! Hurry up now! Away you go! You'll probably pick it up a little south of Arras."

This sounded like a congenial operation—I don't think! Tooling around an old "sausage" is pretty monotonous work, especially if you are going to wait until it lands, or drifts to the other side of the line,—which happened to be our orders.

We took off together in our machines at once, flying straight south and climbing all the time, keeping our eyes peeled for the German sausage that had gone astray.

Now, picking up any special balloon on our side on a fine day is quite a job, especially if it is a "field day"—so called because all the balloons usually come out like flowers in the sun if the weather conditions allow it. It's a very weird sight to look down a 20-mile stretch of the line and see hundreds of balloons in the air all at once. They appear at almost regular intervals and are so placed that they follow the contour of the line; so that if the clouds were to cut you off from the ground and the balloons were to stay above the clouds, you would see almost a reproduction of the line of trenches below.

To pick out any one balloon, even a hostile one, out of such a mess of similar aircraft, was like trying to find a needle in the proverbial haystack. So we thought we had a real job cut out for us that afternoon.

Passing over a large town right on the line, we presently had the satisfaction, however, of spotting the Hun balloon, both by its peculiar sausage shape and because the stray was much higher than the others. We were then at an altitude of 8,000 feet.

I kept straight on for the sausage and eventually passed abreast of it. Lieut. H—— (we'll call him Harry) did likewise. We then throttled our engines down and made a closer inspection of the Hun. I ran quite close to him—within twenty yards—and noticed that the observer in the sausage had apparently attempted to jump out, but had caught his parachute in the rigging. So, abandoning the attempt, he had evidently climbed back into the basket.

Next I took particular notice of the observer, who was clad in a sort of black flying kit. Then I saw that he was frantically waving what I took to be a white handkerchief. He thought, I suppose, from our method of approach, that we were going to shoot him down.

We had our orders though, and for the present he was safe from us anyway; but this he did not realise, being a Hun. Orders would have made little difference in a case like this in the air, to any man who was a bit sporty and had a sense of fair play. No British pilot would have shot the man down under such circumstances, at that stage of his involuntary flight.

So not having any white handkerchief on me, I flew as close to the

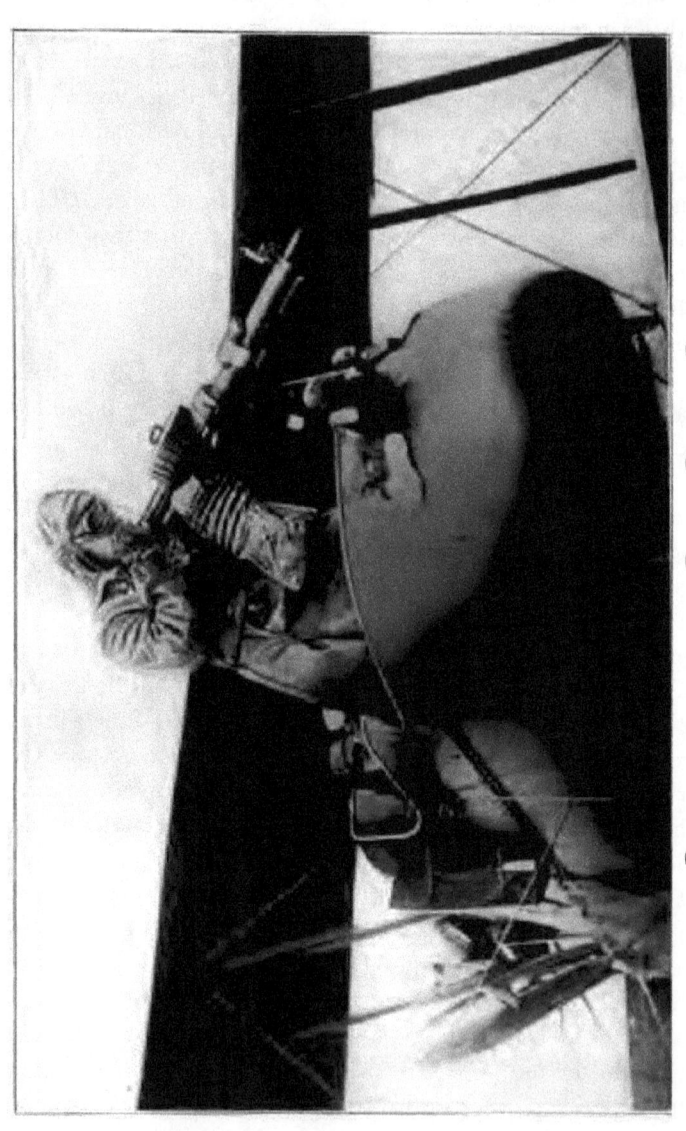

PILOT AND OBSERVER IN A BRITISH BOMBING PLANE.
The observer spotting his Lewis on a Hun.
This machine-gun is so pivoted that it can be fired at almost any angle above, below, or behind

balloon as I dared, the Hun now cowering in his basket, and intimated to him that I understood his signal, making my own signal with the white part of a map, which I waved at him.

As I passed the sausage I noticed that the observer was quite a young fellow, though I could see only a part of his face; also that he was in the act of tying his handkerchief in the rigging. A flag of truce! A surrender!

Then I turned and flew back again. Back and forth—keeping quite close to my captive. The Hun was evidently satisfied now that I was not going to fire on him, for he was busying himself with what I took to be important papers—maps, codes and notebooks. Information for the enemy!

What a wonderful feather in my cap it would be if I could get hold of those papers intact!

I contemplated the idea of changing my drum of ammunition, from "tracer" bullets to ordinary steel bullets, with which to puncture the envelope of his balloon sufficiently to let the gas out and bring him down on our side.

There had been a good breeze on the ground when we took off from the drome, but I had not noticed that the balloon was travelling fast to the north. I was hovering in the rear of the Hun, having taken note of all I could at close range, when I looked around for Harry. I had not observed, in my preoccupation, that he had already fired a green light, having a dud engine—and was going down. But when I spotted him I surmised what had happened, so kept on alone.

Flying at fairly high altitudes is a monotonous job sometimes, especially when there is nothing to occupy your mind in the shape of a hostile patrol that keeps you on the *qui vive*; or some interesting little "strafe" on the ground, which you cannot observe with any degree of accuracy, however, inasmuch as all you see is a few puffs of smoke and perhaps a little barrage now and then.

There being, as they say in the papers, "nothing of importance to report on the western front at this time," I was daydreaming up there and flying around automatically, with one eye on the balloon now and then, knowing I had a long trip ahead of me before that sausage started to descend.

Suddenly, rudely, I was aroused and startled! What had happened to the balloon? What I saw was beyond my understanding.

I looked, and looked harder! Yes, my eyes did not deceive me! There was the balloon, tied in the middle like a figure 8, and descending perceptibly, though not fast. Who or what could have twisted the envelope in that shape?

Now that observer, with his information, has a good chance to get away, I thought, if he happens to land on the Hun side of the line. The Hun side! What had happened flashed across me like a blaze of lightning. Now I could see it all!

Dozing as I must have been, I had not noticed that our own "Archie," usually a little unobservant, even as I had been, had not seen or realised that I was escorting the balloon. True, I had been a little too far behind. So seeing that Mr. Boche and his sausage were crossing the lines—for we had now reached and were almost in the act of crossing the famous Ypres salient—and not wishing Fritz to get away with a whole skin, our fellows on the ground had started "Archieing" him.

I saw that they had been firing diagonally up into the air, and that the balloon must be already in Hun territory. On his own side once more—and dropping with a whole skin!

That roused me to action. Get him I must, now!

At one time, earlier in my experience as a pilot, my finger had itched to pull that trigger on my gun at a Boche, no matter what his disposition might be toward me—whether he was flying a flag of truce or not! But I had conquered that feeling of personal enmity somewhat, and so had waited patiently for a fair opportunity at this particular Hun.

Call it chivalry of the air, if you like—it was still dormant in the most hardhearted of us.

But now there flashed up the thought of my loved ones that had gone; a vision immediately clouded by the sight of blood. I saw red! Surely no man could deny me the right to seek vengeance for what I had suffered and lost. God alone could say me nay and stay my hand.

Then, shutting off my engine, I dived at the balloon. Even as I went I realised that the poor devil was in my power, without an opportunity of any kind of defence. And he was flying a white flag!

But the thought of his defencelessness did not stay me. Somebody must pay! And how about those maps and observation notes? They must be destroyed.

Besides, it was legitimate for me to get him now, I reflected. Flag of truce or no flag of truce, he was on his own side now, and I could not capture him.

I fired a couple of shots, intimating to the Hun what to expect. He realised my meaning at once. Then, still diving straight at the far end of the big twisted gas-bag, I released a drum of tracer ammunition. Straight into the balloon the bullets sped, flame and all! But Archie—for it was he who had tied the sausage into a knot with a solid shell—had let out some of the gas from the envelope, so it did not catch fire readily.

Putting my engine on again, I sped past the balloon, nose still down, and did an "Immelmann" turn. This manoeuvre brought me out almost facing the spot from which I had fired before. Then I released the remainder of my drum, spraying my shots, and had the satisfaction of seeing a small blue flame spurt from the end of the envelope. This I knew would grow larger very quickly, but not quickly enough for me.

We were now getting quite close to the ground, having dropped to about 2,000 feet, and I realised that if the balloon didn't blaze up soon, he would get away! "Get away! I'll be d—d if he will! Not if I know it!"

Changing my spent drum for a fresh one filled with cartridges, and turning again, I looked around for hostile aircraft, for we were now fairly well on the Hun side of the line. There they were, several of them, floating around. Why they did not dive on me I do not know, but I presume there were some of our boys higher up, attending to that.

Diving once more, my object being to hit the Hun observer this time, I saw that he had produced a coil of rope from his basket, and then—seeing his balloon was on fire—he swung out on the rope into midair!

Down, down that rope he went, to the very end, getting as far away from the blazing envelope as he could. God, it did look perilous! Now he looked like a small pendulum, swaying back and forth! That Hun was brave, after all!

Then I noticed that he was carrying a small parcel with him. The papers, of course!

That was enough for me! I must get him! So, dashing down on top of him, I opened fire with tracer bullets. Suddenly I saw him let go! He was hit! Down, down he went, to an awful death.

Now my attention was attracted by the balloon. This was blazing merrily with blue flames from the gas, and emitting dense clouds of smoke. Then what was left of it dropped like a plummet behind the German lines.

While the final act of this little tragedy was being played, to make

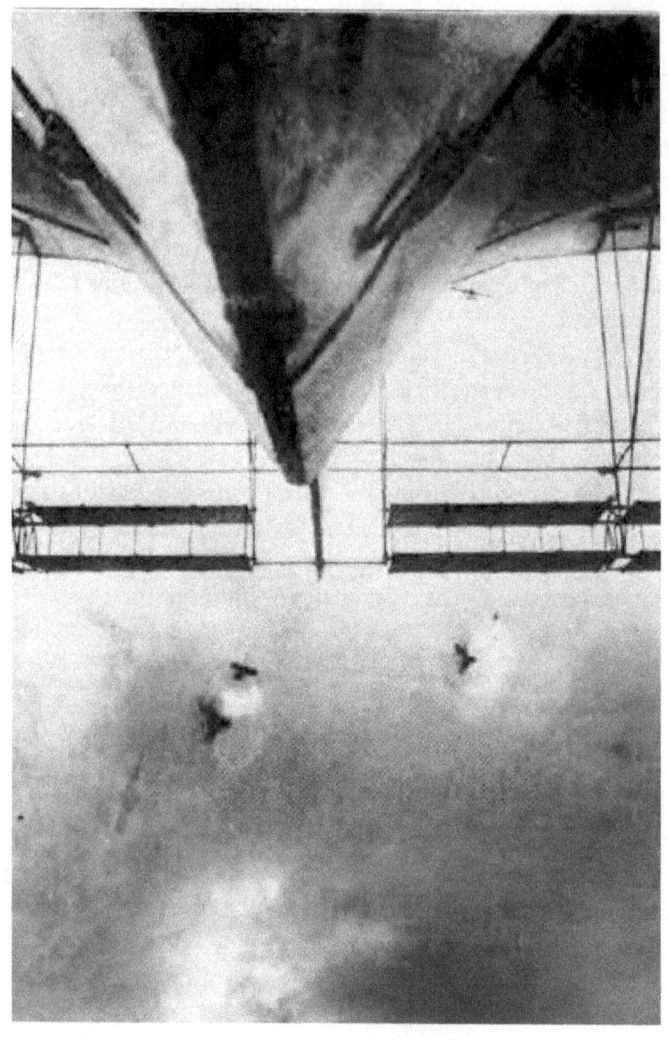

AIR BATTLE IN THE SKY
Photo showing battle in progress, and one of the planes pursuing the "Zepp" from which this was taken.

it more interesting for the spectators—and for me, the Hun "Archie" was strafing, and now the black bursts of gunfire came up with a vengeance. But they failed to reach me, and as my work was done I made a beeline for home, whooping and yelling in exultation as I crossed our lines once more.

Looking into our trenches as I passed over them, I saw the boys below, waving to me and cheering. It sure was good to live for that.

Arrived at the aerodrome, I put in my combat report, the C. O. glancing over my shoulder as I wrote. For once he was pleased. I was thinking of revising my sentiments toward that man,—when Brigade Headquarters rang up, "strafing" us like mad. There was the dickens to pay about my firing on that balloon! Then I was in for it! Instead of being pleased at what I had done, the C. O. gave me everything, word for word, as it came over the wire from the brigade. Gad, they were hot about it! The Hun had been flying a flag of truce, and I had fired on him! Shocking! What would be thought of us now?

I stood stiffly at attention and said nothing while the storm of criticism raged over me, leaving my combat report to speak for me and explain my action. Finally I spoke up:

"Is that all, sir?"

"Yes," he snapped. I saluted and withdrew.

Some time afterward I was told that through my procedure in strafing that balloon the way I did, the "chivalry of the air" was a thing unknown in our sector for several days. However, I thought, "War is war, *n'est-ce pas?*" As the American general said, it is indeed "hell."

Later that afternoon a touring car came up to the aerodrome, where I was standing by. When it pulled up a dapper little officer jumped out. He was neatly booted and breeched, and had the cut of a "regular." I thought I knew him and was not long in doubt, for seeing me he came up and the recognition was mutual.

"Why, hello, Campbell!" he broke out. "What are you doing here? Who'd ever have thought of seeing you again?"

Imagine my surprise to recognise him as C——, a lieutenant in the cavalry when I formerly knew him; now a full-blown major of the Flying Corps.

"Why, hello, Tommy!" I said. "Gad, I'm glad to see you. I beg your pardon, sir!" stiffening up and saluting, recollecting that I was talking to my superior officer.

"Oh, drop that, Campbell. That's all right on parade, but not here. You know that, with me!"

I had only saluted as a "rag," anyway, but you never can tell about some chaps after they are promoted. Dispositions have been known to change with that event.

"Who's the C. O. here?" he asked, and when I replied, "Major L——," he said:

"I've just dropped in on my way up from St. O——. Returning from leave, you know."

"Will you come down to the mess and have some tea?"

"That was my original intention in coming up here to the drome, you know. Jove, I had no lunch, now I come to think of it!"

Chatting briskly, we went down to the mess at the old *château*, where I introduced him to the rest of the boys off duty. We had tea, and in conversation I learned that he was shy a pilot in his squadron. A bright idea occurred to me. "Why not get a transfer?" Any other place would be more to my liking than this, to say the least. So I blurted out:

"Take me!"

"Do you want to come?" asked the major.

"Well, rather!" I replied. "If you think I'm good enough. I hear you've got a crack squadron."

"One of the best—the pet of the brigade!" said its commanding officer, proudly.

I felt elated at the idea of getting down to his squadron. Down to the Somme, where the real fighting was about to take place! For we had heard rumours of the coming offensive, and I was dying for a crack at it.

Then I thought of my present C. O. and my spirits fell. Would he let me go? I explained to my prospective commander that I would rather not mention the matter of a transfer to Major L——, and to my joy he made light of the difficulty.

"I'll look up Colonel H—— at the wing headquarters," he said. "I know I can get you all right."

This he did by wire that same afternoon, getting the necessary order for my transfer to his squadron. With feverish glee I packed my kit, which had finally arrived at the front from England some time before. My orderly dumped my luggage into Major C——'s car, for he had waited for me, and I left without even trying to say goodbye to the C. O., who was absent at A——, though I did not know it, at the time.

Then we set off for my new squadron, down on the Somme! I felt delighted, for a load had been lifted from my mind.

It was a beautiful trip, driving along the smooth French roads a few kilometres behind our lines. We chatted pleasantly along the way, and stopped for an enjoyable dinner at an estaminet in Frévant. Late in the evening we arrived at the —nd Squadron, of which my companion was the gallant C. O.

CHAPTER 12

# An Air Duel on the Somme

The mess of my new squadron was located in a small farmhouse, on one of the main roadways of France. On this road we could see thousands of men of all arms of the service, daily going to and from different positions on the fighting line. It was a little farther back than I had previously been.

I liked this place; it seemed so cheery and nice that it was quite a change from my last billet. The other pilots were congenial fellows and I got along well with them.

It was the most composite crowd of flyers I had seen. Almost every variety of English dialect was represented, from Anglo-Indian to Cockney, and the "bunch" even boasted of an American.

Most of these boys were real fighters, and I took to their society like a duck to water.

I was allotted to "B" flight, under Captain A——. He was a tall, light-complexioned Irish lad, full of sport and a regular soldier, but a strict disciplinarian. Such a leader was what I needed though. I knew it was said of me that if I had a man with a club to stand over me, I would do all right, but that left to myself I was careless and reckless. Probably they were right. So good leadership was invaluable to me.

Everything was well regulated in this squadron. There were no hitches of any kind. I was automatically given a billet the night I arrived, without any trouble on my part to find one. The mess was really wonderful, the food being very good, and altogether everything was "all to the merry."

One chap in particular attracted my attention and I soon acquired a decided liking for him. This pilot was no other than the son of a German baron. Let us call him "Snitz," because that was far from being his name. He was a regular sport and was liked by everybody. I found that he had been in the British Army for twelve years, and had been born in the Argentine Republic. Our liking was mutual, for "Snitz" also took a fancy to me, and many's the game of *vingt-et-un* we had together, and many the "little nip" we shared. Also many a little trip to Amiens we took together, so that we became greatly attached to each other. He was in my "flight."

Of the other two boys in "B" flight (five flyers form a flight) one was a Scotsman like myself and the other an Irishman. Rather a funny combination! Two Scots, two Irishmen, and one German! But one characteristic we had in common—we were fighters all. That I soon found out.

The *esprit-de-corps* in our squadron was something marvellous. To begin with, it had a very good reputation in the air service. Its average for bringing down Huns was very good. Then we had the best amateur dramatic company and had won the brigade handicap cup for football at the front. True, there were a few soreheads. We ran up against them now and then. But usually a quiet little confab, in which you made a good fellow of yourself, changed their minds and brought them into line with the rest of us.

Our aerodrome was a beauty! It was lovely and large and level. Being divided in two by the main roadway on which we lay, our squadron occupied one half of the drome and the Nth Squadron the other half, across the road from us.

Ours was a fighting-scout squadron, the other a bombing squadron. We flew a different type of machine from those I had been used to, and I found it better than my last. I also found a better type of equipment than we had up north, and I determined to help out as much as I could. A willing heart goes a long way in this direction.

Having been allotted a machine, I first flew around the aerodrome and the surrounding country—without any mishaps this time—and made myself familiar with the landmarks. Then, on the fourth day after joining, I was detailed for a "line patrol," the duties of which I have already described. After K——, my companion on this patrol, had given me a few minor instructions and tips, including his methods of signalling, we went up.

What a difference on this part of the line from that farther north! Everything was hustle and bustle behind, in feverish preparation for the coming "push."

I also noticed that there was a vast increase in the number of machines in flight, compared to my old front; and that we had a smaller sector to cover. But it was infinitely more hazardous. Our armies were just about to start the great offensive (which began July 1, 1916) and troops were being massed on both sides.

K—— and I were flying along at about 8,000 feet, when we suddenly noticed black and white "Archie" popping up on our side, and dashed in that direction, K—— leading and I following closely. As we neared the spot, we saw a Fokker biplane—and the Hun was tooling carelessly up and down inside our lines.

Now it doesn't matter how high you get, in dealing with a Fokker. It's perfectly marvellous how he always seems to get a bit higher. So as we went on, straight for that Hun, I finally discovered that he was about 1,500 feet higher than I was; a decided advantage for him. Still, I thought, "If only I can get the opportunity, I'll stick on this man's trail, and follow him into Germany. I want that machine!"

Just then K—— fired a Verey's light, a signal of engine trouble, and I saw him dive off towards home, leaving the Hun to me. Evidently this was the Hun's cue for an attack, for he immediately started diving on K——.

I saw this coming and anticipated the move to such an extent that I was "zooming" at him as he was diving on my comrade, who was practically helpless, with a crippled engine.

As a rule, a Fokker biplane is not a fighting machine, and the Hun's move rather surprised me, now being more or less of an old flyer. So I thought there must be a trick in it. Sure enough, there was!

Our "Archie" had now stopped firing, to avoid hitting us instead of the Hun. An upward glance showed me three more enemy machines "sitting on top." Then I wasted no time. K—— looked as if he was unable to help himself, so standing on my tail as I zoomed, I fired slightly in front of the oncoming Fokker, being then between K—— and the enemy. I hoped against hope that the Hun would run into my shots before I had to put my nose down to gain speed again. And luck was with me!

The next thing I saw was the Hun going into a spinning nose dive and drifting slightly over towards his own lines. K—— meanwhile was still going down, now spinning, now flattening out, and all the time getting to his own side of the line, the fight being directly over the trenches.

But this was no time to watch affairs below. There were the three Huns above, and I determined to fool them if I could. So no sooner had I raised my nose, after gaining some speed, than I looked over my shoulder, pretending not to see them, and gradually working over into Hunland, where I observed a heavy black cloud, a short distance away. This cloud was really my friend!

Clouds are of the greatest assistance to the war flyer at times. They enable you to dodge around on top of them and save yourself from getting "Archied." Or they may be used to ambush an unwary enemy that cannot see you and passes below.

This was my reason for getting near that cloud, although it was in Hunland and my orders were for "line patrol," which means, in effect, "keep on your own side of the line." But I had "urgent private affairs" that way, as we say in the army. And I needed that cloud in my business, so to speak.

Just as I was pulling into the cloud, down dashed the three Hun machines, straight for me. Even then I pretended not to see them, and keeping on the edge of the cloud, I waited for shots to be fired. Then, suddenly doing an "Immelmann turn" into the cloud, and going out of sight for awhile, I kept on turning and dashed out again—just in time to meet the last machine coming on, the other two having passed.

Training the nose of my machine straight at him, both coming head on, I held on till the last minute, trusting that he would "break" before I did. On, on, nearer and nearer, in less time than it takes to tell it—then, "*crack-a-crack-crack!*" I opened fire.

A direct hit, smashing his "prop," as we usually called it; that is, his propeller!

Still I fired! Then, suddenly the most wonderful of all things, it seemed to me, happened. His left wing seemed to collapse, almost at the identical moment that my gun jammed!

Had this occurred a few seconds before, I should have been helpless. As it was—well, I didn't wait to see him go down to death, for at any moment I might have the whole performance to go through again, and without a machine gun it would be most uncomfortable for me.

Let me say here, by the way, that exceptional "scraps" of this kind are the only ones that it is possible for a flyer to describe in detail. Most of the combats in the air are of only a few seconds' duration. The action is so rapid, and the pilot-fighter so engrossed in his work that he has no time to observe the order of details. This particular duel in the air, however, and its features are stamped indelibly in my memory.

Mind you, I do not want to give the impression that I was the only one in the sky at that time. By no means! There were literally hundreds flying around that day, not far away, but most of them were in formations. Hardly any others, so far as I could see, were "on their own," and those that were flying alone were mostly decoys, protected by formation patrols on top.

Now I dashed back to my own lines. On the way I managed to extricate the faulty cartridge from my gun, and finding a fresh drum I felt like going back to seek the other two Huns. But I knew Hun tactics by this time. Once they missed their object, after diving to attack, they did not come back, but usually dashed off with their noses down, going east—that is, home.

The Hun is no sport in this respect, except an occasional one, who will put up a fight and a very good one; though sometimes not "according to Hoyle," or even Marquis of Queensberry rules. But we know the Hun now—what he is and what he is made of—and fair fighting or foul, we shall get the best of him in the long run. For even Von Hindenburg is reported to have said:

> Our armies will win the battles, but the Allies will win the war.

CHAPTER 13

# The Battle that Blinded the Boche

It was splendid flying weather in France, just before the great Allied offensive of July, 1916, on the Somme. This greatly facilitated patrol flights and observation work over the lines.

France is beautiful in summer anyway, though we found the heat intense during the last days of June and the first of July, the period of the greatest air battles of history up to that time. It was up to us of the air service to prepare for the "big push" by blinding the "eyes" of the Boche, if we could. His observers must be driven from the air.

We knew that we had our work cut out for us, because at the outset we were getting pretty well outnumbered in the air, and air supremacy meant much to the boys of the army in general. But all of our pilots kept a stiff upper lip, said little or nothing, and looked forward keenly to our coming engagements. There was a little uncertainty about everything, and this was far from cheering, because it looked for awhile as if we were about to make a last stand against the enemy.

Up to this time our squadron had been fairly lucky, having lost only three missing and two killed of the combatant quota, that is, the pilots. But we knew our time was coming, for stern work was ahead of us. We felt it in the air.

Consequently, the morning our first important orders were received, they sounded like our death knell. We were to go up and face heavy odds, because the Huns were out in force.

When I say "heavy odds" I mean it absolutely. The inherent desire of the Boche to fight in massed formations on the ground had made itself felt in the air. The enemy filled the air.

Now, instead of our ordinary flight patrols, of five machines, it was a case of using whole squadrons to match the Hun formations or at least come somewhere near equal terms with his quota. This was very difficult for us to do then. However, we had the advantage of a good machine for our work, and that was something.

On the morning of June 28, then, we proceeded out with grim determination to dear the air of the Hun. We also wanted to maintain the prestige which the Flying Corps had secured in its infancy, when it was outnumbered and battered about, in the early days of the war. Our squadron and each of us as individuals had this prestige to maintain.

Having left the drome and rendezvoused high over a very prominent landmark, then known as Bootleg Wood, from its shape, we met two other squadrons of fighting patrol. Altogether we numbered between 50 and 60 machines, this being a very heavy fighting patrol for those days.

Our orders were to advance at several different altitudes and sweep everything before us, maintaining this formation throughout the duration of our "trick" in the air. It looked very easy to me, with this number of machines. Nothing in the air can stand against us, I thought, but I was soon to find out that such was not the case.

Crossing the line like so many swarms of bees, at heights ranging from 8,000 to 18,000 feet, we started our campaign of clearing up. It was between 6 and 7 o'clock in the morning, and at first our flight did not offer any excitement, Fritz not appearing in the sky at that hour.

Looking down on crossing the line, I noticed very heavy barrage fire in progress, and spotted several of our contact and reconnaissance planes busily engaged in dealing out destruction to the enemy, through the medium of our batteries, which they were directing.

Although we had three squadrons flying in a formation, the understanding was that if the formation was split up, each squadron could in that event act independently of the others.

I had got quite casual with "Archie" by this time and treated it lightly as a rule, but presently I noticed it coming up furiously. Then, high up in the heavens and away to our right, looking south, I espied an enormous formation of aeroplanes, making directly for a spot which I knew would be of decided advantage for an attack on us. Large as I had thought our own formation that morning, this oncoming lot was much larger, and looked formidable indeed.

Picking out one of the approaching machines, I tried to make out its silhouette, to see if I could recognise it; but found this impossible, as they were travelling in such a manner as to obscure them, getting between us and the sun. But I judged them to be Huns.

Huns they were and with a vengeance, outnumbering us by at least two to one. Now we were in for it!

The storm broke before there was much time to think. Down swooped the enemy at us, firing a fusillade of shots and keeping straight on.

Almost immediately several of my comrades went dropping toward the earth, one in flames and others disabled, spinning downward. What should I do? It seemed impossible to decide what was best.

Like an avalanche they came, and I have a very hazy recollection of what really occurred in this fight, except that all seemed chaos and disorder. The attack came so quickly that a thought even struck me that it could not possibly be the Huns I had seen above, so quickly had they dived.

But the sight of one of our planes collapsing in midair, directly in front and a little to my right, spurred me to action. With a quick glance at my machine-gun, to see that all was in order, and looking at my outstruts, to see that my rockets would be ready for firing, I put my nose down with the intention of running under three Huns that I could now see diving at me. Then doing an "Immelmann," or a sharp turn—whichever seemed best at the time—the Boche, I reckoned, shooting past me, I would turn and come up under him behind.

This feat proved successful, inasmuch as I was aided by a comrade, who anticipated what I was trying to do. This, I afterwards found, was my friend "Snitz." I saw a volley of rockets, six in all, released from his machine. Two of the Huns, catching the full force of the delivery, caught fire.

The other man, being thrown into disorder, did a wild "hoick" or "zoom," to avoid crashing head-on into "Snitz," who held to his course. But the Hun crashed full into one of his own machines, that was diving by at the moment, and the result was a most marvellous spectacle. Two Hun machines splintering as they telescoped into each other, the wings falling off one, and both dropping rapidly to Mother Earth, twisting and turning every conceivable way.

I could almost imagine them catching up with the other two Huns who were going down ablaze just ahead of them, thus making a quartet to add to the family of their friend, the devil.

But I had to act pretty lively now, to avoid colliding with "Snitz," who still held on.

Our formation had broken up considerably by this time, and for the next ten minutes or so there was nothing but chaos. (They say this battle in the air lasted for twenty minutes in all, which seems an age in such encounters.)

All this time you were diving constantly on one enemy after another, only to be dived upon in return. Firing as many shots as you possibly could at one man, you would turn, at the risk of colliding with someone else, and attack the man coming up in your rear. No one seemed to fight single-handed with any other machine. By the time you had picked out an enemy and fired at him, someone else was doing the same thing, with the result that hardly a machine actually dived upon and fired at survived the ordeal.

We were dropping lower and lower all the while, diving and rediving, now this way, now that; side-slipping, zooming, or doing a stiff "bank" to avoid someone in front—if it happened to be one of your own. Always keeping your eye peeled for the black cross of the Hun machines, it seemed to crop up in every position where you least expected it; sometimes from on top, sometimes from the rear, and then again from beneath. You had to be all eyes—and then could not see half enough, or even be sure of what you thought you saw.

At length, turning sharply to my left and following our patrol, part of which, reassembled, I had caught up with, I glanced below. Five of the Huns I saw, going like the very devil, back to their own lines!

Then, looking above and slightly to my rear, I spotted the same old machine that had helped me out before. Now for those Huns below.

Trusting to luck, but feeling that I could not survive that hell in midair much longer, I shut off my engine, throwing my machine over in a "stall" to the rear, and snapping down like a whip, straight at the batch of five retreating Boches. Fondly I hoped that my friend would follow, for the patrols being disorganised, we could now fight independently.

I looked at the enemy. Three of them were of the Albatross type and single-seaters. The other two were Aviatiks, that is, double-seaters, with an observer firing to the rear and up. A pretty mess, I thought.

Still, clinching my teeth, I kept on, and as I drew within the 100-yard range of them, fired my aerial rockets, with the intention of setting them on fire if I could, or at least putting them out a bit.

Away sped my six rockets! Two of them hit an Aviatik, as the observer was in the act of firing up at me. Then I had to turn my attention to an Albatross, which had turned to attack me.

Nosing my machine down a little more, straight at this Albatross, I let loose the whole works, and discharged my gun. He tipped over sidewise, and simultaneously caught fire, a tracer bullet having hit his tank!

Hearing machine guns behind me now, and very plainly, I flattened out a bit, and turning slightly observed the same old friendly machine diving straight at the second Aviatik. Then—*zowie!* He got him.

The other two Albatross machines waited no longer. One of them went into a spin, the other dived like a plummet. I decided to follow, so "stalling" once more, I took an extra long shot and released the remainder of my drum of tracer ammunition. Then, having the bad luck to get a jam in my gun, I flattened out and made straight for our own lines. The battle, of course, had occurred well into Hun territory.

Now looking below, I saw several of our machines flying around as if looking for more of it—dashing madly up and down, back and forth. These I joined, with the friendly machine, which had stuck by me. Good old "Snitz"! As I went I succeeded in extracting the cartridge that had jammed my gun, and loaded and cocked the gun again, ready for action once more.

Tooling up and down with the party I had now joined, I saw another formation above.

This we climbed up to and joined, reinforcing the formation. We were now at about 10,000 feet altitude, with black Archie banging away at us merrily from the enemy lines.

But where were the Huns? Yes, where were they?

They had had as sound a drubbing as ever they got, and there was not a Hun to be seen in the air. Cleared out of the sky! We had won the battle, but at what a cost!

Our losses in the Corps that day were very heavy. Including reconnaissance and fighting machines, they amounted to 64. The Hun official report sounded more like 164, but the Hun has a habit of saying things just to keep up the spirits of the people at home.

Our report for the day in the corps showed that we had brought down over thirty of the enemy, most of them within his own lines. Our losses were heavy, no doubt, but we had fought against great odds and we maintained the field, which the Huns had abandoned to us. Some of our boys, too, had gone down through engine failure—not shot down—and falling in Hunland, were reported "missing," thus increasing our casualty list for the day.

Those who think that the Hun has a superiority in the air because he sometimes brings down more machines than we do in a given time, should learn the truth. The reason why we lose pilots is because we are constantly flying over enemy territory, and are constantly on the offensive, thus poking out the enemy's "eyes" and depriving his artillery of invaluable direction. Then again, our policy of "stand and fight" contributes to the casualty list, while the Hun policy, "attack once and run," often saves the blighter's bacon. Anti-aircraft fire ("Archie," as we usually call it), hostile aircraft, faulty machines, "dud" engines, and above all, the fact that we fight in Hun territory, all help to make our losses at times heavier than those of the Boche. While he, on the other hand, never takes a chance unless he is absolutely driven to it.

We returned to the aerodrome after the battle, saddened by the loss of comrades. Comparing notes in the mess that night, we found that among others poor old Cox and Appleby had pegged out that day; Hunter had gone down in Hunland, and Falconer had been wounded very badly. Major Colby had not yet returned, but one of the boys thought he had seen him land at another drome, so he was probably all right.

But we had cleared the air, and it did feel good in spite of our grief over fallen friends, to know that we had won—and won decisively. How much better it will feel when we win the war—and win it decisively!

The effects of the great aerial battle of June 28 were soon observed on the ground. The enemy—his eyes poked out—knew he would be helpless, and for the first three days of the great Somme offensive, the fighting in the air was sharp, stiff, and hot. Aerial supremacy we must have; and win it we did at last. For ten solid days, while the big push was on, we knocked the devil out of the Hun, both in the sky and on the ground. In the air we decided it for good and all. The Hun's courage and morale were shattered. This we found out later.

Those nine days after our first big battle in the sky, I shall never forget. When the great offensive began, it was particularly interesting to watch the operations from above. We could see our line gradually creeping eastward a few kilos from Albert, then stretching and widening and stretching again; so that when the push came to an end and the line was established for the winter, the gains formed a huge salient. This new line stretched from Peronne on the south, northward to Le Transloy, thence around north and to the west, passing Le Sarr and Miramont, and ending around Beaumont-Hamel. It looked from the air just what it was—a tremendous bite taken out of the enemy terrain.

This salient was a decided advantage to us in the air, for later on our favourite method of attack was to go into the salient as far as possible, cross the line at Le Transloy, go north and east around Bapaume and Cambrai, and then make a beeline due west, thus cutting off any offensive Huns that were hovering around Beaumont-Hamel, which was a particularly sore spot with them.

## Chapter 14

# The Major's "Field Day"

One fine day our major called us all together, and when every available pilot of the squadron was within hearing he said:

"Boys, I think we'll have a field day today."

I have already explained what we called a "field day." It was a day when the weather was particularly fine for aircraft, when all the observation balloons would be up, and lots of Huns might be expected to try crossing the line, to "spy out the land." Hence a day for the Flying Corps to make a clean-up if it could, or at any rate get a good big bag of Huns to its credit for the day. That was the sort of day we liked. It usually meant trouble, but we looked on that kind of trouble as a great lark if the sport was good.

The major having suggested it, he himself accordingly went out that morning, with several others of us. We found little to interest us above, however, so our "field day" soon became a mere line patrol; and while tooling up and down the line I saw all the others drop out and go home, leaving only a pilot named Simcoe and myself with the major.

Presently I sought diversion by diving on a Hun trench and strafing it with machine-gunfire, leaving the other two to their line patrol. For when there was nothing special to do in the sky, we found it really enjoyable to go "contour-chasing" over Hun territory, firing at trenches and raising Cain generally. Such a performance on our part often caused them to shoot up at us what we called "flaming onions." These things are a sort of rocket affair that will go to a height of about 6,000 feet. Each has a lot of hooks attached to it in such fashion that if they catch on your planes, they stick there, and the flaming missile sets your machine on fire.

Having "strafed" enough to suit me for a while, I looked for the major and Simcoe, but they were nowhere to be seen. I was now flying over Mouquet Farm, or "Mucky Farm," as our Tommies called it. Looking away south, I thought I discerned the major and his companion, but also saw something that opened my eyes pretty wide.

What I saw was a "formation" of at least twenty Huns. I spotted them by the silhouettes of several of their machines and by their mannerisms and manoeuvring. These can be recognised by an experienced pilot, because a pilot who has survived several scraps gets to be a wise old bird, just like an old duck that has been hunted for several seasons and shot at by hunters until he decides that it is safer to stay close to the ground than to rise.

These Huns up there "on top" certainly made me sit up and take notice. After clearing the air at the beginning of the great push, we had become somewhat slack in our patrols, while the push was on, for the enemy had made himself scarce in the air. But here was the Hun, out again!

Now I could see several small machines floating about, high in the heavens. Two I spotted as being of my own squadron. The major and Simcoe, I thought!

Like a bolt from high heaven, just as I looked, a most wonderful thing happened. One of our two machines led off by diving to attack the Huns, the other following closely. Can you realise what that meant, against such odds? The enemy had twenty machines to our two. The odds were ten to one against us! But that was the Allied flyer all over.

Now I climbed like mad towards them, my eyes glued on what was taking place. Even before the manoeuvre of the diving machines was finished, first one, then two of the Huns, totally unprepared for the attack of two small fighting machines against their twenty, paid the toll and came crashing down from a height of close on to 15,000 feet. They passed me on their way down, and I saw they were done for!

Still I climbed and watched, first our two little machines and then the remaining Huns, who were now in disorder. Each of them seemed to be getting in the others' line of fire.

"Go it, old boy!" I thought, as I watched the fight. "That's something worthwhile! And it takes a bit of nerve to do, too!"

So interested was I in our leading machine, dodging and dashing about the enemy, that I did not at first notice the other, which now came tumbling down in a violent and erratic manner, first spinning, then falling. "Poor devil!" Which was it, though,—Simcoe or the ma-

FIGHTING SCOUT MACHINE

Note the Lewis gun mounted on the top plane, showing drum of ammunition and the convenient position for use of the fighting scout pilot seated in the cockpit.

jor? I could not make out for sure at the moment, but soon found that it was Simcoe who had been downed.

This spurred me on. I must get there now, to help out the major, if only I could!

Climbing like mad, I hurried my utmost. Then came the satisfaction of seeing two more Huns falling past me, one in flames, the other spinning!

"Marvellous! Marvellous!" Four Huns accounted for—and still the major was up! It looked like madness for him to keep on. In and out he dashed, still in the centre of the enemy, so masking their fire that they could not return his without hitting their fellows. Could his luck possibly last much longer?

Then down he came, spinning and twisting!

"God! He's hit!" burst from me—and then I saw that he had flattened out and poked his nose up once more.

"No! Only a ruse!" And the ruse was successful, for once more a Hun paid with his life.

Nearer and nearer I climbed, and could now see that the pilot of the machine fighting against such terrible odds was indeed the major. There was the streamer on his tail!

Now he was flying merrily around as if nothing at all had happened. I tried to cut in, when once more up went his nose at the nearest Hun, on a "zoom." There was a flash of tracer bullets through the air, and a big black cloud of smoke was the result.

"Another one!" I gasped. "Six!"

The thing was almost too marvellous to believe. But there it was, and I could imagine the eyes, of the whole sector riveted on that wonderful combat. I myself could do nothing but gape.

Again the major tried the trick of shooting up from below, but unsuccessful this time, he still carried on by putting his nose down and doing a very stiff turn, coming out in front of the foremost Hun. For this he paid—and dearly, too!

Like a flash one of them was on him, and I could see the spurt of flame from the Hun's machine gun. His plane wobbled, side-slipped and fell over on its wing-tip. But he steadied himself and turned straight at the oncoming machine, which was still firing.

Then there was a short, sharp burst of fire and the major accounted for his seventh Hun, setting him ablaze!

This was too much for the rest of the Huns, By this time they were completely demoralised. I did my best to catch up, but to no avail. The enemy put their noses down, and made straight off home.

Seeing the major coming for our own lines, I followed, "sitting on his tail." Then, flying closer with the intention of giving him a cheer, I noticed him bending forward in the cockpit, taking no notice of me. I immediately suspected that he was wounded.

Keeping straight on, we soon sighted the drome. I saw there was one machine piled up on the drome already, so waited above, to give the major an opportunity to land before I came down.

He hit the ground and stayed there, right in the middle of the drome. The mechanics ran out, as they always do, to start up the propeller in the event of one stopping before the machine is taxied to its hangar. Then I came down, and saw what followed.

The major was unconscious. They had to pick him out of the machine and carry him into one of the hangars. To the pilots who gathered around I hastily related what had happened, telling the wonderful story of the scrap as well as I could, and filling them with amazement at the major's remarkable work.

Presently a Red Cross ambulance drove up and he was hurried off in it to a dressing station. Later we learned that he had been shot through the right thigh, the bones of the thigh being shattered. He explained that he had had to steer his machine by pushing the lower part of his shattered leg with his hand against the rudder-bar. That, then, I knew, was why I saw him leaning over in the cockpit! Truly, he was a wonderful chap—and as unassuming as he was brave.

That was the last we saw of the major at the aerodrome. But he recovered, and later, reading General Orders, we learned that the "V. C." had been conferred on him for his most valorous deed.

Surely no man was ever more deserving of the Victoria Cross, with its simple but significant inscription—"For Valour."

We also found out later that poor old Simcoe had cashed in. Poor fellow, he, too, was a brave one.

Every day during the big push there seemed to be a new face opposite you in the mess. You could easily tell why. Poor old So-and-So had gone and the stranger had come to fill the gap. This had a very sobering effect on us. You could not help wondering, "When am I going to get it? When will my turn come?"

CHAPTER 14

# Wounded Again—"Napoo!"

Every day now I felt a premonition that I could not go on much longer. Struggle as I might against this feeling, it persisted. Soon it must be "*Napoo*" for me, in the phrase commonly used by our boys to signify the end or finish of anything; the same being the army corruption of the French "*ne plus*," meaning "no more."

Our squadron had been very sorely knocked about and needed reinforcements—only a few of the original twenty pilots being left—when orders came through from wing headquarters that the squadron was to "go into rest," after moving to a new aerodrome.

I had now been on the front quite a while as a fighting scout, and during the period of my service had had three separate "leaves" to England. Every two months it was customary to give the fighting scouts seven days' leave, and such periods of rest from the duties of flying patrol were not only welcome but necessary.

The day our moving orders came, several of us were given leave for England, and I was among the lucky lot. Leaving my kit and personal effects in charge of one of the boys who were staying behind, I joyously bounded off for "Blighty," which, as all the world knows by this time, is the British soldier's favourite name for the tight little island where they keep the home fires burning for him.

This was my fourth leave since joining the Flying Corps at the front, and I had spent all of them most enjoyably in London. Each time, after seven days, I had been glad to get back to the squadron for a rest. This may sound queer, but it is true nevertheless. The laddie who returns from the front is allowed a lot of privileges "at home" and is entertained very freely everywhere; so much so, indeed, that a week of it is about all he can stand at one time, and the old routine of duty was usually welcomed by all of us when our leave expired.

Most of the boys of the squadron spent their leave in London, especially those who felt that there was a good time coming to them, by way of making up for the pleasures they had missed at the front. I well remember how I used to come back from the Colonies and try to squash into two or three weeks in London all the good times I had lost while absent from the big city. It seemed good to get back, therefore, on my fourth leave, though I knew I should be mighty glad to return to duty.

When you go back to the front, after enjoying the hospitalities of home, you feel like repaying in your own little way all that your country and people have done to make your life happy. What if you should lose your life in the effort? After all, you owe your life to your country, and no matter what comes, there is a glorious satisfaction in serving it.

While on leave in London I witnessed one of the Hun bomb raids. These raids, to the English mind, are nothing serious; in fact, they have proved a great stimulus to recruiting and an incentive to revenge. The British fighting man likes a fair fight, and when the miserable Hun tries to strike at the heart of the nation through the medium of its women and children, it only tends to incite the Briton to seek vengeance.

To show how lightly the British nation regards the matter of a small bomb raid, you have only to see how crowded the streets of London are today with provincials, that is, people up from the counties or provinces. They are there for the express purpose of witnessing a bomb raid if they can. Things like these raids are of small importance to the British heart. They do not frighten; they only create a desire for reprisals in one form or another, and a firmer determination to win the war. The bulldog tenacity of purpose inherited from his forefathers still characterizes the Briton, but despite all the Hun atrocities of the present war the great lion-heart of the British public cries out for a fair fight.

On my return to the Squadron, I found it had moved up nearer to the new line established by the "big push" of the previous summer. Our new drome was within a kilometre of the old line, and six or seven kilometres behind the new front. In fact, we were right in the artillery lines, being one of the nearest Flying Corps squadrons to the trenches.

It was just before the Battle of Beaumont-Hamel when I returned from leave, and the prospect of another Allied push was apparent. Everything was being moved up. Batteries were being pushed forward, and new trenches and dugouts were being prepared.

The scene from the air was greatly changed. One peculiarity was that if you looked over into Hunland from an aeroplane, things were so dug in and camouflaged that it was very difficult to observe what was taking place. Looking back at our own lines, on the other hand, it was easy to distinguish batteries, billets, troops, and a nondescript lot of other things, all spread out on the ground with little or no attempt at concealment. This was largely due to our newly-won supremacy in the air. It was remarkable what faith the millions of Allied troops on the ground placed in us, even to the point of thus permitting themselves to remain visible from the air.

My new quarters were anything but pleasant for the first few days, as we had taken over some disused "horse lines," and were sleeping in bell tents. The weather was coming on pretty cold and it was beginning to rain once more. The troops had begun to dig themselves in, establishing the lines for the winter.

Presently our "barrel huts" arrived and we were made more comfortable. These huts in shape resembled a barrel cut longitudinally from end to end and placed with the flat side on the ground, or like the arch of a stone bridge.

Then our life was made miserable for a time by the establishment of several ammunition "dumps" in our neighbourhood. The Hun was particularly anxious to get these, so his shells began to land promiscuously all around us, making our position very uncomfortable indeed.

There being no shellproof dugouts in the near vicinity, I proceeded to make arrangements for one for myself; finding an ideal spot for the purpose in a ravine that ran within a few yards of my hut. The work was done by several German prisoners, whom I obtained from a "cage" situated a few hundred yards from our drome.

This cage was an enclosure surrounded by high barbed-wire entanglements, and a considerable number of German prisoners were kept there for the purpose of filling in shell-holes on the drome and nearby roads, as soon as they were made by the enemy's fire. Holes on the drome had to be filled up promptly, as they made it difficult for our machines to take off.

The prisoners made me an excellent little dugout in the side of the ravine and finished it in one day. Next day I moved in. It was about ten feet square and had a lovely little fireplace in the wall, the whole thing being excavated in solid chalk, such as we used for filling holes in the drome and roads. Altogether I was very comfortable in my little burrow. But I did not occupy it long. My "*Napoo*" was soon to come!

I was now in command of a "flight" of aeroplanes and had been on patrol in the air daily since rejoining the Squadron. One morning, a few days after my dugout was completed, the barrage fire of the guns, which we could hear incessantly now, having started, I was detailed for offensive patrol. The Hun had not been very busy in the air for some time, having been battered about quite a lot, but, as I soon learned to my cost, even a worm will turn sometimes.

Arriving on the line, I was patrolling about, at a height of approximately 12,000 feet, keeping a sharp lookout for hostile aircraft. I was taking advantage of the outline of the trenches below me, and of the wind, which was blowing northward; so by travelling southeast I went into the wind and into the deepest part of the new salient.

My intention was to cross the line at Le Transloy and work northward down wind, thereby getting the added speed of the wind and so baffling "Archie." At the same time, should there be any Huns to the north and west of me, they would have to pass me or else get cut off from their own lines. With this in view I acted accordingly.

While travelling southeast, the sun being up, I observed several Allied planes flying about in front of me, on my right. Paying no more attention to them, I had crossed Le Transloy and was thinking of turning northward, when I espied two more planes. From their silhouettes they looked to me like Allied planes coming towards me, and I thought they were returning from a patrol.

I watched them a minute longer, then saw they were making dead up into the sun, which would be a position very disadvantageous to me should they prove to be Huns.

Paying no more attention to them, however, thinking they were Allies, I turned northward and westward, away from the sun, when suddenly I heard the snap and rattle of a machine gun. Sure enough, I was attacked!

The next thing I knew, my watch disappeared from the dashboard, having been hit by a bullet. The Hun was attacking from the top and rear. Immediately I turned sharply, or did an "Immelmann turn." Then the truth flashed upon me! The two machines I had observed just before were not Allies after all, but Huns. What was worse, they had so fooled me as to get into an advantageous position, between me and the sun, thus blinding me. Imagine my discomfiture—and my plight!

Blindly I held on my course, striving in vain to see my enemy, who was now in the direct orbit of light, or the dead glare of the sun.

Then, as I was pulling my machine over a bit more to the right, with the intention of getting around for a side look at the Hun, without looking into the sun, I felt a sharp twinge of pain in the back of my head, and thought I was hit there.

At the same instant a Hun machine shot past me, and I saw one of my flight open fire on him, I was still turning, now intending to dive at that Hun, when I saw him collapse in midair, his wings crumpling up. Then he dropped rapidly—a very gratifying sight to me!

My patrol had been disorganised by the sudden attack of the enemy, but now assembled once more. While congratulating myself that we had sustained no damage, I grew very faint and had a heavy choking sensation. I wanted to take a deep breath, but found that I couldn't. In fact, I had the greatest difficulty in breathing at all. Then, to add to my horror, I discovered I was spitting blood. I had a haemorrhage—and I was between 10,000 and 12,000 feet up!

Automatically picking out a green light, I fired it and left the patrol. Everything seemed to be growing very black and dim, and a dead heavy sensation was bothering me in the right side of my chest.

I don't remember much of what occurred after that, except that I crossed the line and saw the ground coming closer and closer.

After that, all was oblivion!

It was my "*Napoo!*"

A German Fokker (Monoplane)

The photo was taken from another machine flying behind it. Note the peculiar construction of the under-carriage. This is very noticeable and immediately pronounces it to be of German origin.

Chapter 16

# The Song from a Stretcher

How I landed after receiving my wound I do not know! I had fainted on nearing the ground, but came down behind our own lines.

When I woke up and looked around, it soon became evident that I was in good hands. The atmosphere of the place told me, from previous experience, that I was once more in a hospital cot bed. I saw that I was in a marquee tent, one on the order of a field hospital. Then a spasm of coughing seized me, and the miserable sensation of blood rising in my throat almost strangled me. This brought a Red Cross orderly to my side.

He attended to my immediate needs, and a white-dad nurse very tenderly gave me something to drink. When I could speak, I asked her, "Where am I?" being curious to know my whereabouts.

"That's all right now! Be quiet and go to sleep!" said the nurse, turning to attend to someone else, but glancing back at me the while.

I winked at the orderly, who came to my side once more. Knowing something of the wiles of hospital life, I felt that if I made friends with him, I should probably get the information I wanted. On drawing near, he bent down and whispered: What is it, sir?" Have you got a cigarette?" I asked faintly.

"I don't think you can smoke, sir," he replied.

"That's all right," I said. "One won't hurt me. I must have a cigarette."

He went away, presently coming back with a "gasper," which he placed between my lips and lighted.

If there is one thing the British soldier craves for and that gives him the utmost consolation in any sort of misery or suspense, it is a "gasper," *alias* a "fag," as a cigarette is commonly called in the army.

Drawing in the smoke with a sigh of satisfaction, I once more tinned to the orderly, and managed to get out the words:

"Perhaps you can tell me where I am?"

Knowing that I probably would not rest till I found this out, the man droned out, all in one breath, as if he had repeated it dozens of times before:

"You've in a dressing station—London Women's Auxiliary Hospital unit, field dressing station, at Forceville.—Now go to sleep sir."

I tried to turn over on my side, and was rewarded for my effort by a sharp twinge of pain. So being satisfied to stay the way I was, I kept on smoking till presently I knew no more. I think I must have fallen asleep with that "gasper" in my mouth.

When I awoke I felt that I was moving, and automatically reached for the cigarette, thinking I had just dozed. Disappointed at not finding it, I knew right away, it being dark, that I was in a Red Cross ambulance.

This time, luckily, it was a good ambulance. My experience of the last one I had ridden in, after being wounded at Neuve Chapelle in the early days of the war, was anything but pleasant.

Soon the car stopped. I hung my head over the side of my stretcher and saw the dark form of an orderly at the door. He called out:

"All right in here?"

Three voices answered out of the darkness: "Yes, quite all right."

Then I heard the drawl of one man distinctly: "I say! Have you got a fag?" Just what I wanted myself, consequently I was all eyes and ears, and clamoured out: "Yes, for God's sake, get me one too!"

The orderly produced cigarettes from somewhere, and said:

"Will I light it, sir?"

"Yes, if you don't mind," I blurted out, while the drawling voice said: "I can do that, I think."

Handing me my cigarette, lighted, the orderly disappeared.

I was on the top stretcher of the ambulance, and looking across to see who was my next-door neighbour, I could see nothing but blankness. But the chap who had asked for the cigarette, whom I could not see, was a particularly cheery devil. He kept up a constant little song, interluded now and then with an "Ouch!" or a "Damn!" as a sharp twinge of pain caught him, I suppose.

All along the way he sang, in low tones, but cheerily, the words of his ditty running something like this:

*Oh, a nice little duck and a lot of green peas,*

*A bottle of wine and some Stilton cheese.*

Ending with the refrain:

*Another little drink wouldn't do us any harm!*

It sounded good to me. The song, I knew, was one of a favourite comedian's ditties, in a show popular in London at that time.

I am not ashamed to admit that I agreed with the sentiment of his refrain, I was parched! So, yelling in the darkness as best I could while the ambulance rattled along, and thinking the man across the way would respond, I called out:

"I say, old fellow, have you got a water-bottle of any kind on you, with anything in it fit to drink?"

The singing stopped, and the cheerful voice replied:

"I'm not sure, cocky, but I'll have a look—or rather a feel! Damnably dark here, you know!"

I agreed that it was dark, and asked him:

"Where are you hit?"

"Oh, just in the foot!" he replied. Somewhere down below—not quite certain—except that I know one of those damned blighters' bombs exploded right underneath me."

He passed it off very lightly, and this helped me an awful lot, so when he asked me in turn where I was hit, I said:

"You've got me, old boy! I don't rightly know, but I think it's in the buzzum. All I can say is, it feels damned queer."

I found out afterwards that his foot had been blown off—and he didn't know it! He kept on singing about his "duck and green peas." What a spirit for a fighting man to have! But it is characteristic of our boys.

By and bye we arrived at a railway siding. We could hear engines. "I wonder where we are!" I said.

"Don't talk such platitudes, old man," responded my singing comrade. "You must be a silly fellow! Why, you're in a blinking ambulance, don't you know?"

We stopped and presently some stretcher-bearers came along. The singer was the first to be carried out, calling: "Goodbye, old man! Hope I see you on the train."

"Same here!" was my reply.

Then the other two were carried out. I was last. Out in the cool air, after the foggy ambulance, full of smoke, I tried to take a deep breath. Another sharp twinge in my side, then a fit of coughing! I felt awfully tight in the chest.

It was black as pitch outside, but there were several lights dodging about in the darkness. I heard the rolling of a door being slid back, and a familiar voice quietly singing, "*Another little drink—another little drink—another little drink wouldn't do us any harm.*" What a chap that was!

Then came the blinding glare of the hospital train, as I was carried into it and saw the interior of a wonderful sanitary palace, all enamelled in white!

Sliding me off the stretcher, to the accompaniment of a couple of groans, the bearers placed me on a soft, downy bed on the wall of the car. Immediately I was greeted:

"Here we are again, cocky!" There was my mate,—for I had dubbed him that by now.

"Ah, matey; all fixed up?"

"Yes, quite all right."

Now I got a good look at him. He was a very bright-faced chap, with blue eyes, a little upturned nose, and a small blond moustache, and struck me at first as being Irish. He pulled himself up, to get a better look at me, I suppose, and was rewarded with a good bump on his head that must have made him see stars. A bit bewildered, he lay down, with a few remarks reflecting on the architecture of the train, more especially the roof.

We carried on a conversation for a while, then two orderlies came through the train, dishing out beef tea in big mugs. This was very grateful to me, for I had not eaten for quite a long time. I didn't know just how long I had been "out," but if I had been brought down that morning I had not eaten a thing since; so I felt very hungry and started "grousing" because there wasn't something more to follow. Then we chatted again, with not one word of the battle front being mentioned, and I gradually dozed off again.

A very peculiar thing about the men of the line (especially officers) is that they very seldom "talk shop," even when everything is going smoothly with them, God knows they are glad enough to get away from it, in every sense of the words, though only too anxious to get into it when duty or their country calls. That is, if the man is a human being with red blood in his veins.

When I awoke, I felt the train moving. Presently some hot broth and hardtack was brought around. This I consumed with great avidity—and still felt hungry.

Some time early in the morning, having dozed again, I awoke with a fit of coughing. The train was standing still. There were sounds of activity outside and now and then the screech of a siren and the deep-toned whistle of a boat.

Then they started moving out the boys in our "van." One by one they disappeared through the big doorway. My turn came and I was carried out into the early morning air. Straight across some railway tracks my bearers went to the docks.

The hospital ship for Old Blighty was waiting for us.

## Chapter 17

# Back Home in Blighty

The wounded were toted up a gangplank one after another—a long line of us—on to the hospital ship. Then down into the saloon, where all the orderlies and nurses were busily engaged, dossing wounds and ministering to those in dire need of attention.

Presently my wound was attended to. I had been shot through the lower part of the right lung. The bullet not having come out on the other side, they spent some time trying to figure out where it had gone. No X-ray was available, and they could not do much, except plug up the little hole. I looked at it—not much bigger, if as big as a threepenny-bit—aright between the fourth and fifth ribs.

They made me quite comfortable on the ship. My wound was not such a serious one then, although painful, every breath I took being misery. I looked about for my cheerful acquaintance of the hospital train, but could not find him.

The man on my right lay very still. His face was all bandaged up, only his nose sticking out and two eyeholes visible. The man on the left, in another stretcher, was emitting a few groans as his wounds were being dressed. They were in the region of his neck and he could not talk, nor the chap on my right either. So I composed myself to sleep once more.

An orderly awakened me by bringing some food, in the shape of a few very nice thin sandwiches and a cup of hot tea. It was difficult for me to eat, being in a lying posture, but somehow I managed it. I was getting sorer and stiffer every minute now. God, how it pained!

Alternately dozing and waking, the passage across the Channel ended at last. All was now activity and bustle. The rattle of winches, the shrill whistle of the boatswain, the noise of unloading, all penetrated to the saloon, where, too, there was the hubbub of moving the patients.

Once more I was toted out by two stretcher-bearers, with another cigarette in my mouth, produced by one of the A. M. C. (Army Medical Corps). I came out into bright sunshine and was carried along the dock or quay, into another hospital train.

In Old Blighty once more!

On the way up the quay I noticed dozens of "walking cases"—wounded laddies who could walk—all smoking and joshing each other and cavorting around, feeling very pleased with life and yelling to the curious spectators, "Are we downhearted?" Then would come the answer—a big, hearty "NO!"

On the hospital ship we had all been asked what part of the British Isles our home was in, so as to verify the War Office report to the next of kin, giving the condition of the case, whether serious or otherwise; also that each might be sent to a hospital near his home, or wherever he desired to go.

A couple of hours later the train pulled into Charing Cross station. London at last!

Anxious crowds collect to meet all the hospital trains bearing the wounded back from the front, and as the boys come out through the station exits, walking by themselves, supported by comrades, or borne on stretchers, the people show their heartfelt gratitude; some weeping, others cheering and applauding, and still others trying to express their feelings by kindly words and greetings.

Even the flower "girls"—the old women that sell flowers outside the station—donate the widow's mite—a flower judiciously and tenderly placed on some fighting man's stretcher as he passes.

The "walking cases," on the other hand, cheer for "Old Blighty" and the people, drowning many expressions of sorrow with their never-ending "Are we downhearted?" or with a song, waving their hands in greeting to friends in the crowd.

God knows the people of England do realise that there is a war on! Nine-tenths of the families have been hit or are directly concerned in one way or another. The mothers, sisters, widows, orphans, and families at home really have played, and play today, the hardest part of all in the war. Theirs has been or is the suspense of waiting, waiting—for what? Who knows what day may bring them the fatal little message:

The War Office regrets to announce the death of ———.

Now I was driven up through the Strand, across Trafalgar Square, up Haymarket, along Piccadilly, and thence to a private hospital in Park Lane, followed by the pitying glances of pedestrians who knew what the ambulance meant. Many times I had seen such a trip being made by others, but little did I expect that I myself would ever ride through London in this manner.

The hospital to which I was taken—Dr. S——'s—is one of the best and most up-to-date in London. Why I was sent there I do not know, but I was certainly in luck, having vivid recollections of my former sojourn in a military hospital. This one was homelike.

When I found myself taken up in an elevator to a bright, sunshiny private room, from which I could look out into Hyde Park, the only thing I found lacking was company. The idea of being alone did not appeal to me at all.

Presently entered a very pretty "V. A. D."—a kind of nurse belonging to the Volunteer Auxiliary Department of the Red Cross. The V. A. D.s were very anxious to help wounded soldiers and studied very hard for their part, but were under the supervision of the regular trained nurses. One of their duties was to tidy up your room, and after awhile my room used to be very untidy—on purpose! A pretty V. A. D. was such a comfort in one's loneliness.

But I was a very sick man at first, and wondered when my wound was going to be treated. Then a military doctor entered, looked at my chart, which had been made out and posted on the wall, reading:

G. S. W. (gunshot wound)—right chest.

He looked at me, stripped off the bandages, with the assistance of the nurse (mild curses by the V.A.D. without!) and said:

"We'd better have an X-ray photo of this man taken. I can see no outlet of the bullet."

Then, feeling along my ribs, and prodding, he tried to locate the bullet, asking occasionally, "Does that hurt?" Finally he reached a particularly sore spot, whereat I yelled. This spot he found in my back, two inches from the spine, and deduced from it that the bullet had ricocheted off a rib and gone around.

Next morning I was carried up to the X-ray room and had my photo taken. The bullet was found to be where the doctor had surmised. So I thought I was in for an operation, but surgical science has taken immense strides during this war, and a little electromagnet, judiciously placed, drew the bullet along the course it had taken. Inch by inch, day by day, it came gradually to the surface, until one fine day

WRECKED GERMAN PLANE

Brought down by the British in the Big Push. These planes are distinguished by their black crosses.

it was picked out and handed to me.

All this while the wound had been sprayed and cleansed daily, to keep it antiseptic, but septic poisoning finally set in, and I had a serious time, many of the cells of my lung being affected. But I gradually recovered even from this, and used to take strolls in the park across the way.

After two and a half months in the hospital (thank the Lord the V. A. D. was there!) I was at length discharged, and was sent on convalescent leave.

The day I left Dr. S——'s most excellent establishment, I felt as if I was stepping on air. Out at last, and with three months' solid leave! Wonderful effect leave has on a fellow! I didn't seem to mind my wound at all.

Then I had the good luck to be offered a shooting trip in old Scotland, and returned to London three weeks later, to spend my time cavorting around the metropolis.

On the expiration of my leave I was ordered to report for "light duty" as instructor in flying on Salisbury Plain, where I was delighted to find myself once more. Then, voluntarily getting a non-combatant job in the Flying Corps at the front, I took an aeroplane up one day to a great height, against the advice of the "docs." The result was a haemorrhage and complete breakdown!

I was then placed on the retired officers' list, with the brevet rank of major, having been finally sent home "unfit for active service" in October, 1917.

A few days later I sailed for the United States, with the intention of doing something in the American air service. But I soon found that my flying days in this war were ended.

I was out of it!

# Glossary

Meanings of Technical Words and Phrases, British Army Slang, French Expressions, and Abbreviations used by the Author.

Ac Emma.—An air mechanic, or mechanic of the air service. So called because the initials, A. M., are pronounced "Ac Emma" in the signal code which prevents confusion of letters of similar sound.

Aerodrome.—A piece of level ground set apart for the use of airmen in starting and landing with their machines; usually having facilities for the storage, upkeep, and repair of the machines.

All out.—An aeroplane engine is said to be working "all out" when it is giving its best possible service, or working to its utmost capacity.

A. M. C.—Army Medical Corps.

Archie.—The British Army nickname for anti-aircraft artillery fire.

Backwash.—The condition of the air immediately behind an aeroplane in flight, which often affects the course of a machine following close behind or passing near its tail.

Bank.—To incline an aeroplane sidewise while making a turn.

Blighty.—The British soldier's term of affection for England.

*Bois.*—French for "wood" or "forest."

Bumpy days.—Days when the condition of the weather is such that an aeroplane encounters "bumps" in the air, the effect resembling those when an automobile passes over bumps in a road.

Bus.—The flyer's short term for an aeroplane.

Buzzing.—The sound of the signals made by wireless apparatus.

"*C'est la guerre!*—French for "That is war!"

Checks.—Blocks of wood, etc., placed beneath the wheels of an aeroplane before starting the engine, to keep the machine from moving while the engine is being tested before flight.

Circuit flags.—Flags so placed and flown in an aerodrome as to direct the coarse of a pilot making a circuit of the drome.

C. O.—Commanding officer.

Conk out.—To stop; applied to the working of an engine.

Do in.—An English idiom signifying to kill, stop, or finish; similar to the American "do up."

Drift wires.—In an aeroplane, supporting wires running fore-and-aft of the machine.

Drome.—An aerodrome, or flying-field; the field headquarters of a flying squadron.

Drum—The circular tray from which ammunition is fed to the Lewis machine-gun. Each tray contains 47 cartridges.

Dud.—Poor or defective; a term usually applied ia eontempt to a defective engine or machine.

Emma Gee.—A machine gun. So called because the letters M. G. (machine gun) are pronounced "Emma Gee" is the airman's signal code. (See "Ac Emma.")

Fag.—A cigarette.

Flight commander.—The officer in command of a flight of aeroplanes, usually a unit of five machines.

Fuselage.—The frame of an aeroplane, which carries the wings, tail, rudder, engine, propeller, and nacelle, or body.

Gasper.—A cigarette; the term is mostly used by British officers.

Grousing.—Grumbling or finding fault.

Grummet.—A pilot's name for the large flying helmet usually issued to flying students.

Hangar.—A shed or shelter for a flying-machine.

Hun.—A term of reproach for a German, generally used by the Allies and first suggested by the *Kaiser's* comparison of his troops to the Huns under Attila, who overran Europe in the fifth century. They were an ugly and savage race. The term is also jokingly applied in British flying schools to student flyers in this ease it is a corruption of "young 'un."

Immelmann turn.—A sharp turn, named after a former German pilot, and now a favourite stunt of the fighting scout. It reverses the direction of flight, and places the flyer at a lower altitude very quickly.

Inclinometer.—An instrument which shows the angle at which an aeroplane is inclined, while ascending or descending in the air.

Joyride.—In an aeroplane, a trip of a passenger for pleasure or experience.

Joystick.—The air pilot's nickname for the upright bar with which he controls the upward or downward direction of the aeroplane.

Lewis.—A machine-gun invented by Col. Lewis, an American, and adopted by the British for use on aeroplanes.

Lorry.—A motor truck.

M.P.H.—Miles per hour.

Nacelle.—The body of an aeroplane, exclusive of the framed wings, tail, and under-carriage; the place in which the pilot sits, or the cockpit, forms part of the nacelle.

Napoo.—A corruption of the French "*ne plus*" (no more); used by the British Army in France to express the idea of an end, or the finish of anything. Thus, "*Napoo* for him" means "He is done for."

N'est-ce pas?—French for "Is it not?"

Nose.—The bow, or foremost portion, of the body of a plane.

O. C. plane.—"Officer commanding plane." The pilot of an aeroplane.

Pancake.—To bring (an aeroplane) to the ground in a level position; that is, flattened out like a pancake, so that it lights on its tail as well as the wheels.

Petrol.—Gasoline; so called in England and France.

Pitot tube.—An instrument which registers the speed of an aeroplane in flight.

Plane.—An aeroplane; also, one of the flat surfaces or wings which support the machine in flight.

Prop.—The flyer's abbreviation of "propeller."

Put the wind up.—(English slang.) One is said to "put the wind up" another when he makes the other nervous, or, in American slang, "gets his goat."

Pylons.—Pillars or poles used to outline the limits of an aerodrome or to direct the flight of a pilot in making a circuit of the drome.

Quid—English slang for a gold sovereign, or 20-shilling piece, equivalent to about five dollars.

Revs.—A short term for "revolutions," applied to an engine or propeller.

R.F.C.—Royal Flying Corps.

R.P.M.—Revolutions per minute.

R.E.—Royal Engineers.

Solo flight.—A flight in the air alone, either of a solitary machine or of a pilot without a passenger; a student's flight without an instructor.

Sapper.—A private soldier of the Royal Engineers.

Smoke, or smudge, fires.—Fires of damp fuel built on the ground in an aerodrome or elsewhere, as a day signal to attract the attention of or guide pilots when flying.

Take off.—To leave the ground in beginning a flight in an aeroplane.

Tarmac.—A smooth section of ground in front of a hangar, asphalted or oil surfaced, to prevent the raising of dust by aeroplane propellers and facilitate taking machines in and out of the hangar.

Taxi.—(Taxied, taxiing.) To move an aeroplane on its wheels along the ground, by its own power, as in leaving or approaching a hangar, or in turning into the wind in starting a flight.

Tracer ballet.—A bullet that can be traced through the air by means of its visible trail of fire or smoke.

Van.—An English railway freight car; sometimes applied to the coaches of a hospital train. .

V.A.D,—An amateur nurse, or a member of the Volunteer Auxiliary Department of the British Red Cross.

*Vingt-et-un.*—French for twenty-one. The name of a popular game of cards, so called from the method of counting points.

Windy.—English slang for "nervous" or "agitated."

# Outwitting the Hun

Lieutenant Pat O'Brien
Royal Flying Corps.

# Contents

| | |
|---|---|
| Preface | 141 |
| The Folly of Despair | 143 |
| I Become a Fighting-Scout | 146 |
| Captured by the Huns | 152 |
| Clipped Wings | 159 |
| The Prison-Camp at Courtrai | 170 |
| A Leap for Liberty | 183 |
| Crawling through Germany | 188 |
| Nine Days in Luxembourg | 192 |
| I Enter Belgium | 199 |
| Experiences in Belgium | 208 |
| I Encounter German Soldiers | 214 |
| The Forged Passport | 221 |
| Five Days in an Empty House | 234 |
| A Night of Dissipation | 243 |
| Observations in a Belgian City | 249 |
| I Approach the Frontier | 252 |
| Getting Through the Lines | 257 |
| Experiences in Holland | 264 |

I am Presented to the King 275
Home Again! 279

To
The North Star
Whose Guiding Light Marked the
Pathway to Freedom for a Weary
Fugitive, This Book is Inscribed
In Humble Gratitude
And Abiding Faith

# Preface

There is a common idea that the age of miracles is past. Perhaps it is, but if so, the change must have come about within the past few weeks—after I escaped into Holland. For if anything is certain in this life it is this: this book never would have been written but for the succession of miracles set forth in these pages.

Miracles, luck, coincidence, Providence—it doesn't matter much what you call it—certainly played an important part in the series of hairbreadth escapes in which I figured during my short but eventful appearance in the great drama now being enacted across the seas. Without it, all my efforts and sufferings would have been quite unavailing.

No one realises this better than I do and I want to repeat it right here because elsewhere in these pages I may appear occasionally to overlook or minimise it: without the help of Providence I would not be here today.

But this same Providence which brought me home safely, despite all the dangers which beset me, may work similar miracles for others, and it is in the hope of encouraging other poor devils who may find themselves in situations as hopeless apparently as mine oftentimes were that this book is written.

When this cruel war is over—which I trust may be sooner than I expect it to be—I hope I shall have an opportunity to revisit the scenes of my adventures and to thank in person in an adequate manner every one who extended a helping hand to me when I was a wretched fugitive. All of them took great risks in befriending an escaped prisoner, and they did it without the slightest hope of reward. At the same time I hope I shall have a chance to pay my compliments to those who endeavoured to take advantage of my distress.

In the meanwhile, however, I can only express my thanks in this ineffective manner, trusting that in some mysterious way a copy of this book may fall into the hands of everyone who befriended me. I hope particularly that every good Hollander who played the part of the Good Samaritan to me so bountifully after my escape from Belgium will see these pages and feel that I am absolutely sincere when I say that words cannot begin to express my sense of gratitude to the Dutch people.

It is needless for me to add how deeply I feel for my fellow-prisoners in Germany who were less fortunate than I. Poor, poor fellows!—they are the real victims of the war. I hope that every one of them may soon be restored to that freedom whose value I never fully realised until after I had had to fight so hard to regain it.

Pat O'Brien.

Momence, Illinois, January 14, 1918.

Chapter 1

# The Folly of Despair

Less than nine months ago eighteen officers of the Royal Flying Corps, which had been training in Canada, left for England on the *Megantic*.

If any of them was over twenty-five years of age, he had successfully concealed the fact, because they don't accept older men for the R. F. C.

Nine of the eighteen were British subjects; the other nine were Americans, who, tired of waiting for their own country to take her place with the Allies, had joined the British colours in Canada. I was one of the latter.

We were going to England to earn our "wings"—a qualification which must be won before a member of the R. F. C. is allowed to hunt the Huns on the western front.

That was in May, 1917.

By August 1st most of us were full-fledged pilots, actively engaged at various parts of the line in daily conflict with the enemy.

By December 15th every man Jack of us who had met the enemy in France, with one exception, had appeared on the casualty list. The exception was H. K. Boysen, an American, who at last report was fighting on the Italian front, still unscathed. Whether his good fortune has stood by him up to this time I don't know, but if it has I would be very much surprised.

Of the others five were killed in action—three Americans, one Canadian, and one Englishman. Three more were in all probability killed in action, although officially they are listed merely as "missing." One of these was an American, one a Canadian, and the third a Scotchman. Three more, two of them Americans, were seriously wounded. Another, a Canadian, is a prisoner in Germany. I know nothing of the others.

What happened to me is narrated in these pages. I wish, instead, I could tell the story of each of my brave comrades, for not one of them was downed, I am sure, without upholding the best traditions of the R. F. C. Unfortunately, however, of the eighteen who sailed on the *Megantic* last May, I happened to be the first to fall into the hands of the Huns, and what befell my comrades after that, with one exception, I know only second hand.

The exception was the case of poor, brave Paul Raney—my closest chum—whose last battle I witnessed from my German prison—but that is a story I shall tell in its proper place.

In one way, however, I think the story of my own "big adventure" and my miraculous escape may, perhaps, serve a purpose as useful as that of the heroic fate of my less fortunate comrades. Their story, it is true, might inspire others to deeds of heroism, but mine, I hope, will convey the equally valuable lesson of the folly of despair.

Many were the times in the course of my struggles when it seemed absolutely useless to continue. In a hostile country, where discovery meant death, wounded, sick, famished, friendless, hundreds of miles from the nearest neutral territory the frontier of which was so closely guarded that even if I got there it seemed too much to hope that I could ever get through, what was the use of enduring further agony?

And yet here I am, in the Land of Liberty—although in a somewhat obscure corner, the little town of Momence, Illinois, where I was born—not very much the worse for wear after all I've been through, and, as I write these words, not eight months have passed since my seventeen comrades and I sailed from Canada on the *Megantic!*

Can it be possible that I was spared to convey a message of hope to others who are destined for similar trials? I am afraid there will be many of them.

Years ago I heard of the epitaph which is said to have been found on a child's grave:

*If I was so soon to be done for,*
*O Lord, what was I ever begun for?*

The way it has come to me since I returned from Europe is:

*If, O Lord, I was* not *to be done for,*
*What were my sufferings e'er begun for?*

Perhaps the answer lies in the suggestion I have made.

At any rate, if this record of my adventures should prove instrumental in sustaining others who need encouragement, I shall not feel that my sufferings were in vain.

It is hardly likely that any one will quite duplicate my experiences, but I haven't the slightest doubt that many will have to go through trials equally nerve-racking and suffer disappointments just as disheartening.

It would be very far from the mark to imagine that the optimism which I am preaching now so glibly sustained me through all my troubles. On the contrary, I am free to confess that I frequently gave way to despair and often, for hours at a time, felt so dejected and discouraged that I really didn't care what happened to me. Indeed, I rather hoped that something *would* happen to put an end to my misery.

But, despite all my despondency and hopelessness, the worst never happened, and I can't help thinking that my salvation must have been designed to show the way to others.

CHAPTER 2

# I Become a Fighting-Scout

I started flying, in Chicago, in 1912. I was then eighteen years old, but I had had a hankering for the air ever since I can remember.

As a youngster I followed the exploits of the Wrights with the greatest interest, although I must confess I sometimes hoped that they wouldn't really conquer the air until I had had a whack at it myself. I got more whacks than I was looking for later on.

Needless to say, my parents were very much opposed to my risking my life at what was undoubtedly at that time one of the most hazardous "pastimes" a young fellow could select, and every time I had a smash-up or some other mishap I was ordered never to go near an aviation field again.

So I went out to California. There another fellow and I built our own machine, which we flew in various parts of the state.

In the early part of 1916, when trouble was brewing in Mexico, I joined the American Flying Corps. I was sent to San Diego, where the army flying school is located, and spent about eight months there, but as I was anxious to get into active service and there didn't seem much chance of America ever getting into the war, I resigned and, crossing over to Canada, joined the Royal Flying Corps at Victoria, B. C.

I was sent to Camp Borden, Toronto, first to receive instruction and later to instruct. While a cadet I made the first loop ever made by a cadet in Canada, and after I had performed the stunt I half expected to be kicked out of the service for it. Apparently, however, they considered the source and let it go at that. Later on I had the satisfaction of introducing the loop as part of the regular course of instruction for cadets in the R. F. C, and I want to say right here that Camp Borden has turned out some of the best fliers that have ever gone to France.

In May, 1917, I and seventeen other Canadian fliers left for England on the *Megantic*, where we were to qualify for service in France. Our squadron consisted of nine Americans, C. C. Robinson, H. A. Miller, F. S. McClurg, A. A. Allen, E. B. Garnett, H. K. Boysen, H. A. Smeeton, A. Taylor, and myself; and nine Britishers, Paul H. Raney, J. R. Park, C. Nelmes, C. R. Moore, T. L. Atkinson, F. C. Conry, A. Muir, E. A. L. F. Smith, and A. C. Jones.

Within a few weeks after our arrival in England all of us had won our "wings"—the insignia worn on the left breast by every pilot on the western front.

We were all sent to a place in France known as the Pool Pilots' Mess. Here men gather from all the training squadrons in Canada and England and await assignments to the particular squadron of which they are to become members.

The Pool Pilots' Mess is situated a few miles back of the lines. Whenever a pilot is shot down or killed the Pool Pilots' Mess is notified to send another to take his place.

There are so many casualties every day in the R. F. C. at one point of the front or another that the demand for new pilots is quite active, but when a fellow is itching to get into the fight as badly as I and my friends were I must confess that we got a little impatient, although we realised that every time a new man was called it meant that someone else had, in all probability, been killed, wounded, or captured.

One morning an order came in for a scout pilot, and one of my friends was assigned. I can tell you the rest of us were as envious of him as if it were the last chance any of us were ever going to have to get to the front. As it was, however, hardly more than three hours had elapsed before another wire was received at the mess and I was ordered to follow my friend. I afterward learned that as soon as he arrived at the squadron he had prevailed upon the commanding officer of the squadron to wire for me.

At the Pool Pilots' Mess it was the custom of the officers to wear "shorts"—breeches that are about eight inches long, like the Boy Scouts wear, leaving a space of about eight inches of open country between the top of the *puttees* and the end of the "shorts." The Australians wore them in Salonica and at the Dardanelles.

When the order came in for me, I had these "shorts" on, and I didn't have time to change into other clothes. Indeed, I was in such a sweat to get to the front that if I had been in my pyjamas I think I would have gone that way. As it was, it was raining and I threw an overcoat over me, jumped into the machine, and we made record time to the aerodrome to which I had been ordered to report.

As I alighted from the automobile my overcoat blew open and displayed my manly form attired in "shorts" instead of in the regulation flying breeches, and the sight aroused considerable commotion in camp.

"Must be a Yankee!" I overheard one officer say to another as I approached. "No one but a Yank would have the cheek to show up that way, you know!"

But they laughed good-naturedly as I came up to them and welcomed me to the squadron, and I was soon very much at home.

My squadron was one of four stationed at an aerodrome about eighteen miles back of the Ypres line. There were eighteen pilots in our squadron, which was a scout-squadron, scout-machines carrying but one man.

A scout, sometimes called a fighting-scout, has no bomb-dropping or reconnoitring to do. His duty is just to fight, or, as the order was given to me, "You are expected to pick fights and not wait until they come to you!"

When bomb-droppers go out over the lines in the daytime, a scout-squadron usually convoys them. The bomb-droppers fly at about twelve thousand feet, the scouts a thousand feet or so above them to protect them.

If at any time they should be attacked, it is the duty of the scouts to dive down and carry on the fight, the orders of the bomb-droppers being to go on dropping bombs and not to fight unless they have to. There is seldom a time that machines go out over the lines on this work in the daytime that they are not attacked at some time or other, and so the scouts usually have plenty of work to do. In addition to these attacks, however, the squadron is invariably under constant bombardment from the ground, but that doesn't worry us very much, as we know pretty well how to avoid being hit from that quarter.

On my first flight, after joining the squadron, I was taken out over the lines to get a look at things, map out my location in case I was ever lost, locate the forests, lakes, and other landmarks, and get the general lay of the land.

One thing that was impressed upon me very emphatically was the location of the hospitals, so that in case I was ever wounded and had the strength to pick my landing I could land as near as possible to a hospital. All these things a new pilot goes through during the first two or three days after joining a squadron.

Our regular routine was two flights a day, each of two hours' duration. After doing our regular patrol, it was our privilege to go off on our own hook, if we wished, before going back to the squadron.

I soon found out that my squadron was some hot squadron, our fliers being almost always assigned to special-duty work, such as shooting up trenches at a height of fifty feet from the ground!

I received my baptism into this kind of work the third time I went out over the lines, and I would recommend it to anyone who is hankering for excitement. You are not only apt to be attacked by hostile aircraft from above, but you are swept by machine-gun fire from below. I have seen some of our machines come back from this work sometimes so riddled with bullets that I wondered how they ever held together. Before we started out on one of these jobs we were mighty careful to see that our motors were in perfect condition, because they told us the "war-bread was bad in Germany."

One morning, shortly after I joined the squadron, three of us started over the line on our own accord. We soon observed four enemy machines, two-seaters, coming toward us. This type of machine is used by the Huns for artillery work and bomb-dropping, and we knew they were on mischief bent. Each machine had a machine-gun in front, worked by the pilot, and the observer also had a gun with which he could spray all around.

When we first noticed the Huns our machines were about six miles back of the German lines and we were lying high up in the sky, keeping the sun behind us, so that the enemy could not see us.

We picked out three of the machines and dove down on them. I went right by the man I picked for myself and his observer in the rear seat kept pumping at me to beat the band. Not one of my shots took effect as I went right under him, but I turned and gave him another burst of bullets and down he went in a spinning nose dive, one of his wings going one way and one another. As I saw him crash to the ground I knew that I had got: my first hostile aircraft. One of my comrades was equally successful, but the other, two German machines got away. We chased them back until things got too hot for us by reason of the appearance of other German machines, and then we called it a day.

This experience whetted my appetite for more of the same kind, and I did not have long to wait.

It may be well to explain here just what a spinning nose dive is. A few years ago the spinning nose dive was considered one: of the most dangerous things a pilot could attempt, and many men were killed getting into this spin and not knowing how to come out of it. In fact, lots of pilots thought that when once you got into a spinning nose dive there was no way of coming out of it. It is now used, however, in actual flying.

The machines that are used in France are controlled in two ways, both by hands and by feet, the feet working the yoke or rudder bar which controls the rudder that steers the machine. The lateral controls and fore and aft, which cause the machine to rise or lower, are controlled by a contrivance called a "joy-stick." If, when flying in the air, a pilot should release his hold on this stick, it will gradually come back toward the pilot.

In that position the machine will begin to climb. So if a pilot is shot and loses control of this "joy-stick" his machine begins to ascend, and climbs until the angle formed becomes too great for it to continue or the motor to pull the plane; for a fraction of a second it stops, and the motor then being the heaviest, it causes the nose of the machine to fall forward, pitching down at a terrific rate of speed and spinning at the same time. If the motor is still running, it naturally increases the speed much more than it would if the motor were shut off, and there is great danger that the wings will double up, causing the machine to break apart. Although spins are made with the motor on, you are dropping like a ball being dropped out of the sky and the velocity increases with the power of the motor.

This spinning nose dive has been frequently used in "stunt" flying in recent years, but is now put to practical use by pilots in getting away from hostile machines, for when a man is spinning, it is almost impossible to hit him, and the man making the attack invariably thinks his enemy is going down to certain death in the spin.

This is all right when a man is over his own territory, because he can right his machine and come out of it; but if it happens over German territory, the Huns would only follow him down, and when he came out of the spin they would be above him, having all the advantage, and would shoot him down with ease.

It is a good way of getting down into a cloud, and is used very often by both sides, but it requires skill and courage by the pilot making it if he ever expects to come out alive.

A spin being made by a pilot intentionally looks exactly like a spin that is made by a machine actually being shot down, so one never knows whether it is forced or intentional until the pilot either rights his machine and comes out of it or crashes to the ground.

Another dive similar to this one is known as just the plain "dive." Assume, for instance, that a pilot flying at a height of several thousand feet is shot, loses control of his machine, and the nose of the plane starts down with the motor full on. He is going at a tremendous speed and in many instances is going so straight and swiftly that the speed is too great for the machine, because it was never constructed to withstand the enormous pressure forced against the wings, and they consequently crumple up.

If, too, in an effort to straighten the machine, the elevators should become affected, as often happens in trying to bring a machine out of a dive, the strain is again too great on the wings, and there is the same disastrous result. Oftentimes, when the petrol-tank is punctured by a tracer-bullet from another machine in the air, the plane that is hit catches on fire and either gets into a spin or a straight dive and heads for the earth, hundreds of miles an hour, a mass of flame, looking like a brilliant comet in the sky.

The spinning nose dive Is used to greater advantage by the Germans than by our own pilots, for the reason that when a fight gets too hot for the German he will put his machine in a spin, and as the chances are nine out of ten that we are fighting over German territory, he simply spins down out of our range, straightens out before he reaches the ground, and goes on home to his aerodrome. It is useless to follow him down inside the German lines, for you would in all probability be shot down before you could attain sufficient altitude to cross the line again.

It often happens that a pilot will be chasing another machine when suddenly he sees it start to spin. Perhaps they are fifteen or eighteen thousand feet in the air, and the hostile machine spins down for thousands of feet. He thinks he has hit the other machine and goes home happy that he has brought down another Hun. He reports the occurrence to the squadron, telling how he shot down his enemy; but when the rest of the squadron come in with their report, or some artillery observation balloon sends in a report, it develops that when a few hundred feet from the ground the supposed dead man in the spin has come out of the spin and gone merrily on his way for his own aerodrome.

## Chapter 3

# Captured by the Huns

I shall not easily forget the 17th of August, 1917. I killed two Huns in a double-seated machine in the morning, another in the evening, and then I was captured myself. I may have spent more eventful days in my life, but I can't recall any just now.

That morning, in crossing the line on early morning patrol, I noticed two German balloons. I decided that as soon as my patrol was over I would go off on my own hook and see what a German balloon looked like at close quarters.

These observation balloons are used by both sides in conjunction with the artillery. A man sits up in the balloon with a wireless apparatus and directs the firing of the guns. From his point of vantage he can follow the work of his own artillery with a remarkable degree of accuracy and at the same time he can observe the enemy's movements and report them.

The Germans are very good at this work and they use a great number of these balloons. It was considered a very important part of our work to keep them out of the sky.

There are two ways of going after a balloon in a machine. One of them is to cross the lines at a low altitude, flying so near the ground that the man with the antiaircraft gun can't bother you. You fly along until you get to the level of the balloon, and if, in the mean time, they have not drawn the balloon down, you open fire on it and the bullets you use will set it on fire if they land.

The other way is to fly over where you know the balloons to be, put your machine in a spin so that they can't hit you, get above them, spin over the balloon, and then open fire. In going back over the line you cross at a few hundred feet.

This is one of the hardest jobs in the service. There is less danger in attacking an enemy's aircraft.

Nevertheless, I had made up my mind either to get those balloons or make them descend, and I only hoped that they would stay on the job until I had a chance at them.

When our two hours' duty was up, therefore, I dropped out of the formation as we crossed the lines and turned back again.

I was at a height of fifteen thousand feet, considerably higher than the balloons. Shutting my motor off, I dropped down through the clouds, thinking to find the balloons at about five or six miles behind the German lines.

Just as I came out of the cloud-banks I saw below me, about a thousand feet, a two-seater hostile machine doing artillery observation and directing the German guns. This was at a point about four miles behind the German lines.

Evidently the German artillery saw me and put out ground signals to attract the Hun machine's attention, for I saw the observer quit his work and grab his gun, while the pilot stuck the nose of his machine straight down.

But they were too late to escape me. I was diving toward them at a speed of probably two hundred miles an hour, shooting all the time as fast as possible. Their only chance lay in the possibility that the force of my dive might break my wings. I knew my danger in that direction, but as soon as I came out of my dive the Huns would have their chance to get me, and I knew I had to get them first and take a chance on my wings holding out.

Fortunately, some of my first bullets found their mark and I was able to come out of my dive at about four thousand feet. They never came out of theirs!

But right then came the hottest situation in the air I had experienced up to that time. The depth of my dive had brought me within reach of the machineguns from the ground and they also put a "barrage" around me of shrapnel from anti-aircraft guns, and I had an opportunity to "ride the barrage," as they call it in the R. F. C. To make the situation more interesting, they began shooting "flaming onions" at me.

"Flaming onions" are rockets shot from a rocket-gun. They are used to hit a machine when it is flying low and they are effective up to about five thousand feet.

Sometimes they are shot up one after another in strings of about eight, and they are one of the hardest things to go through. If they hit the machine it is bound to catch fire and then the jig is up.

All the time, too, I was being attacked by "Archi"—the anti-aircraft fire. I escaped the machine-guns and the "flaming onions," but "Archie" got me four or five times. Every time a bullet plugged me, or rather my machine, it made a loud bang, on account of the tension on the material covering the wings.

None of their shots hurt me until I was about a mile from our lines, and then they hit my motor. Fortunately I still had altitude enough to drift on to our own side of the lines, for my motor was completely out of commission. They just raised the dickens with me all the time I was descending, and I began to think I would strike the ground before crossing the line, but there was a slight wind in my favour and it carried me two miles behind our lines. There the balloons I had gone out to get had the satisfaction of "pin-pointing" me. Through the directions which they were able to give to their artillery, they commenced shelling my machine where it lay.

Their particular work is to direct the fire of their artillery, and they are used just as the artillery observation airplanes are. Usually two men are stationed in each balloon. They ascend to a height of several thousand feet about five miles behind their own lines and are equipped with wireless and signalling apparatus. They watch the burst of their own artillery, check up the position, get the range, and direct the next shot.

When conditions are favourable they are able to direct the shots so accurately that it is a simple matter to destroy the object of their attack. It was such a balloon as this that got my position, marked me out, called for an artillery shot, and they commenced shelling my machine where it lay. If I had got the two balloons instead of the airplane, I probably would not have lost my machine, for he would in all probability have gone on home and not bothered about getting my range and causing the destruction of my machine.

I landed in a part of the country that was literally covered with shell-holes. Fortunately my machine was not badly damaged by the forced landing. I leisurely got out, walked around it to see what the damage was, and concluded that it could be easily repaired. In fact, I thought, if I could find a space long enough between shell-holes to get a start before leaving the ground, that I would be able to fly on from there.

I was still examining my plane and considering the matter of a few slight repairs, without any particular thought for my own safety in that unprotected spot, when a shell came whizzing through the air, knocked me to the ground, and landed a few feet away. It had no sooner struck than I made a run for cover and crawled into a shell-hole. I would have liked to have got farther away, but I didn't know where the next shell would burst, and I thought I was fairly safe there, so I squatted down and let them blaze away.

The only damage I suffered was from the mud which splattered up in my face and over my clothes. That was my introduction to a shell-hole, and I resolved right there that the infantry could have all the shell-hole fighting they wanted, but it did not appeal to me, though they live in them through many a long night and I had only sought shelter there for a few minutes.

After the Germans had completely demolished my machine and ceased firing I waited there a short time, fearing perhaps they might send over a lucky shot, hoping to get me, after all. But evidently they concluded enough shells had been wasted on one man. I crawled out cautiously, shook the mud off, and looked over in the direction where my machine had once been. There wasn't enough left for a decent souvenir, but nevertheless I got a few, such as they were, and, readily observing that nothing could be done with what was left, I made my way back to infantry headquarters, where I was able to telephone in a report.

A little later one of our automobiles came out after me and took me back to our aerodrome. Most of my squadron thought I was lost beyond a doubt and never expected to see me again; but my friend, Paul Raney, had held out that I was all right, and, as I was afterward told, "Don't send for another pilot; that Irishman will be back if he has to walk."

And he knew that the only thing that kept me from walking was the fact that our own automobile had been sent out to bring me home.

I had lots to think about that day, and I had learned many things; one was not to have too much confidence in my own ability. One of the men in the squadron told me that I had better not take those chances; that it was going to be a long war and I would have plenty of opportunities to be killed without deliberately "wishing them on" myself. Later I was to learn the truth of his statement.

That night my "flight"—each squadron is divided into three flights consisting of six men each—got ready to go out again. As I started to put on my tunic I noticed that I was not marked up for duty as usual.

I asked the commanding officer, a major, what the reason for that was, and he replied that he thought I had done enough for one day. However, I knew that if I did not go, someone else from another "flight" would have to take my place, and I insisted upon going up with my patrol as usual, and the major reluctantly consented. Had he known what was in store for me I am sure he wouldn't have changed his mind so readily.

As it was, we had only five machines for this patrol, anyway, because as we crossed the lines one of them had to drop out on account of motor trouble. Our patrol was up at 8 p.m., and up to within ten minutes of that hour it had been entirely uneventful.

At 7.50 p.m., however, while we were flying at a height of sixteen thousand feet, we observed three other English machines which were about three thousand feet below us pick a fight with nine Hun machines.

I knew right then that we were in for it, because I could see over toward the ocean a whole flock of Hun machines which evidently had escaped the attention of our scrappy comrades below us.

So we dove down on those nine Huns.

At first the fight was fairly even. There were eight of us to nine of them. But soon the other machines which I had seen in the distance, and which were flying even higher than we were, arrived on the scene, and when they, in turn, dove down on us, there was just twenty of them to our eight!

Four of them singled me out. I was diving and they dove right down after me, shooting as they came. Their tracer-bullets were coming closer to me every moment. These tracer-bullets are balls of fire which enable the shooter to follow the course his bullets are taking and to correct his aim accordingly. They do no more harm to a pilot if he is hit than an ordinary bullet, but if they hit the petrol-tank, good-night! When a machine catches fire in flight there is no way of putting it out. It takes less than a minute for the fabric to burn off the wings, and then the machine drops like an arrow, leaving a trail of smoke like a comet.

As their tracer-bullets came closer and closer to me I realised that my chances of escape were nil. Their very next shot, I felt, must hit me.

Once, some days before, when I was flying over the line I had watched a fight above me. A German machine was set on fire and dove down through our formation in flame on its way to the ground. The Hun was diving at such a sharp angle that both his wings came

The aeroplane which Lieutenant O'Brien used in his last battle with the Huns when he was brought down and made prisoner.

off, and as he passed within a few hundred feet of me I saw the look of horror upon his face.

Now, when I expected any moment to suffer a similar fate, I could not help thinking of that poor Hun's last look of agony.

I realised that my only chance lay in making an Immermann turn. This manoeuvre was invented by a German—one of the greatest who ever flew and who was killed in action some time ago. This turn, which I made successfully, brought one of their machines right in front of me, and as he sailed along barely ten yards away I had "the drop" on him, and he knew it.

His white face and startled eyes I can still see. He knew beyond question that his last moment had come, because his position prevented his taking aim at me, while my gun pointed straight at him. My first tracer-bullet passed within a yard of his head, the second looked as if it hit his shoulder, the third struck him in the neck, and then I let him have the whole works and he went down in a spinning nose dive.

All this time the three other Hun machines were shooting away at me. I could hear the bullets striking my machine one after another. I hadn't the slightest idea that I could ever beat off those three Huns, but there was nothing for me to do but fight, and my hands were full.

In fighting, your machine is dropping, dropping all the time. I glanced at my instruments and my altitude was between eight and nine thousand feet. While I was still looking at the instruments the whole blamed works disappeared. A burst of bullets went into the instrument board and blew it to smithereens, another bullet went through my upper lip, came out of the roof of my mouth and lodged in my throat, and the next thing I knew was when I came to in a German hospital the following morning at five o'clock, German time.

I was a prisoner of war!

CHAPTER 4

# Clipped Wings

The hospital in which I found myself on the morning after my capture was a private house made of brick, very low and dirty, and not at all adapted for use as a hospital. It had evidently been used but a few days, on account of the big push that was taking place at that time of the year, and in all probability would be abandoned as soon as they had found a better place.

In all, the house contained four rooms and a stable, which was by far the largest of all. Although I never looked into this "wing" of the hospital, I was told that it, too, was filled with patients, lying on beds of straw around on the ground. I do not know whether they, too, were officers or privates.

The room in which I found myself contained eight beds, three of which were occupied by wounded German officers. The other rooms, I imagined, had about the same number of beds as mine. There were no Red Cross nurses in attendance, just orderlies, for this was only an emergency hospital and too near the firing-line for nurses. The orderlies were not old men nor very young boys, as I expected to find, but young men in the prime of life, who evidently had been medical students. One or two of them, I discovered, were able to speak English, but for some reason they would not talk. Perhaps they were forbidden by the officer in charge to do so.

In addition to the bullet wound in my mouth, I had a swelling from my forehead to the back of my head almost as big as my shoe—and that is saying considerable. I couldn't move an inch without suffering intense pain, and when the doctor told me that I had no bones broken I wondered how a fellow would feel who had.

German officers visited me that morning and told me that my machine went down in a spinning nose dive from a height of between eight and nine thousand feet, and they had the surprise of their lives when they discovered that I had not been dashed to pieces. They had to cut me out of my machine, which was riddled with shots and shattered to bits.

A German doctor removed the bullet from my throat, and the first thing he said to me when I came to was, "You are an American!"

There was no use denying it, because the metal identification disk on my wrist bore the inscription, "Pat O'Brien, U. S. A. Royal Flying Corps."

Although I was suffering intense agony, the doctor, who spoke perfect English, insisted upon conversing with me.

"You may be all right as a sportsman," he declared, "but you are a damned murderer just the same for being here. You Americans who got into this thing before America came into the war are no better than common murderers and you ought to be treated the same way!"

The wound in my mouth made it impossible for me to answer him, and I was suffering too much pain to be hurt very much by anything he could say.

He asked me if I would like an apple! I could just as easily have eaten a brick.

When he got no answers out of me he walked away disgustedly.

"You don't have to worry any more," he declared, as a parting shot; "for you the war is over!"

I was given a little broth later in the day, and as I began to collect my thoughts I wondered what had happened to my comrades in the battle which had resulted so disastrously to me. As I began to realise my plight I worried less about my physical condition than the fact that, as the doctor had pointed out, for me the war was practically over. I had been in it but a short time, and now I would be a prisoner for the duration of the war!

The next day some German flying officers visited me, and I must say they treated me with great consideration. They told me of the man I had brought down. They said he was a Bavarian and a fairly good pilot. They gave me his hat as a souvenir and complimented me on the fight I had put up.

My helmet, which was of soft leather, was split from front to back by a bullet from a machine gun and they examined it with great interest. When they brought me my uniform I found that the star of my rank which had been on my right shoulder-strap had been shot off clean. The one on my left shoulder-strap they asked me for as a souve-

The identification disc worn by Lieutenant O'Brien when he was captured by the Huns. It revealed to them that he was an American.

nir, as also my R. F. C. badges, which I gave them. They allowed me to keep my "wings," which I wore on my left breast, because they were aware that that is the proudest possession of a British flying officer.

I think I am right in saying that the only chivalry in this war on the German side of the trenches has been displayed by the officers of the German Flying Corps, which comprises the pick of Germany. They pointed out to me that I and my comrades were fighting purely for the love of it, whereas they were fighting in defence of their country, but still, they said, they admired us for our sportsmanship. I had a notion to ask them if dropping bombs on London and killing so many innocent people was in defence of their country, but I was in no position or condition to pick a quarrel at that time.

That same day a German officer was brought into the hospital and put in the bunk next to mine. Of course, I casually looked at him, but did not pay any particular attention to him at that time. He lay there for three or four hours before I did take a real good look at him. I was positive that he could not speak English, and naturally I did not say anything to him.

Once when I looked over in his direction his eyes were on me and to my surprise he said, very sarcastically, "What the hell are you looking at?" and then smiled. At this time I was just beginning to say a few words, my wound having made talking difficult, but I said enough to let him know what I was doing there and how I happened to be there. Evidently he had heard my story from some of the others, though, because he said it was too bad I had not broken my neck; that he did not have much sympathy with the Flying Corps, anyway. He asked me what part of America I came from, and I told him "California."

After a few more questions he learned that I hailed from San Francisco, and then added to my distress by saying, "How would you like to have a good juicy steak right out of the Hofbräu?" Naturally, I told him it would "hit the spot," but I hardly thought my mouth was in shape just then to eat it. I immediately asked, of course, what he knew about the Hofbräu, and he replied, "I was connected with the place a good many years, and I ought to know all about it."

After that this German officer and I became rather chummy—that is, as far as I could be chummy with an enemy, and we whiled away a good many long hours talking about the days we had spent in San Francisco, and frequently in the conversation one of us would mention some prominent Californian, or some little incident occurring there, with which we were both familiar.

He told me when war was declared he was, of course, intensely patriotic and thought the only thing for him to do was to go back and aid in the defence of his country. He found that he could not go directly from San Francisco because the water was too well guarded by the English, so he boarded a boat for South America. There he obtained a forged passport and in the guise of a Montevidean took passage for New York and from there to England.

He passed through England without any difficulty on his forged passport, but concluded not to risk going to Holland, for fear of exciting too much suspicion, so went down through the Strait of Gibraltar to Italy, which was neutral at that time, up to Austria, and thence to Germany. He said when they put in at Gibraltar, after leaving England, there were two suspects taken off the ship, men that he was sure were neutral subjects, but much to his relief his own passport and credentials were examined and passed O. K.

The Hun spoke of his voyage from America to England as being exceptionally pleasant, and said he had had a fine time because he associated with the English passengers on board, his fluent English readily admitting him to several spirited arguments on the subject of the war which he keenly enjoyed.

One little incident he related revealed the remarkable tact which our enemy displayed in his associations at sea, which no doubt resulted advantageously for him. As he expressed it, he "made a hit" one evening when the crowd had assembled for a little music by suggesting that they sing "God Save the King." Thereafter his popularity was assured and the desired effect accomplished, for very soon a French officer came up to him and said, "It's too bad that England and ourselves haven't men in our army like you." It was too bad, he agreed, in telling me about it, because he was confident he could have done a whole lot more for Germany if he had been in the English Army.

In spite of his apparent loyalty, however, the man didn't seem very enthusiastic over the war and frankly admitted one day that the old political battles waged in California were much more to his liking than the battles he had gone through over here. On second thought he laughed as though it were a good joke, but he evidently intended me to infer that he had taken a keen interest in politics in San Francisco.

When my "chummy enemy" first started his conversation with me the German doctor in charge reprimanded him for talking to me, but he paid no attention to the doctor, showing that some real Americanism had soaked into his system while he had been in the U. S. A.

I asked him one day what he thought the German people would do after the war; if he thought they would make Germany a republic, and, much to my surprise, he said, very bitterly, "If I had my way about it, I would make her a republic today and hang the damned *Kaiser* in the bargain." And yet he was considered an excellent soldier. I concluded, however, that he must have been a German Socialist, though he never told me so.

On one occasion I asked him for his name, but he said that I would probably never see him again and it didn't matter what his name was. I did not know whether he meant that the Germans would starve me out or just what was on his mind, for at that time I am sure he did not figure on dying. The first two or three days I was in the hospital I thought surely he would be up and gone long before I was, but blood poisoning set in about that time and just a few hours before I left for Courtrai he died.

One of those days, while my wound was still very troublesome, I was given an apple; whether it was just to torment me, knowing that I could not eat it, or whether for some other reason, I do not know. But, anyway, a German flying officer there had several in his pockets and gave me a nice one. Of course, there was no chance of my eating it, so when the officer had gone and I discovered this San Francisco fellow looking at it rather longingly I picked it up, intending to toss it over to him. But he shook his head and said, "If this was San Francisco, I would take it, but I cannot take it from you here." I was never able to understand just why he refused the apple, for he was usually sociable and a good fellow to talk to, but apparently he could not forget that I was his enemy. However, that did not stop one of the orderlies from eating the apple.

One practice about the hospital which impressed me particularly was that if a German soldier did not stand much chance of recovering sufficiently to take his place again in the war, the doctors did not exert themselves to see that he got well. But if a man had a fairly good chance of recovering and they thought he might be of some further use, everything that medical skill could possibly do was done for him. I don't know whether this was done under orders or whether the doctors just followed their own inclinations in such cases.

My teeth had been badly jarred up from the shot, and I hoped that I might have a chance to have them fixed when I reached Courtrai, the prison where I was to be taken. So I asked the doctor if it would be possible for me to have this work done there, but he very curtly told me that though there were several dentists at Courtrai, they were busy enough fixing the teeth of their own men without bothering about mine. He also added that I would not have to worry about my teeth; that I wouldn't be getting so much food that they would be put out of commission by working overtime. I wanted to tell him that from the way things looked he would not be wearing his out very soon, either.

My condition improved during the next two days and on the fourth day of my captivity I was well enough to write a brief message to my squadron reporting that I was a prisoner of war and "feeling fine," although, as a matter of fact, I was never so depressed in my life. I realised, however, that if the message reached my comrades, it would be relayed to my mother in Momence, Illinois, and I did not want to worry her more than was absolutely necessary. It was enough for her to know that I was a prisoner. She did not have to know that I was wounded.

I had hopes that my message would be carried over the lines and dropped by one of the German flying officers. That is a courtesy which is usually practised on both sides. I recalled how patiently we had waited in our aerodrome for news of our men who had failed to return, and I could picture my squadron speculating on my fate.

That is one of the saddest things connected with service in the R. F. C. You don't care much what happens to you, but the constant casualties among your friends is very depressing.

You go out with your "flight" and get into a muss. You get scattered and when your formation is broken up you finally wing your way home alone.

Perhaps you are the first to land. Soon another machine shows in the sky, then another, and you patiently wait for the rest to appear. Within an hour, perhaps, all have shown up save one, and you begin to speculate and wonder what has happened to him.

Has he lost his way? Has he landed at some other aerodrome? Did the Huns get him?

When darkness comes you realise that, at any rate, he won't be back that night, and you hope for a telephone-call from him telling of his whereabouts.

If the night passes without sign or word from him he is reported as missing, and then you watch for his casualty to appear in the war-office lists.

One day, perhaps a month later, a message is dropped over the line by the German Flying Corps with a list of pilots captured or killed by the Huns, and then, for the first time, you know definitely why it was your comrade failed to return the day he last went over the line with his squadron.

I was still musing over this melancholy phase of the scout's life when an orderly told me there was a beautiful battle going on in the air, and he volunteered to help me outside the hospital that I might witness it, and I readily accepted his assistance.

That afternoon I saw one of the gamest fights I ever expect to witness.

There were six of our machines against perhaps sixteen Huns. From the type of the British machines I knew that they might possibly be from my own aerodrome. Two of our machines had been apparently picked out by six of the Huns and were bearing the brunt of the fight. The contest seemed to me to be so unequal that victory for our men was hardly to be thought of, and yet at one time they so completely outmanoeuvred the Huns that I thought their superior skill might save the day for them, despite the fact that they were so hopelessly outnumbered. One thing I was sure of: they would never give in.

Of course it would have been a comparatively simple matter for our men, when they saw how things were going against them, to have turned their noses down, landed behind the German lines, and given themselves up as prisoners, but that is not the way of the R. F. C.

A battle of this kind seldom lasts many minutes, although every second seems like an hour to those who participate in it and even onlookers stiffer more thrills in the course of the struggle than they would ordinarily experience in a lifetime. It is apparent even to a novice that the loser's fate is death.

Of course the Germans around the hospital were all watching and rooting for their comrades, but the English, too, had one sympathizer in that group who made no effort to stifle his admiration for the bravery his comrades were displaying.

The end came suddenly. Four machines crashed to earth almost simultaneously. It was an even break—two of theirs and two of ours. The others apparently returned to their respective lines.

The wound in my mouth was bothering me considerably, but by means of a pencil and paper I requested one of the German officers to find out for me who the English officers were who had been shot down.

A little later he returned and handed me a photograph taken from the body of one of the victims. It was a picture of Paul Raney, of Toronto, and myself, taken together! Poor Raney! He was the best friend I had and one of the best and gamest men who ever fought in France!

It was he, I learned long after, who, when I was reported missing, had checked over all my belongings and sent them back to England with a signed memorandum—which is now in my possession. Poor fellow, he little realised then that but a day or two later he would be engaged in his last heroic battle, with me a helpless onlooker!

The same German officer who brought me the photograph also drew a map for me of the exact spot, where Raney was buried in Flanders. I guarded it carefully all through my subsequent adventures and finally turned it over to his father and mother when I visited them in Toronto to perform the hardest and saddest duty I have ever been called upon to execute—to confirm to them in person the tidings of poor Paul's death.

The other British pilot who fell was also from my squadron and a man I knew well—Lieutenant Keith, of Australia. I had given him a picture of myself only a few hours before I started on my own disastrous flight. He was one of the star pilots of our squadron and had been in many a desperate battle before, but this time the odds were too great for him. He put up a wonderful fight and he gave as much as he took.

The next two days passed without incident and I was then taken to the Intelligence Department of the German Flying Corps, which was located about an hour from the hospital. There I was kept two days, during which time they put a thousand and one questions to me. While I was there I turned over to them the message I had written in the hospital and asked them to have one of their fliers drop it on our side of the line.

They asked me where I would like it dropped, thinking perhaps I would give my aerodrome away, but when I smiled and shook my head they did not insist upon an answer.

"I'll drop it over ——," declared one of them, naming my aerodrome, which revealed to me that their flying corps is as efficient as other branches of the service in the matter of obtaining valuable information.

And right here I want to say that the more I came to know of the enemy the more keenly I realised what a difficult task we're going to

LIEUT. PAUL H. RANEY OF TORONTO AND LIEUT. PAT O BRIEN
(Raney was killed in action before the eyes of O'Brien,
who was a prisoner of war. This picture, found on the
body of Raney when he fell behind the German lines,
was handed to O'Brien to identify the victim.)

have to lick him. In all my subsequent experience the fact that there is a heap of fight left in the Huns still was thoroughly brought home to me. We shall win the war eventually, if we don't slow up too soon in the mistaken idea that the Huns are ready to lie down.

The flying officers who questioned me were extremely anxious to find out all they could about the part America is going to play in the war, but they evidently came to the conclusion that America hadn't taken me very deeply into her confidence, judging from the information they got, or failed to get, from me.

At any rate, they gave me up as a bad job and I was ordered to the officers' prison at Courtrai, Belgium.

CHAPTER 5

# The Prison-Camp at Courtrai

From the Intelligence Department I was conveyed to the officers' prison-camp at Courtrai in an automobile. It was about an hour's ride. My escort was one of the most famous flyers in the world, barring none. He was later killed in action, but I was told by an English airman who witnessed his last combat that he fought a game battle and died a hero's death.

The prison, which had evidently been a civil prison of some kind before the war, was located right in the heart of Courtrai. The first building we approached was large, and in front of the archway, which formed the main entrance, was a sentry box. Here we were challenged by the sentry, who knocked on the door; the guard turned the key in the lock and I was admitted. We passed through the archway and directly into a courtyard, on which faced all of the prison buildings, the windows, of course, being heavily barred.

After I had given my pedigree—my name, age, address, etc.—I was shown to a cell with bars on the windows overlooking this courtyard. I was promptly told that at night we were to occupy these rooms, but I had already surveyed the surroundings, taken account of the number of guards and the locked door outside, and concluded that my chances of getting away from some other place could be no worse than in that particular cell.

As I had no hat, my helmet being the only thing I wore over the lines, I was compelled either to go bareheaded or wear the red cap of the Bavarian whom I had shot down on that memorable day. It can be imagined how I looked attired in a British uniform and a bright red cap. Wherever I was taken, my outfit aroused considerable curiosity among the Belgians and German soldiers.

When I arrived at prison that day I still wore this cap, and as I was taken into the courtyard, my overcoat covering my uniform, all that the British officers who happened to be sunning themselves in the courtyard could see was the red cap. They afterward told me they wondered who the "big Hun" was with the bandage on his mouth. This cap I managed to keep with me, but was never allowed to wear it on the walks we took. I either went bareheaded or borrowed a cap from some other prisoner.

At certain hours each day the prisoners were allowed to mingle in the courtyard, and on the first occasion of this kind I found that there were eleven officers imprisoned there besides myself.

They had here interpreters who could speak all languages. One of them was a mere boy who had been born in Jersey City, New Jersey, and had spent all his life in America until the beginning of 1914. Then he moved with his folks to Germany, and when he became of military age the Huns forced him into the army. I think if the truth were known he would much rather have been fighting for America than against her.

I found that most of the prisoners remained at Courtrai only two or three days. From there they were invariably taken to prisons in the interior of Germany.

Whether it was because I was an American or because I was a flier, I don't know, but this rule was not followed in my case. I remained there two weeks.

During that period, Courtrai was constantly bombed by our airmen. Not a single day or night passed without one or more air raids. In the two weeks I was there I counted twenty-one of them. The town suffered a great deal of damage. Evidently our people were aware that the Germans had a lot of troops concentrated in this town, and, besides, the headquarters staff was stationed there. The *Kaiser* himself visited Courtrai while I was in the prison, I was told by one of the interpreters, but he didn't call on me and, for obvious reasons, I couldn't call on him.

The courtyard was not a very popular place during air raids. Several times when our airmen raided that section in the daytime I went out and watched the machines and the shrapnel bursting all around; but the Germans did not crowd out there, for their own anti-aircraft guns were hammering away to keep our planes as high in the sky as possible, and shells were likely to fall in the prison yard any moment. Of course, I watched these battles at my own risk.

Many nights from my prison window I watched with peculiar

interest the air raids carried on, and it was a wonderful sight with the German searchlights playing on the sky, the "flaming onions" fired high and the burst of the anti-aircraft guns, but rather an uncomfortable sensation when I realised that perhaps the very next minute a bomb might be dropped on the building in which I was a prisoner. But perhaps all of this was better than no excitement at all, for prison life soon became very monotonous.

One of the hardest things I had to endure throughout the two weeks I spent there was the sight of the Hun machines flying over Courtrai, knowing that perhaps I never would have another chance to fly, and I used to sit by the hour watching the German machines manoeuvring over the prison, as they had an aerodrome not far away, and every afternoon the students—I took them for students because their flying was very poor—appeared over the town.

One certain Hun seemed to find particular satisfaction in flying right down over the prison nightly, for my special discomfort and benefit it seemed, as if he knew an airman imprisoned there was vainly longing to try his wings again over their lines. But I used to console myself by saying, "Never mind, old boy; there was never a bird whose wings could not be clipped if they got him just right, and your turn will come some day."

One night there was an exceptionally heavy air raid going on. A number of German officers came into my room, and they all seemed very much frightened. I jokingly remarked that it would be fine if our airmen hit the old prison—the percentage would be very satisfactory—one English officer and about ten German ones. They didn't seem to appreciate the joke, however, and, indeed, they were apparently too much alarmed at what was going on overhead to laugh even at their own jokes. Although these night raids seemed to take all the starch out of the Germans while they were going on, the officers were usually as brave as lions the next day and spoke contemptuously of the raid of the night before.

I saw thousands of soldiers in Courtrai, and although they did not impress me as having very good or abundant food, they were fairly well clothed. I do not mean to imply that conditions pointed to an early end of the war. On the contrary, from what I was able to observe on that point, unless the Huns have an absolute crop failure, they can, in my opinion, go on for years! The idea of our being able to win the war by starving them out strikes me as ridiculous. This is a war that must be won by *fighting*, and the sooner we realise that fact the sooner it will be over.

Rising-hour in the prison was seven o'clock. Breakfast came at eight. This consisted of a cup of coffee and nothing else. If the prisoner had the foresight to save some bread from the previous day, he had bread for breakfast also, but that never happened in my case. Sometimes we had two cups of coffee—that is, near-coffee. It was really chicory or some cereal preparation. We had no milk or sugar.

For lunch they gave us boiled sugar-beets or some other vegetable, and once in a while some kind of pickled meat, but that happened very seldom. We also received a third of a loaf of bread—war-bread. This war-bread was as heavy as a brick, black, and sour. It was supposed to last us from noon one day to noon the next. Except for some soup, this was the whole lunch menu.

Dinner came at 5.30 p.m., when we sometimes had a little jam made out of sugar-beets, and a preparation called tea which you had to shake vigorously or it settled in the bottom of the cup and then about all you had was hot water. This "tea" was a sad blow to the Englishmen. If it hadn't been called tea, they wouldn't have felt so badly about it, perhaps, but it was adding insult to injury to call that stuff "tea" which, with them, is almost a national institution.

Sometimes with this meal they gave us butter instead of jam, and once in a while we had some kind of canned meat.

This comprised the usual run of eatables for the day—I can eat more than that for breakfast! In the days that were to come, however, I was to fare considerably worse.

We were allowed to send out and buy a few things, but as most of the prisoners were without funds, this was but an empty privilege. Once I took advantage of the privilege to send my shoes to a Belgian shoemaker to be half-soled. They charged me twenty *marks*—five dollars!

Once in a while a Belgian Ladies' Relief Society visited the prison and brought us handkerchiefs, American soap—which sells at about one dollar and fifty cents a bar in Belgium—toothbrushes, and other little articles, all of which were American-made, but whether they were supplied by the American Relief Committee or not I don't know. At any rate, these gifts were mighty useful and were very much appreciated.

One day I offered a button off my uniform to one of these Belgian ladies as a souvenir, but a German guard saw me and I was never allowed to go near the visitors afterward.

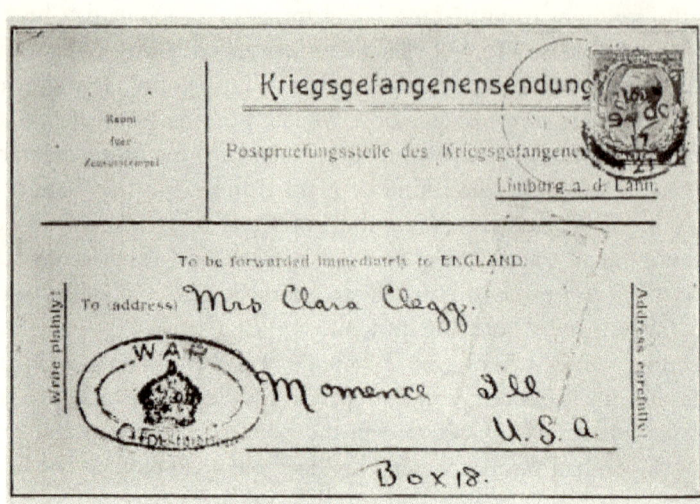

MAILING-CARD SENT BY GERMAN GOVERNMENT TO PAT O'BRIEN'S SISTER, MRS. CLARA CLEGG OF MOMENCE, ILLINOIS

OBVERSE SIDE OF CARD SHOWN ABOVE

The sanitary conditions in this prison-camp were excellent as a general proposition. One night, however, I discovered that I had been captured by "cooties."

This was a novel experience to me and one that I would have been very willing to have missed, because in the Flying Corps our aerodromes are a number of miles back of the lines and we have good billets, and our acquaintance with such things as "cooties" and other unwelcome visitors is very limited.

When I discovered my condition I made a holler and roused the guard, and right then I got another example of German efficiency.

This guard seemed to be even more perturbed about my complaint than I was myself, evidently fearing that he would be blamed for my condition.

The *commandant* was summoned, and I could see that he was very angry. Someone undoubtedly got a severe reprimand for it.

I was taken out of my cell by a guard with a rifle and conducted about a quarter of a mile from the prison to an old factory building which had been converted into an elaborate fumigating plant. There I was given a pickle bath in some kind of solution, and while I was absorbing it my clothes, bedclothes, and whatever else had been in my cell were being put through another fumigating process.

While I was waiting for my things to dry—it took, perhaps, half an hour—I had a chance to observe about one hundred other victims of "cooties"—German soldiers who had become infested in the trenches. We were all nude, of course, but apparently it was not difficult for them to recognise me as a foreigner even without my uniform on, for none of them made any attempt to talk to me, although they all were very busy talking *about* me. I could not understand what they were saying, but I know I was the butt of most of their jokes, and they made no effort to conceal the fact that I was the subject of their conversation.

When I got back to my cell I found that it had been thoroughly fumigated, and from that time on I had no further trouble with "cooties" or other visitors of the same kind.

As we were not allowed to write anything but prison cards, writing was out of the question; and as we had no reading-matter to speak of, reading was nil. We had nothing to do to pass away the time, so consequently cards became our only diversion, for we did, fortunately, have some of those.

There wasn't very much money, as a rule, in circulation, and I think for once in my life I held most of that, not due to any particular ability on my part in the game, but I happened to have several hundred *francs* in my pockets when shot down. But we held a lottery there once a day, and I don't believe there was ever another lottery held that was watched with quite such intense interest as that. The drawing was always held the day before the prize was to be awarded, so we always knew the day before who was the lucky man. There was as much speculation as to who would win the prize as if it had been the finest treasure in the world. The great prize was one-third of a loaf of bread.

Through some arrangement which I never quite figured out, it happened that among the eight or ten officers who were there with me there was always one-third of a loaf of bread over. There was just one way of getting that bread, and that was to draw lots. Consequently that was what started the lottery. I believe if a man had ever been inclined to cheat he would have been sorely tempted in this instance, but the game was played absolutely square, and if a man had been caught cheating, the chances are that he would have been shunned by the rest of the officers as long as he was in prison. I was fortunate enough to win the prize twice.

One man—I think he was the smallest eater in the camp—won it on three successive days, but it was well for him that his luck deserted him on the fourth day, for he probably would have been handled rather roughly by the rest of the crowd, who were growing suspicious. But we handled the drawing ourselves and knew there was nothing crooked about it, so he was spared.

We were allowed to buy pears, and, being small and very hard, they were used as the stakes in many a game. But the interest in these little games was as keen as if the stakes had been piles of money instead of two or three half-starved pears. No man was ever so reckless, however, in all the betting, as to wager his own rations.

By the most scheming and sacrificing I ever did in my life I managed to hoard two pieces of bread (grudgingly spared at the time from my daily rations), but I was preparing for the day when I should escape—if I ever should. It was not a sacrifice easily made, either, but instead of eating bread I ate pears until I finally got one piece of bread ahead; and when I could force myself to stick to the pear diet again I saved the other piece from that day's allowance, and in days to come I had cause to credit myself fully for the foresight.

Whenever a new prisoner came in and his German hosts had satisfied themselves as to his life history and taken down all the details—

that is, all he would give them—he was immediately surrounded by his fellow-prisoners, who were eager for any bit of news or information he could possibly give them, and as a rule he was glad to tell us because, if he had been in the hands of the Huns for any length of time, he had seen very few English officers.

The conditions of this prison were bad enough when a man was in normally good health, but it was barbarous to subject a wounded soldier to the hardships and discomforts of the place. However, this was the fate of a poor private we discovered there one day in terrific pain, suffering from shrapnel in his stomach and back. All of us officers asked to have him sent to a hospital, but the doctors curtly refused, saying it was against orders. So the poor creature went on suffering from day to day and was still there when I left, another victim of German cruelty.

At one time in this prison-camp there were a French marine, a French flying officer, and two Belgian soldiers, and of the United Kingdom one from Canada, two from England, three from Ireland, a couple from Scotland, one from Wales, a man from South Africa, one from Algeria, and a New-Zealander, the last being from my own squadron, a man whom I thought had been killed, and he was equally surprised, when brought into the prison, to find me there. In addition there were a Chinaman and myself from the U. S. A.

It was quite a cosmopolitan group, and as one typical Irishman said, "Sure, and we have every nation that's worth mentioning, including the darn Germans, with us whites." Of course, this was not translated to the Germans, nor was it even spoken in their hearing, or we probably would not have had quite so cosmopolitan a bunch. Each man in the prison was ready to uphold his native country in any argument that could possibly be started, and it goes without saying that I never took a back seat in any of them with my praise for America, with the Canadian and Chinaman chiming in on my side. But they were friendly arguments; we were all in the same boat and that was no place for quarrelling.

Every other morning, the weather allowing, we were taken to a large swimming-pool and were allowed to have a bath. There were two pools, one for the German officers and one for the men. Although we were officers, we had to use the pool occupied by the men. While we were in swimming a German guard with a rifle across his knees sat at each corner of the pool and watched us closely as we dressed and undressed. English interpreters accompanied us on all of these trips, so at no time could we talk without their knowing what was going on.

Whenever we were taken out of the prison for any purpose they always paraded us through the most crowded streets—evidently to give the populace an idea that they were getting lots of prisoners. The German soldiers we passed on these occasions made no effort to hide their smiles and sneers.

The Belgian people were apparently very curious to see us, and they used to turn out in large numbers whenever the word was passed that we were out. At times the German guards would strike the women and children who crowded too close to us. One day I smiled and spoke to a pretty Belgian girl, and when she replied a German made a run for her. Luckily she stepped into the house before he reached her or I am afraid my salutation would have resulted seriously for her and I would have been powerless to have assisted her.

Whenever we passed a Belgian home or other building which had been wrecked by bombs dropped by our airmen our guards made us stop a moment or two while they passed sneering remarks among themselves.

One of the most interesting souvenirs I have of my imprisonment at Courtrai is a photograph of a group of us taken in the prison courtyard. The picture was made by one of the guards, who sold copies of it to those of us who were able to pay his price—one *mark* apiece.

As we faced the camera, I suppose we all tried to look our happiest, but the majority of us, I am afraid, were too sick at heart to raise a smile even for this occasion. One of our Hun guards is shown in the picture seated at the table. I am standing directly behind him, attired in my flying tunic, which they allowed me to wear all the time I was in prison, as is the usual custom with prisoners of war. Three of the British officers shown in the picture, in the foreground, are clad in "shorts."

Through all my subsequent adventures I was able to retain a print of this interesting picture, and although when I gaze at it now it only serves to increase my gratification at my ultimate escape, it fills me with regret to think that my fellow-prisoners were not so fortunate. All of them, by this time, are undoubtedly eating their hearts up in the prison-camps of interior Germany. Poor fellows!

Despite the scanty fare and the restrictions we were under in this prison, we did manage on one occasion to arrange a regular banquet. The planning which was necessary helped to pass the time.

A GROUP OF PRISONERS OF WAR IN THE PRISON-CAMP AT COURTRAI, BELGIUM

(Lieutenant O'Brien, in his R.F.C. flying tunic, is standing in the centre behind the German guard seated at the table. This picture was taken by one of the German guards and sold to Lieutenant O'Brien for one mark.)

At this time there were eight of us. We decided that the principal thing we needed to make the affair a success was potatoes, and I conceived a plan to get them. Every other afternoon they took us for a walk in the country, and it occurred to me that it would be a comparatively simple matter for us to pretend to be tired and sit down when we came to the first potato-patch.

It worked out nicely. When we came to the first potato-patch that afternoon we told our guards that we wanted to rest a bit and we were allowed to sit down. In the course of the next five minutes each of us managed to get a potato or two. Being Irish, I got six.

When we got back to the prison I managed to steal a handkerchief full of sugar which, with some apples that we were allowed to purchase, we easily converted into a sort of jam.

We now had potatoes and jam, but no bread. It happened that the Hun who had charge of the potatoes was a great musician. It was not very difficult to prevail upon him to play us some music, and while he went out to get his zither I went into the bread pantry and stole a loaf of bread.

Most of us had saved some butter from the day before and we used it to fry our potatoes. By bribing one of the guards he bought some eggs for us. They cost twenty-five cents apiece, but we were determined to make this banquet a success, no matter what it cost.

The cooking was done by the prison cook, whom, of course, we had to bribe.

When the meal was ready to serve it consisted of scrambled eggs, fried potatoes, bread and jam, and a pitcher of beer which we were allowed to buy.

That was the 29th of August. Had I known that it was to be the last real meal that I was to eat for many weeks I might have enjoyed it even more than I did, but it was certainly very good.

We had cooked enough for eight, but while we were still eating another joined us. He was an English officer who had just been brought in on a stretcher. For seven days, he told us, he had lain in a shell-hole, wounded, and he was almost famished, and we were mighty glad to share our banquet with him.

We called on each man for a speech, and one might have thought that we were at a first-class club meeting. A few days after that our party was broken up and some of the men I suppose I shall never see again.

One of the souvenirs of my adventure is a check given me during this "banquet" by Lieut. James Henry Dickson, of the Tenth Royal Irish Fusiliers, a fellow-prisoner. It was for twenty *francs* and was made payable to the order of "Mr. Pat O'Brien, 2nd Lieut." Poor Jim forgot to scratch out the "London" and substitute "Courtrai" on the date line, but its value as a souvenir is just as great. When he gave it to me he had no idea that I would have an opportunity so soon afterward to cash it in person, although I am quite sure that whatever financial reverses I may be destined to meet my want will never be great enough to induce me to realise on that check.

There was one subject that was talked about in this prison whenever conversation lagged, and I suppose it is the same in the other prisons, too. What were the chances of escape?

Every man seemed to have a different idea and one way I suppose was about as impracticable as another. None of us ever expected to get a chance to put our ideas into execution, but it was interesting speculation, and, anyway, one could never tell what opportunities might present themselves.

One suggestion was that we disguise ourselves as women. "O'Brien would stand a better chance disguised as a horse!" declared another, referring to the fact that my height (I am six feet two inches) would make me more conspicuous as a woman than as a man.

Another suggested that we steal a German Gotha—a type of aeroplane used for long-distance bombing. It is these machines which are used for bombing London. They are manned by three men, one sitting in front with a machine-gun, the pilot sitting behind him, and an observer sitting in the rear with another machine-gun. We figured that at a pinch perhaps seven or eight of us could make our escape in a single machine. They have two motors of very high horse-power, fly very high and make wonderful speed. But we had no chance to put this idea to the test.

I worked out another plan by which I thought I might have a chance if I could ever get into one of the German aerodromes. I would conceal myself in one of the hangars, wait until one of the German machines started out, and as he taxied along the ground I would rush out, shout at the top of my voice, and point excitedly at his wheels. This, I figured, would cause the pilot to stop and get out to see what was wrong. By that time I would be up to him and as he stooped over to inspect the machine I could knock him senseless, jump into the machine, and be over the lines before the Huns could make up their minds just what had happened.

It was a fine dream, but my chance was not to come that way.

There were dozens of other ways which we considered. One man would be for endeavouring to make his way right through the lines. Another thought the safest plan would be to swim some river that crossed the lines.

The idea of making one's way to Holland, a neutral country, occurred to everyone, but the one great obstacle in that direction, we all realised, was the great barrier of barbed and electrically charged wire which guards every foot of the frontier between Belgium and Holland and which is closely watched by the German sentries.

This barrier was a threefold affair. It consisted first of a barbed-wire wall six feet high. Six feet beyond that was a nine-foot wall of wire powerfully charged with electricity. To touch it meant electrocution. Beyond that, at a distance of six feet was another wall of barbed wire six feet high.

Beyond the barrier lay Holland and liberty, but how to get there was a problem which none of us could solve and few of us ever expected to have a chance to try.

Mine came sooner than I expected.

CHAPTER 6

# A Leap for Liberty

I had been in prison at Courtrai nearly three weeks when, on the morning of September 9th, I and six other officers were told that we were to be transferred to a prison-camp in Germany.

One of the guards told me during the day that we were destined for a reprisal camp in Strassburg. They were sending us there to keep our airmen from bombing the place.

He explained that the English carried German officers on hospital-ships for a similar purpose, and he excused the German practice of torpedoing these vessels on the score that they also carried munitions! When I pointed out to him that France would hardly be sending munitions to England, he lost interest in the argument.

Some days before I had made up my mind that it would be a very good thing to get hold of a map of Germany which I knew was in the possession of one of the German interpreters, because I realised that if ever the opportunity came to make my escape such a map might be of the greatest assistance to me.

With the idea of stealing this map, accordingly, a lieutenant and I got in front of this interpreter's window one day and engaged in a very hot argument as to whether Heidelberg was on the Rhine or not, and we argued back and forth so vigorously that the German came out of his room, map in hand, to settle it. After the matter was entirely settled to our satisfaction he went back into his room and I watched where he put the map.

When, therefore, I learned that I was on my way to Germany I realised that it was more important than ever for me to get that map, and, with the help of my friend, we got the interpreter out of his room on some pretext or another, and while he was gone I confiscated the map from the book in which he kept it and concealed it in my sock underneath my legging. As I had anticipated, it later proved of the utmost value to me.

I got it none too soon, for half an hour later we were on our way to Ghent. Our party consisted of five British officers and one French officer. At Ghent, where we had to wait for several hours for another train to take us direct to the prison in Germany, two other prisoners were added to our party.

In the interval we were locked in a room at a hotel, a guard sitting at the door with a rifle on his knee. It would have done my heart good for the rest of my life if I could have got away then and fooled that Hun, he was so cocksure.

Later we were marched to the train that was to convey us to Germany. It consisted of some twelve coaches, eleven of them containing troops going home on leave, and the twelfth reserved for us. We were placed in a fourth-class compartment, with old, hard, wooden seats, a filthy floor, and no lights save a candle placed there by a guard. There were eight of us prisoners and four guards.

As we sat in the coach we were an object of curiosity to the crowd who gathered at the station.

"Hope you have a nice trip!" one of them shouted, sarcastically.

"Drop me a line when you get to Berlin, will you?" shouted another in broken English.

"When shall we see you again?" asked a third.

"Remember me to your friends, will you? You'll find plenty where you're going!" shouted another.

The German officers made no effort to repress the crowd; in fact, they joined in the general laughter which followed every sally.

I called to a German officer who was passing our window.

"You're an officer, aren't you?" I asked, respectfully enough.

"Yes. What of it?" he rejoined.

"Well, in England," I said, "we let your officers who are prisoners ride first-class. Can't you fix it so that we can be similarly treated, or be transferred at least to a second-class compartment?"

"If I had my way," he replied, "you'd ride with the hogs!"

Then he turned to the crowd and told them of my request and how he had answered me, and they all laughed hilariously.

This got me pretty hot.

"That would be a damned sight better than riding with the Germans!" I yelled after him, but if he considered that a good joke, too, he didn't pass it on to the crowd.

Some months later when I had the honour of telling my story to King George he thought this incident was one of the best jokes he had ever heard. I don't, believe he ever laughed harder in his life.

Before our train pulled out our guards had to present their arms for inspection, and their rifles were loaded in our presence to let us know that they meant business.

From the moment the train started on its way to Germany the thought kept coming to my head that unless I could make my escape before we reached that reprisal camp I might as well make up my mind that, as far as I was concerned, the war was over.

It occurred to me that if the eight of us in that car could jump up at a given signal and seize those four Hun guards by surprise, we'd have a splendid chance of besting them and jumping off the train when it first slowed down, but when I passed the idea on to my comrades they turned it down. Even if the plan had worked out as gloriously as I had pictured, they pointed out, the fact that so many of us had escaped would almost inevitably result in our recapture. The Huns would have scoured Belgium till they had got us and then we would all be shot. Perhaps they were right.

Nevertheless, I was determined that, no matter what the others decided to do, I was going to make one bid for freedom, come what might.

As we passed through village after village in Belgium and I realised that we were getting nearer and nearer to that dreaded reprisal camp, I concluded that my one and only chance of getting free before we reached it was through the window! I would have to go through that window while the train was going full speed, because if I waited until it had slowed up or stopped entirely, it would be a simple matter for the guards to overtake or shoot me.

I opened the window. The guard who sat opposite me—so close that his feet touched mine and the stock of his gun which he held between his knees occasionally struck my foot—made no objection, imagining, no doubt, that I found the car too warm or that the smoke, with which the compartment was filled, annoyed me.

As I opened the window the noise the train was making as it thundered along grew louder. It seemed to say: "You're a fool if you do; you're a fool if you don't! You're a fool if you do; you're a fool if you don't!" And I said to myself, "The 'no's' have it," and closed down the window again.

As soon as the window was closed the noise of the train naturally subsided and its speed seemed to diminish, and my plan appealed to me stronger than ever.

I knew the guard in front of me didn't understand a word of English, and so, in a quiet tone of voice, I confided to the English officer who sat next me what I planned to do.

"For God's sake, Pat, chuck it!" he urged. "Don't be a lunatic! This railroad is double-tracked and rock-ballasted and the other track is on your side. You stand every chance in the world of knocking your brains out against the rails, or hitting a bridge or a whistling post, and, if you escape those, you will probably be hit by another train on the other track. You haven't one chance in a thousand to make it!"

There was a good deal of logic in what he said, but I figured that, once I was in that reprisal camp, I might never have even one chance in a thousand to escape, and the idea of remaining a prisoner of war indefinitely went against my grain. I resolved to take my chance now even at the risk of breaking my neck.

The car was full of smoke. I looked across at the guard. He was rather an old man, going home on leave, and he seemed to be dreaming of what was in store for him rather than paying any particular attention to me. Once in a while I had smiled at him and I figured that he hadn't the slightest idea of what was going through my mind all the time we had been travelling.

I began to cough as though my throat were badly irritated by the smoke, and then I opened the window again. This time the guard looked up and showed his disapproval, but did not say anything.

It was then four o'clock in the morning and would soon be light. I knew I had to do it right then or never, as there would be no chance to escape in the daytime.

I had on a trench coat that I had used as a flying-coat and wore a knapsack which I had constructed out of a gas-bag brought into Courtrai by a British prisoner. In this I had two pieces of bread, a piece of sausage, and a pair of flying-mittens. All of them had to go with me through the window.

The train was now going at a rate of between thirty and thirty-five miles an hour, and again it seemed to admonish me, as it rattled along over the ties:

"You're a fool if you do; you're a fool if you don't! You're a fool if you don't; you're a fool if you do! You're a fool if you don't—"

I waited no longer. Standing up on the bench as if to put the bag on the rack, and taking hold of the rack with my left hand and a strap that hung from the top of the car with my right, I pulled myself up, shoved my feet and legs out of the window, and let go!

There was a prayer on my lips as I went out and I expected a bullet between my shoulders, but it was all over in an instant.

I landed on my left side and face, burying my face in the rock ballast, cutting it open and closing my left eye, skinning my hands and shins and straining my ankle. For a few moments I was completely knocked out, and if they shot at me through the window, in the first moments after my escape, I had no way of knowing.

Of course, if they could have stopped the train right then, they could easily have recaptured me, but at the speed it was going and in the confusion which must have followed my escape, they probably didn't stop within half a mile from the spot where I lay.

I came to within a few minutes, and when I examined myself and found no bones broken I didn't stop to worry about my cuts and bruises, but jumped up with the idea of putting as great a distance between me and that track as possible before daylight came. Still being dazed, I forgot all about the barbed-wire fence along the right-of-way and ran full tilt into it. Right there I lost one of my two precious pieces of bread, which fell out of my knapsack, but I could not stop to look for it then.

The one thing that was uppermost in my mind was that for the moment I was free and it was up to me now to make the most of my liberty.

## Chapter 7

# Crawling through Germany

The exact spot at which I made my desperate leap I don't know. Perhaps, after the war is over, some one on that train will be good enough to tell me, and then I may go back and look for the dent I must have made in the rock ballast.

As I have said, I didn't stop very long that morning after I once regained my senses.

I was bleeding profusely from the wounds caused by the fall, but I checked it somewhat with handkerchiefs I held to my face and I also held the tail of my coat so as to catch the blood as it fell and not leave telltale traces on the ground.

Before I stopped I had gone about a mile. Then I took my course from the stars and found that I had been going just opposite to the direction I should be making, but I could not go back across the track there.

Heading west, therefore, I kept this course for about two and a half hours, but as I was very weak from loss of blood I didn't cover very much ground in that time. Just before daylight I came to a canal which I knew I had to cross, and I swam it with everything I had on.

This swim, which proved to be the first of a series that I was destined to make, taught me several things.

In the first place, I had forgotten to remove my wristwatch. This watch had been broken in my fall from the air, but I had had it repaired at Courtrai. In the leap from the train the crystal had been broken again, but it was still going and would probably have been of great service to me in my subsequent adventures, but the swim across the canal ruined it.

Then, too, I had not thought to take my map out of my sock, and the water damaged that, too.

Thereafter, whenever I had any swimming to do, I was careful to take such matters into consideration, and my usual practice was to make a bundle of all the things that would be damaged by water and tie it to my head. In this way I was able to keep them dry.

It was now daylight and I knew that it would be suicidal for me to attempt to travel in the daytime. My British uniform would have been fatal to me. I decided to hide in the daytime and travel only at night.

Not far from the canal I could see a heavily wooded piece of ground, and I made my way there. By this time I had discovered that my left ankle had been strained in my leap from the train, and when I got to the woods I was glad to lie down and rest. The wound in my mouth had been opened, too, when I jumped, and it would have been difficult for me to have swallowed had not the piece of bread, which was to serve for my breakfast, got wet when I swam the canal. I found a safe hiding-place in which to spend the day and I tried to dry some of my clothes, but a slight drizzling rainfall made that out of the question. I knew that I ought to sleep, as I planned to travel at night, but, sore as I was, caked with mud and blood, my clothing soaked through, and my hunger not nearly appeased, sleep was out of the question. This seemed to me about the longest day I had ever spent, but I was still to learn how long a day can really be and how much longer a night!

When night came I dragged myself together and headed northeast.

My clothing consisted of my Flying Corps uniform, two shirts, no underwear, leather leggings, heavy shoes, a good pair of wool socks, and a German cap. I had a wallet containing several hundred *francs* in paper money and various other papers. I also had a jack-knife which I had stolen one day from the property-room at Courtrai where all the personal effects taken from prisoners were kept. For a day or two I carried the knapsack, but as I had nothing to carry in it I discarded it.

I travelled rapidly, considering my difficulties, and swam a couple of canals that night, covering in all perhaps ten miles before daylight. Then I located in some low bushes, lying there all day in my wet clothes and finishing my sausage for food. That was the last of my rations.

That night I made perhaps the same distance, but became very hungry and thirsty before the night was over.

For the next six days I still figured that I was in Germany, and I was living on nothing but cabbage, sugar-beets, and an occasional carrot, always in the raw state, just as I got them out of the fields. The water

I drank was often very rank, as I had to get it from canals and pools. One night I lay in a cabbage-patch for an hour lapping the dew from the leaves with my tongue!

Dining this period I realised that I must avoid meeting any one at all hazards. I was in the enemy's country and my uniform would have been a dead give-away. Anyone who captured me or who gave information from which my capture resulted might have been sure of a handsome reward. I knew that it was necessary for me to make progress as fast as possible, but the main consideration was to keep out of sight, even if it took me a year to get to Holland, which was my objective. From my map, I estimated that I was about thirty-five miles from Strassburg when I made my leap from the train, and if I could travel in a straight line I had perhaps one hundred and fifty miles to travel. As it was, however, I was compelled to make many detours, and I figured that two hundred and fifty miles was nearer the extent of the journey ahead of me.

In several parts of this country I had to travel through forests of young pine-trees about twelve feet high. They were very close together and looked almost as if they had been set out. They proved to be a serious obstacle to me, because I could not see the stars through them, and I was relying upon the heavens to guide me to freedom. I am not much of an astronomer, but I know the Pole Star when I see it. But for it I wouldn't be here today!

I believe it rained every night and day while I was making my way through Germany to Luxembourg.

My invariable program at this stage of my journey was to travel steadily all night until about six in the morning, when I would commence looking around for a place wherein to hide during the day. Low bushes or woods back from the road, as far as possible from the travelled pathway, usually served me for this purpose. Having found such a spot, I would drop down and try to sleep. My overcoat was my only covering, and that was usually soaked through either from the rain or from swimming.

The only sleep I got during those days was from exhaustion, and it usually came to me toward dusk when it was time for me to start again.

It was a mighty fortunate thing for me that I was not a smoker. Somehow I have never used tobacco in any form and I was now fully repaid for whatever pleasure I had foregone in the past as a result of my habits in that particular, because my sufferings would certainly have been intensified now if in addition to lack of food and rest I had had to endure a craving for tobacco.

About the sixth night I was so drowsy and exhausted when the time came for me to be on the move that I was very much tempted to sleep through the night. I knew, however, that that would be a bad precedent to establish and I wouldn't give in.

I plugged wearily along and about eleven o'clock, after I had covered perhaps four miles, I sat down to rest for a moment on a shock of brush which was sheltered from the drizzle somewhat by other shocks which were stacked there. It was daylight when I awoke, and I found myself right in a German's backyard. You can imagine that I lost no time getting out of that neighbourhood, and I made up my mind right then that I would never give way to that "tired feeling" again.

In the daytime, in my hiding-place, wherever it happened to be, I had plenty of opportunity to study my map, and before very long I knew it almost by heart. Unfortunately, however, it did not show all the rivers and canals which I encountered, and sometimes it fooled me completely.

It must have been about the ninth night that I crossed into Luxembourg, but while this principality is officially neutral, it offered me no safer a haven than Belgium would. The Huns have violated the neutrality of both and discovery would have been followed by the same consequences as capture in Germany proper.

In the nine days I had covered perhaps seventy-five miles and I was that much nearer liberty, but the lack of proper food, the constant wearing of wet clothes, and the loss of sleep and rest had reduced me to a very much weakened condition. I doubted very much whether I would be able to continue, but I plugged along.

Chapter 8

# Nine Days in Luxembourg

I was now heading northwest and I thought that by keeping that course I would get out of Luxembourg and into Belgium, where I expected to be a little better off, because the people in Luxembourg were practically the same as Germans.

One of the experiences I had in Luxembourg which I shall never forget occurred the first day that I spent there. I had travelled all night and I was feeling very weak. I came to a small wood with plenty of low underbrush, and I picked out a thick clump of bushes which was not in line with any paths, crawled in, and lay down to spend the day.

The sun could just reach me through an opening in the trees above, and I took off all my clothes except my shirt and hung them on the bushes to dry in the sun. As the sun moved I moved the clothes around correspondingly, because, tired as I was, I could take only catnaps.

That afternoon I awoke from one of these naps with a start. There were voices not a dozen feet from me! My first impulse was to jump to my feet and sell my life as dearly as I could, but on second thoughts I decided to look before I leaped. Peeping through the underbrush, I could just discern two men calmly chopping down a tree and conversing as they worked. I thanked my lucky stars that I had not jumped up on my first impulse, for I was apparently quite safe as long as I lay where I was.

It then occurred to me that if the tree upon which they were working should happen to fall in my direction it would crush me to death! It was tall enough to reach me and big enough to kill me if it landed in my direction, and as I could see only the heads of the men who were chopping it down, I was unable to tell which way they planned to have it fall.

There was this much in my favour: the chances of the tree falling in just my direction were not very great and there was more than an even chance that the men would be wise enough to fell it so that it would not, because if it landed in the bushes the task of trimming the branches off the trunk would be so much harder.

But, even without this feeling of security, there was really nothing else I could do but wait and see what fate had in store for me. I lay there watching the top of the tree for more than an hour. Time and again I saw it sway and fancied it was coming in my direction, and it was all I could do to keep my place, but a moment later I would hear the crash of the men's axes and I knew that my imagination had played me a trick.

I was musing on the sorry plight I was in—weak, nearly starving to death, a refugee in a hostile country and waiting patiently to see which way a tree was going to fall—when there came a loud crack and I saw the top of the tree sway and fall almost opposite to the place where I lay! I had guessed right.

Later I heard some children's voices, and again peering through the underbrush, I saw that they had brought the men their lunch. You can't realise how I felt to see them eating their lunch so near at hand and to know that, hungry as I was, I could have none of it. I was greatly tempted to go boldly up to them and take a chance of getting a share, but I did not know whether they were Germans or not, and I had gone through too much to risk my liberty even for food. I swallowed my hunger instead.

Shortly afterward it began to rain, and about four o'clock the men left. I crawled out as fast as I could, and scurried around looking for crumbs, but found none, and when darkness came I went on my way once more.

That night I came to a river, and as it was the first time my clothes had been dry for a long time, I thought I would try to keep them that way as long as possible. I accordingly took off all my things and made them into two bundles, planning to carry one load across and then swim back for the other.

The river was quite wide, but I am a fairly good swimmer, and I figured I could rest awhile after the first trip before going back for the second bundle.

The first swim was uneventful. When I landed on the other side I drank till my thirst was quenched, and then swam back. After resting awhile I started across a third time, with my shoes and several other things firmly tied to my head. Just about ten feet from the opposite bank one of the shoes worked its way loose and sank in about eight feet of water. There was nothing to do but finish the trip and then go back and dive for the missing shoe, as I could not go on with a single shoe.

Diving in my weakened condition was considerable strain, but I had to have that shoe, and I kept at it for nearly an hour before I eventually found it, and I was pretty nearly all in by that time.

That was the last time I ever took my shoes off, for my feet were becoming so swollen that I figured if I took my shoes off I might be unable to get them on again.

This stunt of crossing the river and diving for the lost shoe had consumed about three hours, and after resting some fifteen minutes I went on my way again. I had hardly gone a mile when I came to another river, about the same size as the one I had just crossed. I walked along the bank awhile, thinking that I might be lucky enough to find a boat or a bridge, but after walking about half an hour I received one of those disappointments which "come once in a lifetime." I found that this river was the one I had just swum! I had swum it on the bend and was still on the wrong side! Had I made only a short detour in the first place, I would have avoided all the annoyance of the past three hours and saved my strength and time. I was never so mad in my life at myself as I was to think that I had not paid more attention to the course of the stream before I undertook to cross it, but, as a matter of fact, there was really no way of telling. The river was not shown on my map at all.

Now I *had* to cross it, whereas before I could have turned it. I walked boldly into the water, not bothering to take my clothes off this time, nor did I ever bother to take them off afterward when swimming canals or rivers. I found it was impossible to keep them dry, anyway, and so I might just as well swim in them and save time.

All the next day I spent in a forest, to which my night's travel had brought me about five o'clock in the morning. I kept on my way through the woods until daylight came, and then, thinking the place would afford fairly good concealment, I concluded to rest until night.

The prospects of even a good sleep were dismal, however, for about the time the sun's face should have appeared a drizzling rain began and I gave up my search for a dry spot which would serve as a bed. Some of the leaves were beginning to fall, but of course there were not enough of them to have formed a covering for the ground, and the dampness seemed to have penetrated everywhere.

I wandered around through the woods for two or three hours, looking for shelter, but without any success, for, though the trees were large, the forest was not dense and there was practically no brush or shrubbery. Consequently, one could get a fairly clear view for some distance, and I knew it would be unwise to drop off to sleep just any place, or some one would surely happen onto me.

Once I came very near the edge of the woods and heard voices of men driving by in a wagon, but I couldn't make out just what they were, and instinct told me I had better not come out of the woods, so I turned back. Here and there small artificial ditches had been dug, which at a dry season might have cradled a weary-fugitive, but now they, too, were filled with water. Once I singled out a good big tree with large branches and thought I might climb into it and go to sleep, but the longer I looked at it the more I realised that it would require more energy than I had in my present weak and exhausted condition, so I didn't attempt that.

Finally I chose a spot that looked a bit drier than the rest, concluded to take a chance on being discovered, and threw myself down for a nap. I was extremely nervous, though, throughout that whole day and would scarcely get settled into a comfortable position and doze off for a few minutes when, startled by some sound in the woods, I would suddenly waken.

After what seemed like a year or more, night finally came, and with it a "dud" sky, low-hanging clouds, and still more rain. There was not a star in the sky, of course, and that made it very bad, because without the aid of the stars I had absolutely no way of knowing in which direction I was going. It was just a case of taking a chance. I probably would have been better off if I had simply picked out a place and stayed there until the weather improved, but naturally I was impatient to be on my way when each day without food only lessened my strength and my ultimate chances of reaching the frontier.

So I left the woods and struck off in the direction which I thought was north. I hadn't been at all sure of my bearings the day before, and as it had rained the sun failed entirely to help me out; but I was almost sure I had the right direction, and trusted to luck. That night I found more rivers, canals, and swamps than I ever found in my life before, but I had the good fortune to stumble on to some celery, and after my diet of beets it surely was a treat. Perhaps it's unnecessary to add that I took on a good supply of celery, and for days I went along chewing celery like a cow would a cud.

Along toward morning, when I supposed I had got in a fairly good lap of my journey—perhaps seven or eight miles—I began to recognise certain objects as familiar landmarks. At least, I thought I had seen them before, and as I travelled along I knew positively I had seen certain objects very recently. Off at my right—not over a quarter of a mile—I noticed some fairly good-sized woods, and thought I would go over there to hide that day, because it looked as though the sun was going to shine, and I hoped to get my clothes dry and perhaps get a decent sleep. I had this celery and a large beet, so I knew I would be able to live the day through.

Finally, I made my way over to the woods. It was still too dark in among the trees to do much in the way of selecting my quarters for the day, and I could not go a step farther. So I waited on the edge of the forest until dawn and then set out to explore the place with a view to finding some nook where I might sleep. Imagine my disgust and discouragement, too, when, an hour or so later, I came upon the exact place where I had spent the day before, and I realised that all night long I had been circling the very woods I was trying to get away from. I think perhaps I had gone all of a quarter of a mile in the right direction, but then had lost my bearings entirely and daylight found me with nothing accomplished.

The sun, however, did come out that day, and I welcomed its warm rays as they perhaps have never been welcomed before. I was very tired—just about all in—but I spent a better day in the woods than the previous one.

That night the stars came out; I located my friend, the North Star, and tried to make up for lost time. But when one is making only seven or eight miles a day, or rather a night, one night lost means a whole lot, especially when each day keeps him from freedom. Such ill fortune and discouragements as this were harder to endure, I believe, than the actual hunger, and the accompanying worry naturally reduced my weight. At times I was furiously angry with myself for the mistakes I made and the foolish things I did, but I always tried to see something funny about the situation, whatever it might be, that relieved the strain a bit and helped to pass the time. I think if a man is overburdened with a sense of humour and wants to get rid of it, this trip I took would be an excellent remedy for it. Right at this time I would have welcomed anything for a companion; I believe even a snake would have been a godsend to me.

With a name as Irish as mine, it is only natural that I looked for goats along the way, thinking that I might be able to milk them. There are very few cows in this country, and the opportunities for milking them fewer than the cows themselves, because they are housed in barns adjoining the homes and always alertly watched by their fortunate owners. I did hope that I might find a goat staked out some place in the fields, but in all my travels I never saw a goat or a pig, and only a few cows. Several times I searched nests for eggs, but somebody always had beaten me to it, as I never even found so much as a nest egg.

There was no chance of getting away with any "bullying" stuff in Luxembourg, I knew, because the young men have not been forced into the army and are still at home, and as they are decidedly pro-German, it would have been pretty hard for me to demand anything in that part of the country. It was not like taking things away from old men and women or robbing people that could not stop me if they chose to do so. I thought at this time that I was suffering about the worst hardships any human being could ever be called upon to endure, but I was later to find out that the best of my journey was made along about this time. There were plenty of vegetables, even though they were raw, and these were much better than the things I was afterward compelled to eat or go without.

We frequently hear of men who have lived for a certain number of days on their own resources in the woods just on a bet or to prove that the "back to nature" theory still has its merits and will still work. My advice to some of those nature-seekers is to, if in the future they wish to make a real good record, try the little countries of Luxembourg and Belgium, with a slice of Germany thrown in.

I suppose that during this experience of mine I made many mistakes and travelled many unnecessary miles which one with a knowledge of woodsmanship might have avoided, and I failed to take advantage of many things which would have been quite apparent to one who knew. It must not be forgotten, however, that I did not undertake this adventure voluntarily. It was "wished on me." I simply had to make the most of the knowledge I had.

At about this time blisters began to appear on my legs and my knees swelled. In addition I was pretty well convinced that I had lost the sight of my left eye. I hadn't seen a thing out of it since my leap from the train.

When I imagine the villainous appearance I must have presented at this time—my unhealed wounds, eighteen days' growth of beard, and general haggard and unkempt visage—I think the fear I felt about meeting strangers was perhaps unwarranted. The chances are they would have been infinitely more scared than I!

As it was, I was nearly out of Luxembourg before I really came face to face with anyone. It was about six o'clock in the morning and I was travelling along a regular path. Just as I approached a cross-path I heard footsteps coming down it. I stopped short, stooped over, and pretended to be adjusting my shoe-lace, figuring that if the stranger turned into my path he would probably pass right by me. As luck would have it, he continued on his way and never noticed me at all.

After that I frequently noticed groups of Luxembourg peasants in the distance, but I usually saw them first and managed to avoid them.

About the eighteenth day after my leap from the train I crossed into Belgium. It had taken me just nine days to get through Luxembourg—a distance which a man could ordinarily cover in two, but, considering the handicaps under which I laboured, I was very well satisfied with my progress.

## Chapter 9

# I Enter Belgium

I have said it was about the eighteenth day after my escape that I entered Belgium, but that is more or less guesswork. I was possibly well into that country before I realised that I had crossed the line.

About the third day after I figured I was in Belgium I started to swim a canal just before daylight. I was then heading due north in the direction of the German lines. I was just about to wade into the canal when I heard a German yelling violently, and for the first time I knew I was being followed!

I ran up the bank of the canal quite a distance and then swam to the opposite side, as I reasoned they would not be looking for me there. I found a sheltered clump of bushes in a swamp near the canal, and in the driest part that I could find I crawled in and made myself as comfortable as possible. The sun came up soon and kept me warm, and I planned to camp right there, food or no food, until the Huns got tired of searching for me. I think I heard them once or twice that day, and my heart nearly stopped on each occasion, but evidently they decided to look in some other direction and I was not further molested.

At the same time I figured that it was absolutely necessary for me to change my course even at the expense of going somewhat out of my way. Certainly if I went north they would get me. I decided to go due west, and I kept in that direction for four days.

As I was in a very weak condition, I did not cover more than five miles a night. I kept away from the roads and did all my journeying through fields, beet patches, woods, swamps—anywhere, provided I was not likely to be seen and captured. Food was an important consideration to me, but it was secondary to concealment.

At last I brought up at the Meuse River at a place between Namur and Huy, and it was here that I came nearest of all to giving up the struggle.

The Meuse at this point is about half a mile wide—as wide as the Hudson River at West Point. Had I been in normal condition I wouldn't have hesitated a moment to swim across. San Diego Bay, California, is a mile and a half wide, and I had often swum across and back, and the San Joaquin, which is also a mile and a half wide, had never proved an obstacle to me.

In the wretched shape in which I then was, however, the Meuse looked like the Atlantic Ocean to me. I looked for a boat, but could find none. I tried to get a piece of wood upon which I hoped to ferry across, but I was equally unsuccessful.

Get across I must, and I decided there was nothing to do but swim it.

It was then about three o'clock in the morning. I waded in and was soon in beyond my depth and had to swim. After about an hour of it I was very much exhausted and I doubted whether I could make the opposite bank, although it was not more than thirty or forty feet away. I choked and gasped and my arms and legs were completely fagged out. I sank a little and tried to touch bottom with my feet, but the water was still beyond my depth.

There are times when every one will pray, and I was no exception. I prayed for strength to make those few wicked yards, and then, with all the will power I could summon, struck out for dear life. It seemed a lifetime before I finally felt the welcome mud of bottom and was able to drag myself up to the bank, but I got there. The bank was rather high, and I was shaking so violently that when I took hold of the grass to pull myself up, the grass shook out of my hands. I could not retain my grip. I was afraid I would faint then and there, but I kept pulling and crawling frantically up that infernal bank, and finally made it.

Then, for the first time in my life, I fainted—fainted from utter exhaustion.

It was now about four o'clock in the morning and I was entirely unprotected from observation. If anyone had come along I would have been found lying there dead to the world.

Possibly two hours passed before I regained consciousness, and then, no doubt, only because the rain was beating in my face.

I knew that I had to get away, as it was broad daylight. Moreover, there was a towpath right there and any minute a boat might come along and find me. But it was equally dangerous for me to attempt to travel very far. Fortunately, I found some shrubbery near by, and I hid there all day, without food or drink.

That night I made a little headway, but when day broke I had a dreadful fever and was delirious. I talked to myself and thereby increased my chances of capture. In my lucid intervals, when I realised that I had been talking, the thought sent a chill through me, because in the silent night even the slightest sound carries far across the Belgian country. I began to fear that another day of this would about finish me.

I have a distinct recollection of a ridiculous conversation I canned on with an imaginary Pat O'Brien—a sort of duplicate of myself. I argued with him as I marched drearily along, and he answered me back in kind, and when we disagreed I called upon my one constant friend, the North Star, to stand by me. I cried, aloud:

> There you are, you old North Star! You want me to get to Holland, don't you? But this Pat O'Brien—this Pat O'Brien who calls himself a soldier—he's got a yellow streak—North Star—and he says it can't be done! He wants me to quit—to lie down here for the Huns to find me and take me back to Courtrai—after all you've done, North Star, to lead me to liberty. Won't you make this coward leave me. North Star? I don't want to follow him—I just want to follow you—because you—you are taking me away from the Huns and this Pat O'Brien—this fellow who keeps after me all the time and leans on my neck and wants me to lie down—this yellow Pat O'Brien wants me to go back to the Huns!

After a spell of foolish chatter like that my senses would come back to me for a while and I would trudge along without a word until the fever came on me again.

I knew that I had to have food because I was about on my last legs. I was very much tempted to lie down then and there and call it a heat. Things seemed to be getting worse for me the farther I went, and all the time I had before me the spectre of that electric barrier between Belgium and Holland, even if I ever reached there alive. What was the use of further suffering when I would probably be captured in the end, anyway?

Before giving up, however, I decided upon one bold move. I would approach one of the houses in the vicinity and get food there or die in the effort!

I picked out a small house, because I figured there would be less likelihood of soldiers being billeted there.

Then I wrapped a stone in my khaki handkerchief as a sort of camouflaged weapon, determined to kill the occupant of the house, German or Belgian, if that step were necessary in order to get food. I tried the well in the yard, but it would not work, and then I went up to the door and knocked.

It was one o'clock in the morning. An old lady came to the window and looked out. She could not imagine what I was, probably, because I was still attired in that old overcoat. She gave a cry, and her husband and a boy came to the door.

They could not speak English and I could not speak Flemish, but I pointed to my flying-coat and then to the sky and said *"fleger"* ("flier"), which I thought would tell them what I was.

Whether they understood or were intimidated by my hard-looking appearance, I don't know, but certainly it would have to be a brave old man and boy who would start an argument with such a villainous-looking character as stood before them that night! I had not shaved for a month, my clothes were wet, torn, and dirty, my leggings were gone—they had got so heavy I had discarded them—my hair was matted, and my cheeks were flushed with fever. In my hand I carried the rock in my handkerchief, and I made no effort to conceal its presence or its mission.

Anyway, they motioned me indoors and gave me my first hot meal in more than a month. True, it consisted only of warm potatoes. They had been previously cooked, but the old woman warmed them up in milk in one of the dirtiest kettles I had ever seen. I asked for bread, but she shook her head, although I think it must have been for lack of it rather than because she begrudged it to me. For if ever a man showed he was famished, I did right. I swallowed those warm potatoes ravenously and I drank four glasses of water one after another. It was the best meal I had had since the "banquet" in the prison at Courtrai.

The woman of the house was probably seventy-five years old and had evidently worn wooden shoes all her life, for she had a callous spot on the side of her foot the size of half a dollar, and it looked so hard that I doubt whether you could have driven a nail into it with a hammer.

As I sat there drying myself—for I was in no hurry to leave the first human habitation I had entered in four weeks—I reflected on my unhappy lot and the unknown troubles and dangers that lay ahead of me. Here, for more than a month, I had been leading the life of a hunted animal—yes, worse than a hunted animal, for Nature clothes her less favoured creatures more appropriately for the life they lead than I was clothed for mine—and there was not the slightest reason to hope that conditions would grow better.

Perhaps the first warm food I had eaten for over a month had released unused springs of philosophy in me, as food sometimes does for a man.

I pointed to my torn and water-soaked clothes and conveyed to them as best I could that I would be grateful for an old suit, but apparently they were too poor to have more than they actually needed themselves, and I rose to go. I had roused them out of bed, and I knew I ought not to keep them up longer than was absolutely necessary.

As I approached the door I got a glance at myself in a mirror. I was the awfulest sight I had ever laid eyes on! The glimpse I got of myself startled me almost as much as if I had seen a dreaded German helmet! My left eye was fairly well healed by this time, and I was beginning to regain the sight of it, but my face was so haggard and my beard so long and unkempt that I looked like Santa Claus on a "bat."

As they let me out of the door I pointed to the opposite direction to the one I intended taking and started off in the direction I had indicated. Later I changed my course completely to throw off any possible pursuit.

The next day I was so worn out from exposure and exhaustion that I threw away my coat, thinking that the less weight I had to carry the better it would be for me, but when night came I regretted my mistake, because the nights were now getting colder. I thought at first it would be best for me to retrace my steps and look for the coat I had so thoughtlessly discarded, but I decided to go on without it.

I then began to discard everything that I had in my pocket, finally throwing my wrist-watch into a canal. A wristwatch does not add much weight, but when you plod along and have not eaten for a month it finally becomes rather heavy. The next thing I discarded was a pair of flying-mittens.

These mittens I had got at Camp Borden, in Canada, and had become quite famous, as my friends termed them "snowshoes." In fact, they were a ridiculous pair of mittens, but the best pair I ever had, and I really felt worse when I lost those mittens than anything else. I could not think of anybody else ever using them, so I dug a hole in the mud and buried them, and could not help but laugh at the thought of what my friends would say had they seen me burying my mittens, because they were a standing joke in Canada, England, and France.

I had on two shirts, and as they were always both wet and didn't keep me warm, it was useless to wear both. One of these was a shirt that I had bought in France, the other an American army shirt. They were both khaki and one as apt to give me away as the other, so I discarded the French shirt. The American army shirt I brought back with me to England, and it is still in my possession.

When I escaped from the train I still had that Bavarian cap of bright red in my pocket and wore it for many nights, but I took great care that no one saw it. It also had proved very useful when swimming rivers, for I carried my map and a few other belongings in it, and I had fully made up my mind to bring it home as a souvenir. But the farther I went the heavier my extra clothing became, so I was compelled to discard even the cap. I knew that it would be a telltale mark if I simply threw it away, so one night after swimming a river I dug a hole in the soft mud on the bank and buried it, too, with considerably less ceremony than my flying-mittens had received, perhaps; and that was the end of my Bavarian hat.

My experience at the Belgian's house whetted my appetite for warm food, and I figured that what had been done once could be done again. Sooner or later I realised I would probably approach a Belgian and find a German instead, but in such a contingency I was determined to measure my strength against the Hun's if necessary to effect my escape.

As it was, however, most of the Belgians to whom I applied for food gave it to me readily enough, and if some of them refused me it was only because they feared I might be a spy or that the Germans would shoot them if their action were subsequently found out.

About the fifth day after I had entered Belgium I was spending the day as usual in a clump of bushes when I discerned in the distance what appeared to be something hanging on a line. All day long I strained my eyes trying to decide what it could be and arguing with myself that it might be something that I could add to my inadequate wardrobe, but the distance was so great that I could not identify it. I had a great fear that before night came it would probably be removed.

As soon as darkness fell, however, I crawled out of my hiding-place and worked up to the line and got a pair of overalls for my industry. It was a mighty joyful night for me. That pair of overalls was the first bit of civilian clothes I had thus far picked up, with the exception of a civilian cap which I had found at the prison and concealed on my person and which I still had. The overalls were rather small and very short, but when I put them on I found that they hung down far enough to cover my breeches.

It was perhaps three days later that I planned to search another house for further clothes. Entering Belgian houses at night is anything but a safe proposition, because their families are large and sometimes as many as seven or eight sleep in a single room. The barn is usually connected with the house proper, and there was always the danger of disturbing some dumb animal, even if the inmates of the house were not aroused.

Frequently I took a chance of searching a backyard at night in the hope of finding food scraps, but my success in that direction was so slight that I soon decided it wasn't worth the risk, and I continued to live on the raw vegetables that I could pick with safety in the fields and the occasional meal that I was able to get from the Belgian peasants in the daytime.

Nevertheless, I was determined to get more in the way of clothing, and when night came I picked out a house that looked as though it might furnish me with what I wanted. It was a moonlight night, and if I could get in the barn I would have a fair chance of finding my way around by the moonlight which would enter the windows.

The barn adjoined the main part of the house, but I groped around very carefully and soon I touched something hanging on a peg. I didn't know what it was, but I confiscated it and carried it out into the fields. There in the moonlight I examined my booty and found it was an old coat. It was too short as an overcoat and too long for an ordinary coat, but nevertheless I made use of it. It had probably been an overcoat for the Belgian who had worn it.

Some days later I got a scarf from a Belgian peasant, and with this equipment I was able to conceal my uniform entirely.

Later on, however, I decided that it was too dangerous to keep the uniform on anyway, and when night came I dug a hole and buried it.

I never realised until I had to part with it just how much I thought of that uniform. It had been with me through many hard trials, and I felt as if I were abandoning a friend when I parted with it. I was tempted to keep the wings off the tunic, but thought that that would be a dangerous concession to sentiment in the event that I was ever captured. It was the only distinction I had left, as I had given the Royal Flying Corps badges and the stars of my rank to the German Flying Officers as souvenirs, but I felt that it was safer to discard it. As it finally turned out, through all my subsequent experiences my escape would never have been jeopardized had I kept my uniform, but, of course, I had no idea what was in store for me.

There was one thing which surprised me very much as I journeyed through Belgium, and that was the scarcity of dogs. Apparently most of them have been taken by the Germans, and what are left are beasts of burden who are too tired at night to bark or bother intruders. This was a mighty good thing for me, for I would certainly have stirred them up in passing through backyards, as I sometimes did when I was making a short cut.

One night as I came out of a yard it was so pitch dark I could not see ten feet ahead of me, and I was right in the back of a little village, although I did not know it. I crawled along, fearing I might come to a crossroads at which there would in all probability be a German sentry.

My precaution served me in good stead, for I had come out in the main street of a village and within twenty feet of me, sitting on some bricks where they were building a little store, I could see the dim outline of a German spiked helmet!

I could not cross the street and the only thing to do was to backtrack. It meant making a long detour and losing two hours of precious time and effort, but there was no help for it, and I plodded wearily back, cursing the Huns at every step.

The next night while crossing some fields I came to a road. It was one of the main roads of Belgium and was paved with cobblestones. On these roads you can hear a wagon or horse about a mile or two away. I listened intently before I moved ahead, and, hearing nothing, concluded that the way was clear.

As I emerged from the field and got my first glimpse of the road I got the shock of my life! In either direction, as far as I could see, the road was lined with German soldiers!

What they were doing in that part of Belgium I did not know, but you can be mighty sure I didn't spend any time trying to find out.

Again it was necessary to change my course and lose a certain amount of ground, but by this time I had become fairly well reconciled to these reverses and they did not depress me as much as they had at first.

At this period of my adventure if a day or a night passed without its thrill I began to feel almost disappointed, but such disappointments were rather rare.

One evening as I was about to swim a canal about two hundred feet wide I suddenly noticed, about one hundred yards away, a canal-boat moored to the side.

It was a sort of out-of-the-way place, and I wondered what the canal-boat had stopped for. I crawled up to see. As I neared the boat five men were leaving it, and I noticed them cross over into the fields. At a safe distance I followed them, and they had not gone very far before I saw what they were after. They were committing the common but heinous crime of stealing potatoes!

Without the means to cook them, potatoes didn't interest me a bit, and I thought that the boat itself would probably yield me more than the potato-patch. Knowing that the canal hands would probably take their time in the fields, I climbed up the stem of the boat leisurely and without any particular pains to conceal myself. Just as my head appeared above the stem of the boat I saw, silhouetted against the sky, the dreaded outline of a German soldier—spiked helmet and all! A chill ran down my spine as I dropped to the bank of the canal and slunk away. Evidently the sentry had not seen me or, if he had, he had probably figured that I was one of the foraging party, but I realised that it wouldn't pay in future to take anything for granted.

CHAPTER 10

# Experiences in Belgium

I think that one of the worst things I had to contend with in my journey through Belgium was the number of small ditches. They intercepted me at every half-mile or so, sometimes more frequently. The canals and the big rivers I could swim. Of course, I got soaked to the skin every time I did it, but I was becoming hardened to that.

These little ditches, however, were too narrow to swim and too wide to jump. They had perhaps two feet of water in them and three feet of mud, and it was almost invariably a case of wading through. Some of them, no doubt, I could have jumped if I had been in decent shape, but with a bad ankle and in the weakened condition in which I was, it was almost out of the question.

One night I came to a ditch about eight or nine feet wide. I thought I was strong enough to jump it, and it was worth trying, as the discomfort I suffered after wading these ditches was considerable. Taking a long run, I jumped as hard as I could, but I missed it by four or five inches and landed in about two feet of water and three feet more of mud. Getting out of that mess was quite a job. The water was too dirty and too scanty to enable me to wash off the mud with which I was covered and it was too wet to scrape off. I just had to wait until it dried and scrape it off then.

In many sections of Belgium through which I had to pass I encountered large areas of swamp and marshy ground, and, rather than waste the time involved in looking for better under-footing—which I might not have found, anyway—I used to plod right through the mud. Apart from the discomfort of this method of travelling and the slow time I made, there was an added danger to me in the fact that the "squash-squash" noise which I made might easily be overheard by Belgians and Germans and give my position away. Nobody would cross a swamp or marsh in that part of the country unless he was trying to get away from somebody, and I realised my danger, but could not get around it.

It was a common sight in Belgium to see a small donkey and a common, ordinary milch cow hitched together, pulling a wagon. When I first observed the unusual combination I thought it was a donkey and ox or bull, but closer inspection revealed to me that cows were being used for the purpose.

From what I was able to observe, there must be very few horses left in Belgium except those owned by the Germans. Cows and donkeys are now doing the work formerly done by horses and mules. Altogether I spent nearly eight weeks wandering through Belgium and in all that time I don't believe I saw more than half a dozen horses in the possession of the native population.

One of the scarcest things in Germany, apparently, is rubber, for I noticed that their motor trucks, or lorries, unlike our own, had no rubber tires. Instead, heavy iron bands were employed. I could hear them come rumbling along the stone roads for miles before they reached the spot where I happened to be in hiding. When I saw these military roads in Belgium for the first time, with their heavy cobblestones that looked as if they would last for centuries, I realised at once why it was that the Germans had been able to make such a rapid advance into Belgium at the start of the war.

I noticed that the Belgians used dogs to a considerable extent to pull their carts, and I thought many times that if I could have stolen one of those dogs it would have made a very good companion for me, and might, if the occasion arose, help me out in a fight. But I had no way of feeding it and the animal would probably have starved to death. I could live on vegetables which I could always depend upon finding in the fields, but a dog couldn't, and so I gave up the idea.

The knack of making fire with two pieces of dry wood I had often read about, but I had never put it to a test, and for various reasons I concluded that it would be unsafe for me to build a fire even if I had matches. In the first place, there was no absolute need for it. I didn't have anything to cook, nor utensils to cook it in even if I had. While the air was getting to be rather cool at night, I was usually on the go at the time and didn't notice it. In the daytime, when I was resting or sleeping, the sun was usually out.

To have borrowed matches from a Belgian peasant would have been feasible, but when I was willing to take the chance of approaching any one it was just as easy to ask for food as matches.

In the second place, it would have been extremely dangerous to have built a fire even if I had needed it. You can't build a fire in Belgium, which is the most thickly populated country in Europe, without every one knowing it, and I was far from anxious to advertise my whereabouts.

The villages in the part of Belgium through which I was making my course were so close together that there was hardly ever an hour passed without my hearing some clock strike. Every village has its clock. Many times I could hear the clocks striking in two villages at the same time.

But the hour had very little interest to me. My program was to travel as fast as I could from sunset to sunrise and pay no attention to the hours in between, and in the daytime I had only two things to worry about: keep concealed and get as much sleep as possible.

The cabbage that I got in Belgium consisted of the small heads that the peasants had not cut. All the strength had concentrated in these little heads and they would be as bitter as gall. I would have to be pretty hungry today before I could ever eat cabbage again, and the same observation applies to carrots, turnips, and sugar-beets—especially sugar-beets.

It is rather a remarkable thing that today even the smell of turnips, raw or cooked, makes me sick, and yet a few short months ago my life depended upon them.

Night after night, as I searched for food, I was always in hopes that I might come upon some tomatoes or celery—vegetables which I really liked, but with the exception of once, when I found some celery, I was never so fortunate. I ate so much of the celery the night I came upon it that I was sick for two days thereafter, but I carried several bunches away with me and used to chew on it as I walked along.

Of course, I kept my eyes open all the time for fruit trees, but apparently it was too late in the year for fruit, as all that I ever was able to find were two pears which I got out of a tree. That was one of my red-letter days, but I was never able to repeat it.

In the brooks and ponds that I passed I often noticed fish of different kinds. That was either in the early morning, just before I turned in for the day, or on moonlight nights when the water seemed as clear in spots as in the daytime. It occurred to me that it would be a simple matter to rig a hook and line and catch some of the fish, but I had no means of cooking them and it was useless to fish for the sake of it.

One night in Belgium my course took me through a desolate stretch of country which seemed to be absolutely uncultivated. I must have covered twelve miles during the night without passing a single farm or cultivated field. My stock of turnips which I had plucked the night before was gone and I planned, of course, to get enough to carry me through the following day.

The North Star was shining brightly that night and there was absolutely nothing to prevent my steering an absolutely direct course for Holland and liberty, but my path seemed to lie through arid pastures. Far to the east or to the west I could hear faintly the striking of village bells, and I knew that if I changed my course I would undoubtedly strike farms and vegetables, but the North Star seemed to plead with me to follow it, and I would not turn aside.

When daylight came the consequence was I was empty-handed, and I had to find a hiding-place for the day. I thought I would approach the first peasant I came to and ask for food, but that day I had misgivings—a hunch—that I would get into trouble if I did, and I decided to go without food altogether for that day.

It was a foolish thing to do, I found, because I not only suffered greatly from hunger all that day, but it interfered with my sleep. I would drop off to sleep for half an hour, perhaps, and during that time I would dream that I was free, back home, living a life of comparative ease, and then I would wake up with a start and catch a glimpse of the bushes surrounding me, feel the hard ground beneath me and the hunger pangs gnawing at my insides, and then I would realise how far from home I really was, and I would lie there and wonder whether I would ever really see my home again. Then I would fall asleep again and dream this time, perhaps, of the days I spent in Courtrai of my leap from the train window, of the Bavarian pilot whom I sent to eternity in my last air-fight, of my tracer-bullets getting closer and closer to his head, and then I would wake up again with a start and thank the Lord that I was only dreaming it all again instead of living through it!

That night I got an early start because I knew I had to have food, and I decided that, rather than look for vegetables, I would take a chance and apply to the first Belgian peasant I came to.

It was about eight o'clock when I came to a small house. I had picked up a heavy stone and had bound it in my handkerchief, and I was resolved to use it as a weapon if it became necessary. After all I had gone through I was resolved to win my liberty eventually at whatever cost.

As it happened, I found that night the first real friend I had encountered in all my travelling. When I knocked timidly on the door it was opened by a Belgian peasant, about fifty years of age. He asked me in Flemish what I wanted, but I shook my head and, pointing to my ears and mouth, intimated that I was deaf and dumb, and then I opened and closed my teeth several times to show him that I wanted food.

He showed me inside and sat me at the table. He apparently lived alone, for his ill-furnished room had but one chair, and the plate and knife and fork he put before me seemed to be all he had. He brought me some cold potatoes and several slices of stale bread, and he warmed me some milk on a small oil-stove.

I ate ravenously, and all the time I was engaged I knew that he was eying me closely.

Before I was half through he came over to me, touched me on the shoulder, and, stooping over so that his lips almost touched my ear, he said, in broken English, "You are an Englishman—I know it—and you can hear and talk if you wish. Am I not right?"

There was a smile on his face and a friendly attitude about him that told me instinctively that he could be trusted, and I replied, "You have guessed right—only I am an American, not an Englishman."

He looked at me pityingly and filled my cup again with warm milk.

His kindness and apparent willingness to help me almost overcame me, and I felt like warning him of the consequences he would suffer if the Huns discovered he had befriended me. I had heard that twenty Belgians had been shot for helping Belgians to escape into Holland, and I hated to think what might happen to this Good Samaritan if the Huns ever knew that he had helped an escaped American prisoner.

After my meal was finished I told him in as simple language as I could command of some of the experiences I had gone through, and I outlined my future plans.

"You will never be able to get to Holland," he declared, "without a passport. The nearer you get to the frontier the more German soldiers you will encounter, and without a passport you will be a marked man."

I asked him to suggest a way by which I could overcome this difficulty.

He thought for several moments and studied me closely all the time—perhaps endeavouring to make absolutely sure that I was not a German spy—and then, apparently deciding in my favour, told me what he thought it was best for me to do.

"If you will call on this man," mentioning the name of a Belgian in a city through which I had to pass, he advised, "you will be able to make arrangements with him to secure a passport, and he will do everything he can to get you out of Belgium."

He told me where the man in question could be found and gave me some useful directions to continue my journey, and then he led me to the door. I thanked him a thousand times and wanted to pay him for his kindness and help, but he would accept nothing. He did give me his name, and you may be sure I shall never forget it, but to mention it here might, of course, result in serious consequences for him. When the war is over, however, or the Germans are thrown out of Belgium, I shall make it my duty to find that kind Belgian, if to do it I have to go through again all that I have suffered already.

## Chapter 11

# I Encounter German Soldiers

What the Belgian had told me about the need of a passport gave me fresh cause for worry. Suppose I should run into a German sentry before I succeeded in getting one?

I decided that until I reached the big city which the Belgian had mentioned—and which I cannot name for fear of identifying some of the people there who befriended me—I would proceed with the utmost precaution. Since I had discarded my uniform and had obtained civilian clothes I had not been quite as careful as I was at first. While I had done my travelling at night, I had not gone into hiding so early in the morning as before, and I had sometimes started again before it was quite dark, relying upon the fact that I would probably be mistaken for a Belgian on his way to or from work, as the case might be. From now on, I resolved, however, I would take no more chances.

That evening I came to a river perhaps seventy-five yards wide, and I was getting ready to swim it when I thought I would walk a little way to find, if possible, a better place to get to the river from the bank. I had not walked more than a few hundred feet when I saw a boat. It was the first time I had seen a boat in all my experiences.

It was firmly chained, but as the stakes were sunk in the soft bank it was not much of a job to pull them out. I got in, drank to my heart's content, shoved over to the other side, got out, drove a stake into the ground, and moored the boat. It would have been a simple matter to have drifted down the river, but the river was not shown on my map and I had no idea where it might lead me. Very reluctantly, therefore, I had to abandon the boat and proceed on foot.

I made several miles that night and before daylight found a safe place in which to hide for the day. From my hiding-place I could see through the bushes a heavy thick wood only a short distance away. I decided that I would start earlier than usual, hurry over to the wood, and perhaps in that way I could cover two or three miles in the daytime and gain just so much time. Travelling through the wood would be comparatively safe. There was a railroad going through the wood, but I did not figure that that would make it any the less safe.

About three o'clock that afternoon, therefore, I emerged from my hiding-place and hurried into the wood. After proceeding for half a mile or so I came to the railroad. I took a sharp look in both directions and, seeing no signs of trains or soldiers, I walked boldly over the tracks and continued on my way.

I soon came upon a clearing and knew that some one must be living in the vicinity. As I turned a group of trees I saw a small house and in the distance an old man working in a garden. I decided to enter the house and ask for food, figuring the woman would probably be old and would be no match for me even if she proved hostile. The old woman who came to the door in response to my knock was older even than I had expected. If she wasn't close to a hundred years, I miss my guess very much.

She could not speak English and I could not speak Flemish, of course, but, nevertheless, I made her understand that I wanted something to eat. She came out of the door and hollered for her husband in a shrill voice that would have done credit to a girl of eighteen. The old man came in from his garden and between the two of them they managed to get the idea that I was hungry, and they gave me a piece of bread—a, very small piece—which was quite a treat.

The house they lived in consisted of just two rooms—the kitchen and a bedroom. The kitchen was perhaps fourteen feet square, eight feet of one side of it being taken up by an enormous fireplace. What was in the bedroom I had no way of telling, as I did not dare to be too inquisitive.

I made the old couple understand that I would like to stay in their house all night, but the old man shook his head. I bade them goodbye and disappeared into the woods, leaving them to speculate as to the strange foreigner they had entertained.

From the greater density of the population in the section through which I was now passing I realised that I must be in the outskirts of the big city which the Belgian had mentioned and where I was to procure a passport.

Village after village intercepted me, and, although I tried to skirt them wherever possible, I realised that I would never make much progress if I continued that course. To gain a mile I would sometimes have to make a detour of two or three. I decided that I would try my luck in going straight through the next village I came to.

As I approached it I passed numbers of peasants who were ambling along the road. I was afraid to mingle with them because it was impossible for me to talk to them and it was dangerous to arouse suspicion even among the Belgians. For all I knew, one of them might be treacherous enough to deliver me to the Germans in return for the reward he might be sure of receiving.

About nine o'clock that evening I came to a point where ahead of me on the right was a Belgian police station—I knew it from its red lights—and on the other side of the street were two German soldiers in uniform leaning against a bicycle.

Here was a problem which called for instant decision. If I turned back, the suspicion of the soldiers would be instantly aroused, and if I crossed the road so as not to pass so closely to them, they might be equally suspicious. I decided to march bravely by the Huns, bluff my way through, and trust to Providence. If anybody imagines, however, that I was at all comfortable as I approached those soldiers, he must think that I am a much braver man than I claim to be. My heart beat so loud I was afraid they would hear it. Every step I took brought me so much nearer to what might prove to be the end of all my hopes. It was a nerve-racking ordeal.

I was now within a few feet of them. Another step and—

They didn't turn a hair! I passed right by them—heard what they were saying, although, of course, I didn't understand it, and went right on. I can't say I didn't walk a little faster as I left them behind, but I tried to maintain an even gait so as not to give them any idea of the inward exultation I was experiencing. No words can explain, however, how relieved I really felt—to know that I had successfully passed through the first of a series of similar tests which I realised were in store for me—although I did not know then how soon I was to be confronted with the second.

As it was, however, the incident gave me a world of confidence. It demonstrated to me that there was nothing in my appearance, at any rate, to attract the attention of the German soldiers. Apparently I looked like a Belgian peasant, and if I could only work things so that I would never have to answer questions and thus give away my nationality, I figured I would be tolerably safe.

As I marched along I felt so happy I couldn't help humming the air of one of the new patriotic songs that we used to sing at the aerodrome back of Ypres.

In this happy fame of mind I covered the next three miles in about an hour, and then I came to another little village. My usual course would have been to go around it—through fields, backyards, woods, or whatever else lay in my way—but I had gained so much time by going through the last village instead of detouring around it, and my appearance seemed to be so unsuspicious, that I decided to try the same stunt again.

I stopped humming and kept very much on the alert, but, apart from that, I walked boldly through the main street without any feeling of alarm.

I had proceeded perhaps a mile along the main street when I noticed ahead of me three German soldiers standing at the curb.

Again my heart started to beat fast, I must confess, but I was not nearly so scared as I had been an hour or so before. I walked ahead, determined to follow my previous procedure in every particular.

I had got to about fifteen feet away from the soldiers when one of them stepped onto the sidewalk and shouted:

"*Halt!*"

My heart stopped beating fast—for a moment, I believe, it stopped beating altogether! I can't attempt to describe my feelings. The thought that the jig was up, that all I had gone through and all I had escaped would now avail me nothing, mingled with a feeling of disgust with myself because of the foolish risk I had taken in going through the village, combined to take all the starch out of me, and I could feel myself wilting as the soldier advanced to the spot where I stood rooted in my tracks.

I had a bottle of water in one pocket and a piece of bread in the other, and as the Hun advanced to search me I held the bottle up in one hand and the piece of bread in the other so that he could see that was all I had.

It occurred to me that he would "frisk" me—that is, feel me over for arms or other weapons, then place me under arrest and march me off to the guard-house. I had not the slightest idea but that I was captured, and there didn't seem to be much use in resisting, unarmed as I was and with two other German soldiers within a few feet of us.

Like a flash it suddenly dawned on me, however, that for all this soldier could have known I was only a Belgian peasant and that his object in searching me, which he proceeded to do, was to ascertain whether I had committed the common "crime" of smuggling potatoes!

The Belgians are allowed only a certain amount of potatoes, and it is against the laws laid down by the Huns to deal in vegetables of any kind except under the rigid supervision of the authorities. Nevertheless, it was one of. the principal vocations of the average poor Belgian to buy potatoes out in the country from the peasants and then smuggle them into the large cities and sell them clandestinely at a high price.

To stop this traffic in potatoes the German soldiers were in the habit of subjecting the Belgians to frequent search, and I was being held up by this soldier for no other reason than that he thought I might be a potato-smuggler!

He felt of my outside clothes and pockets, and, finding no potatoes, seemed to be quite satisfied. Had he but known who I was he could have earned an iron cross! Or perhaps, in view of the fact that I had a heavy water-bottle in my uplifted hand, it might have turned out to be a *wooden* cross!

He said something in German, which, of course, I did not understand, and then some Belgian peasants came along and seemed to distract his attention. Perhaps he had said, "It's all right, you may go on," or he may have been talking to the others in Flemish, but, at any rate, observing that he was more interested in the others than he was in me at the moment, I put the bottle in my pocket and walked on.

After I walked a few steps I took a furtive glance backward and noticed the soldier who had searched me rejoin his comrades at the curb and then stop another fellow who had come along, and then I disappeared in the darkness.

I cannot say that the outcome of this adventure left me in the same confident frame of mind that followed the earlier one. It was true I had come out of it all right, but I could not help thinking what a terribly close shave I had.

Suppose the soldier had questioned me? The ruse I had been following in my dealings with the Belgian peasants—pretending I was deaf and dumb—might possibly have worked here, too, but a soldier—a, German soldier—might not so easily have been fooled. It was more than an even chance that it would at least have aroused his suspicions and resulted in further investigation. A search of my clothing would have revealed a dozen things which would have established my identity, and all my shamming of deafness would have availed me nothing.

As I wandered along I knew that I was now approaching the big city which my Belgian friend had spoken of and which I would have to enter if I was to get the passport, and I realised now how essential it was to have something to enable me to get through the frequent examinations to which I expected to be subjected.

While I was still debating in my mind whether it was going to be possible for me to enter the city that night, I saw in the distance what appeared to be an arc-light, and as I neared it that was what it turned out to be. Beneath the light I could make out the forms of three guards, and the thought of having to go through the same kind of ordeal that I had just experienced filled me with misgivings. Was it possible that I could be fortunate enough to get by again?

As I slowed up a little, trying to make up my mind what was best to do, I was overtaken by a group of Belgian women who were shuffling along the road, and I decided to mingle with them and see if I couldn't convey the impression that I was one of their party.

As we approached the arc-light the figures of those three soldiers with their spiked helmets loomed up before me like a regiment. I felt as if I were walking right into the jaws of death. Rather than go through what was in store for me I felt that I would infinitely prefer to be fighting again in the air with those four desperate Huns who had been the cause of my present plight; then, at least, I would have a chance to fight back, but now I had to risk my life and take what was coming to me without a chance to strike a blow in my own defence.

I shall never forget my feelings as we came within the shaft of light projected by that great arc-light, nor the faces of those three guards as we passed by them. I didn't look directly at them, but out of the corner of my eye I didn't miss a detail. I held a handkerchief up to my face as we passed them, and endeavoured to imitate the slouching gait of the Belgians as well as I could; and apparently it worked. We walked right by those guards and they paid absolutely no attention to us.

If ever a fellow felt like going down on his knees and praying, I did at that moment, but it wouldn't have done to show my elation or gratitude in that conspicuous way.

It was then well after eleven o'clock, and I knew it would be unsafe for me to attempt to find a lodging-place in the city, and the only thing for me to do was to locate the man whose name the Belgian had given me. He had given me a good description of the street and had directed me how to get there, and I followed his instructions closely.

After walking the streets for about half an hour I came upon one of the landmarks my friend had described to me, and ten minutes afterward I was knocking at the door of the man who was to make it possible for me to reach Holland—and liberty. At least that was what I hoped.

CHAPTER 12

# The Forged Passport

For obvious reasons I cannot describe the man to whom I applied for the passport, nor the house in which he lived. While, in view of what subsequently happened, I would not be very much concerned if he got into trouble for having dealt with me, I realise that the hardships he had endured in common with all the other inhabitants of that conquered city may possibly have distorted his ideas of right and justice, and I shall not deliberately bring further disaster on him by revealing his identity.

This man—we will call him Huyliger, because that is as unlike his name as it is mine—was very kind to me on that memorable night when I aroused him from his sleep and in a few words of explanation told him of my plight.

He invited me inside, prepared some food for me, and, putting on a dressing-gown, came and sat by me while I ate, listening with the greatest interest to the short account I gave him of my adventures.

He could speak English fluently, and he interrupted me several times to express his sympathy for the sufferings I had endured.

"O'Brien," he said, after I had concluded my story, "I am going to help you. It may take several days—perhaps as long as two weeks, but eventually we will provide the means to enable you to get into Holland!"

I thanked him a thousand times and told him that I didn't know how I could possibly repay him.

"Don't think of that," he replied; "the satisfaction of knowing that I have aided in placing one more victim of the Huns beyond their power to harm him will more than repay me for all the risk I shall run in helping you. You'd better turn in now, O'Brien, and in the morning I'll tell you what I plan to do."

He showed me to a small room on the second floor, shook hands with me, and left me to prepare for the first real night's rest I had been able to take in nearly two months.

As I removed my clothes and noticed that my knees were still swollen to twice their normal size, that my left ankle was black and blue from the wrench I had given it when I jumped from the train, and that my ribs showed through my skin, I realised what a lot I had been through. As a matter of fact, I could not have weighed more than one hundred and fifty pounds at that time, whereas I had tipped the scales at one hundred and ninety when I was with my squadron in France.

I lost no time in getting into bed and still less in getting to sleep. I don't know what I dreamed of that night, but I had plenty of time to go through the experiences of my whole life, for when I was aroused by a knock on the door, and Huyliger came in, in response to my invitation to enter, he told me that it was nearly noon. I had slept for nearly twelve hours. I cannot say that the thought did not run through my head that perhaps, after all, I was living in a fool's paradise, and that when Huyliger reappeared it would be with a couple of German soldiers behind him, but I dismissed such misgivings summarily, realising that I was doing Huyliger an injustice to let such things enter my head even for an instant. I had no right to doubt his sincerity, and it would do me no good to entertain such suspicions. If he was going to prove treacherous to me, I was powerless, anyway, to cope with him.

In a few moments my host appeared with a tray containing my breakfast. I don't suppose I shall ever forget that meal. It consisted of a cup of coffee—real coffee, not the kind I had had at Courtrai—several slices of bread, some hot potatoes, and a dish of scrambled eggs.

Every mouthful of that meal tasted like angel-food to me, and Huyliger sat on the edge of the bed and watched me enjoying the meal, at the same time outlining the plans he had made for my escape.

In brief, the scheme was to conceal me in a convent until conditions were ripe for me to make my way to the border. In the meanwhile I was to be dressed in the garb of a priest, and when the time came for me to leave the city I was to pretend that I was a Spanish sailor, because I could speak a little Spanish, which I had picked up on the coast. To attempt to play the part of a Belgian would become increasingly difficult, he pointed out, and would bring inevitable disaster in the event that I was called upon to speak.

Huyliger said I would be given sufficient money to bribe the German guards at the Dutch frontier, and he assured me that everything would work out according to schedule, he declared:

> Yours is not the first case, O'Brien, we have handled successfully. Only three weeks ago I heard from an English merchant who had escaped from a German detention camp and come to me for assistance, and whom I had been able to get through the lines. His message telling me of his safe arrival in Rotterdam came to me in an indirect way, of course, but the fact that the plans we had made carried through without mishap makes me feel that we ought to be able to do as much for you.

I told Huyliger I was ready to follow his instructions and would do anything he suggested.

"I want to rejoin my squadron as soon as I possibly can, of course," I told him, "but I realise that it will take a certain length of time for you to make the necessary arrangements, and I will be as patient as I can."

The first thing to do, Huyliger told me, was to prepare a passport. He had a blank one and it was a comparatively simple matter to fill in the spaces, using a genuine passport which Huyliger possessed as a sample of the handwriting of the passport clerk. My occupation was entered as that of a sailor. My birthplace we gave as Spain, and we put my age at thirty. As a matter of fact, at that time I could easily have passed for thirty-five, but we figured that with proper food and a decent place to sleep in at night I would soon regain my normal appearance and the passport would have to serve me, perhaps, for several weeks to come.

Filling in the blank spaces on the passport was, as I have said, a comparatively easy matter, but that did not begin to fill the bill. Every genuine passport bore an official rubber stamp, something like an elaborate postmark, and I was at a loss to know how to get over that difficulty.

Fortunately, however, Huyliger had half of a rubber stamp which had evidently been thrown away by the Germany, and he planned to construct the other half out of the cork from a wine bottle. He was very skilful with a penknife, and although he spoiled a score or more of corks before he succeeded in getting anything like the result he was after, the finished article was far better than our most sanguine expectations. Indeed, after we had pared it over here and there and removed whatever imperfections our repeated tests disclosed, we had

THE FORGED PASSPORT PREPARED IN A BELGIAN CITY TO AID LIEUTENANT O'BRIEN'S ESCAPE INTO HOLLAND, BUT WHICH WAS NEVER USED a stamp which made an impression so closely resembling the original that, without a magnifying-glass, we were sure it would have been impossible to tell that it was a counterfeit.

Huyliger procured a camera and took a photograph of me to paste on the passport in the place provided for that purpose, and we then had a passport which was entirely satisfactory to both of us and would, we hoped, prove equally so to our friends the Huns.

It had taken two days to fix up the passport. In the meanwhile, Huyliger informed me that he had changed his plans about the convent, and that instead he would take me to an empty house where I could remain in safety until he told me it was advisable for me to proceed to the frontier.

This was quite agreeable to me, as I had had some misgivings as to the kind of a priest I would make, and it seemed to me to be safer to remain aloof from everyone in a deserted house than to have to mingle with people or come in contact with them even with the best of disguises.

That night I accompanied Huyliger to a fashionable section of the city where the house in which I was to be concealed was located.

This house turned out to be a four-storey structure of brick. Huyliger told me that it had been occupied by a wealthy Belgian before the war, but since 1914 it had been uninhabited save for the occasional habitation of some refugee whom Huyliger was befriending.

Huyliger had a key and let me in, but he did not enter the house with me, stating that he would visit me in the morning.

I explored the place from top to bottom as well as I could without lights. The house was elaborately furnished, but, of course, the dust lay a quarter of an inch thick almost everywhere. It was a large house, containing some twenty rooms. There were two rooms in the basement, four on the first floor, four on the second, five on the third, and five on the top. In the days that were to come I was to have plenty of opportunity to familiarise myself with the contents of that house, but at the time I did not know it, and I was curious enough to want to know just what the house contained.

Down in the basement there was a huge pantry, but it was absolutely bare, except of dust and dirt. A door which evidently led to a sub-basement attracted my attention, and I thought it might be a good idea to know just where it led in case it became necessary for me to elude searchers.

In that cellar I found case after case of choice wine—Huyliger subsequently told me that there were eighteen hundred bottles of it. I was so happy at the turn my affairs had taken and in the rosy prospects which I now entertained that I was half inclined to indulge in a little celebration then and there. On second thoughts, however, I remembered the old warning of the folly of shouting before you are well out of the woods, and I decided that it would be just as well to postpone the festivities for a while and go to bed instead.

In such an elaborately furnished house I had naturally conjured up ideas of a wonderfully large bed, with thick hair mattresses, downy quilts, and big soft pillows. Indeed, I debated for a while which particular bedroom I should honour with my presence that night. Judge of my disappointment, therefore, when, after visiting bedroom after bedroom, I discovered that there wasn't a bed in any one of them that was in a condition to sleep in. All the mattresses had been removed and the rooms were absolutely bare of everything in the way of wool, silk, or cotton fabrics. The Germans had apparently swept the house clean.

There was nothing to do, therefore, but to make myself as comfortable as I could on the floor, but as I had grown accustomed by this time to sleeping under far less comfortable conditions I swallowed my disappointment as cheerfully as I could and lay down for the night.

In the morning Huyliger appeared and brought me some breakfast, and after I had eaten it he asked me what connections I had in France or England from whom I could obtain money.

I told him that I banked at Cox & Co., London, and that if he needed any money I would do anything I could to get it for him, although I did not know just how such things could be arranged.

"Don't worry about that, O'Brien," he replied. "We'll find a way of getting at it, all right. What I want to know is how far you are prepared to go to compensate me for the risks I am taking and for the service I am rendering you."

The change in the man's attitude stunned me. I could hardly believe my ears.

"Of course, I shall pay you as well as I can for what you have done, Huyliger," I replied, trying to conceal as far as possible the disappointment his demand had occasioned me. "But don't you think that this is hardly the proper time or occasion to talk of compensation? All I have on me, as you know, is a few hundred francs, and that, of course, you are welcome to, and when I get back, if I ever do, I shall not easily forget the kindness you have shown me. I am sure you need have no concern about my showing my gratitude in a substantial way."

"That's all right, O'Brien," he insisted, looking at me in a knowing sort of way. "You may take care of me afterward, and then again you may not. I'm not satisfied to wait. I want to be taken care of *now!*"

"Well, what do you want me to do? How much do you expect in the way of compensation? How can I arrange to get it to you? I am willing to do anything that is reasonable."

"I want —— pounds!" he replied, and he named a figure that staggered me. If I had been Lord Kitchener instead of just an ordinary lieutenant in the R. F. C, he would hardly have asked a larger sum. Perhaps he thought I was.

"Why, my dear man," I said, smilingly, thinking that perhaps he was joking, "you don't really mean that, do you?"

"I certainly do, O'Brien, and what is more," he threatened, "I intend to get every cent I have asked, and you are going to help me get it!"

He pulled out an order calling for the payment to him of the amount he had mentioned, and demanded that I sign it.

I waved it aside.

"Huyliger," I said, "you have helped me out so far, and perhaps you have the power to help me further. I appreciate what you have done for me, although now, I think, I see what your motive was, but I certainly don't intend to be blackmailed, and I tell you right now that I won't stand for it!"

"Very well," he said. "It is just as you say. But before you make up your mind so obstinately I would advise you to think it over. I'll be back this evening."

My first impulse, after the man had left, was to get out of that house just as soon as I could. I had the passport he had prepared for me, and I figured that even without further help from him I could now get to the border without very much difficulty, and when I got there I would have to use my own ingenuity to get through.

It was evident, however, that Huyliger still had an idea that I might change my mind with regard to the payment he had demanded, and I decided that it would be foolish to do anything until he paid me a second visit.

At the beginning of my dealings with Huyliger I had turned over to him some pictures, papers, and other things that I had on me when I entered his house, including my identification disk, and I was rather afraid that he might refuse to return them to me.

All day long I remained in the house without a particle of food other than the breakfast Huyliger had brought to me. From the windows I could see plenty to interest me and help pass the time away, but of my experiences while in that house I shall tell in detail later on, confining my attention now to a narration of my dealings with Huyliger.

That night he appeared, as he had promised.

"Well, O'Brien," he asked, as he entered the room where I was awaiting him, "what do you say? Will you sign the order or not?"

It had occurred to me during the day that the amount demanded was so fabulous that I might have signed the order without any danger of its ever being paid, but the idea of this man, who had claimed to be befriending me, endeavouring to make capital out of my plight galled me so that I was determined not to give in to him, whether I could do so in safety or not.

"No, Huyliger," I replied. "I have decided to get along as best I can without any further assistance from you. I shall see that you are reasonably paid for what you have done, but I will not accept any further assistance from you at any price, and, what is more, I want you to return to me at once all the photographs and other papers and belongings of mine which I turned over to you a day or two ago!"

"I'm sorry about that, O'Brien," he retorted, with a show of apparent sincerity, "but that is something I cannot do."

"If you don't give me back those papers at once," I replied, hotly, "I will take steps to get them and damned quick, too!"

"I don't know just what you could do, O'Brien," he declared, coolly, "but as a matter of fact the papers and pictures you refer to are out of the country. I could not give them back to you if I wanted to."

Something told me the man was lying.

"See here, Huyliger!" I threatened, advancing toward him, putting my hand on his shoulder and looking him straight in the eye, "I want those papers and I want them here before midnight tonight. If I don't get them, I shall sleep in this place just once more, and then, at eight o'clock tomorrow morning, I shall go to the German authorities, give myself up, show them the passport that you fixed up for me, tell them how I got it, and explain everything!"

Huyliger paled. We had no lights in the house, but we were standing near a landing at the time and the moonlight was streaming through a stained-glass window.

The Belgian turned on his heel and started to go down the stairs.

"Mind you," I called after him, "I shall wait for you till the city clock strikes twelve, and if you don't show up with those papers by that time, the next time you will see me is when you confront me before the German authorities! I am a desperate man, Huyliger, and I mean every word I say!"

He let himself out of the door and I sat on the top stair and wondered just what he would do. Would he try to steal a march on me and get in a first word to the authorities, so that my story would be discredited when I put it to them?

Of course my threat to give myself up to the Huns was a pure bluff. While I had no desire to lose the papers which Huyliger had, and which included the map of the last resting-place of my poor chum Raney, I certainly had no intention of cutting off my nose to spite my chin by surrendering to the Germans. I would have been shot, as sure as fate, for, after all I had been able to observe behind the German lines, I would be regarded as a spy and treated as such.

At the same time I thought I had detected a yellow streak in Huyliger, and I figured that he would not want to take the risk of my carrying out my threat, even though he believed there was but a small chance of my doing so. If I did, he would undoubtedly share my fate, and the pictures and papers he had of mine were really of no use to him, and I have never been able to ascertain why it was he wished to retain them unless they contained something—some information about me—which accounted for his complete change of attitude toward me in the first place, and he wanted the papers as evidence to account to his superiors or associates for his conduct toward me.

When he first told me that the plan of placing me in a convent disguised as a priest had been abandoned he explained it by saying that the cardinal had issued orders to the priests to help no more fugitives, and I have since wondered whether there was anything in my papers which had turned him against me and led him to forsake me after all he had promised to do for me.

For perhaps two hours I sat on that staircase musing about the peculiar turn in my affairs, when the front door opened and Huyliger ascended the stairs.

"I have brought you such of your belongings as I still had, O'Brien," he said, softly. "The rest, as I told you, I cannot give you. They are no longer in my possession."

I looked through the little bunch he handed me. It included my identification disk, most of the papers I valued, and perhaps half of the photographs.

"I don't know what your object is in retaining the rest of my pictures, Huyliger," I replied, "but, as a matter of fact, the ones that are missing were only of sentimental value to me, and you are welcome to them if you want them. We'll call it a heat."

I don't know whether he understood the idiom, but he sat down on the stairs just below me and cogitated for a few moments.

"O'Brien," he started, finally, "I'm sorry things have gone the way they have. I feel sorry for you and I would really like to help you. I don't suppose you will believe me, but the matter of the order which I asked you to sign was not of my doing. However, we won't go into that. The proposition was made to you and you turned it down, and that's an end of it. At the same time, I hate to leave you to your own resources and I'm going to make one more suggestion to you for your own good. I have another plan to get you into Holland, and if you will go with me to another house I will introduce you to a man who I think will be in a position to help you."

"How many millions of pounds will he want for his trouble?" I asked, sarcastically.

"You can arrange that when you see him. Will you go?"

I suspected there was something fishy about the proposition, but I felt that I could take care of myself and decided to see the thing through. I knew Huyliger would not dare to deliver me to the authorities because of the fact that I had the telltale passport, which would be his death-knell as well as my own.

Accordingly I said I would be quite willing to go with him whenever he was ready, and he suggested that we go the next evening.

I pointed out to him that I was entirely without food and asked him whether he could not arrange to bring or send me something to eat while I remained in the house.

"I'm sorry, O'Brien," he replied, "but I'm afraid you'll have to get along as best you can. When I brought you your breakfast this morning I took a desperate chance. If I had been discovered by one of the German soldiers entering this house with food in my possession, I would not only have paid the penalty myself, but you would have been discovered, too. It is too dangerous a proposition. Why don't you go out by yourself and buy your food at the stores? That would give you confidence, and you'll need plenty of it when you continue your journey to the border."

There was a good deal of truth in what he said, and I really could not blame him for not wanting to take any chances to help me, in view of the relations between us.

"Very well," I said; "I've gone without food for many hours at a time before and I suppose I shall be able to do so again. I shall look for you tomorrow evening."

The next evening he came and I accompanied him to another house not very far from the one in which I had been staying and not unlike it in appearance. It, too, was a substantial dwelling-house which had been untenanted since the beginning, save perhaps for such occasional visits as Huyliger and his associates made to it.

Huyliger let himself in and conducted me to a room on the second floor, where he introduced me to two men. One, I could readily see by the resemblance, was his own brother. The other was a stranger.

Very briefly they explained to me that they had procured another passport for me—a genuine one—which would prove far more effective in helping to get me to the frontier than the counterfeit one they had manufactured for me.

I think I saw through their game right at the start, but I listened patiently to what they had to say.

"Of course, you will have to return to us the passport we gave you before we can give you the real one," said Huyliger's brother.

"I haven't the slightest objection," I replied, "if the new passport is all you claim for it. Will you let me see it?"

There was considerable hesitation on the part of Huyliger's brother and the other chap at this.

"Why, I don't think that's necessary at all, Mr. O'Brien," said the former. "You give us the old passport and we will be very glad to give you the new one for it. Isn't that fair enough?"

"It may be fair enough, my friends," I retorted, seeing that it was useless to conceal further the fact that I was fully aware of their whole plan and why I had been brought to this house. "It may be fair enough, my friends," I said, "but you will get the passport that I have here," patting my side and indicating my inside breast pocket, "only off my dead body!"

I suppose the three of them could have made short work of me then and there if they had wanted to go the limit, and no one would ever have been the wiser, but I had gone through so much and I was feeling so mean toward the whole world just at that moment that I was determined to sell my life as dearly as possible.

"I have that passport here," I repeated, "and I'm going to keep it.

If you gentlemen think you can take it from me, you are welcome to try!"

To tell the truth, I was spoiling for a fight and I half wished they would start something. The man who had lived in the house had evidently been a collector of ancient pottery, for the walls were lined with great pieces of earthenware which had every earmark of possessing great value. They certainly possessed great weight. I figured that if the worst came to the worst that pottery would come in mighty handy. A single blow with one of those big vases would put a man out as neatly as possible, and as there was lots of pottery and only three men I believed I had an excellent chance of holding my own in the combat which I had invited.

I had already picked out in my mind what I was going to use, and I got up, stood with my back to the wall, and told them that if they ever figured on getting the passport, then would be their best chance.

Apparently they realised that I meant business and they immediately began to expostulate at the attitude I was taking.

One of the men spoke excellent English. In fact, he told me that he could speak five languages, and if he could lie in the others as well I know he did in my own tongue, he was not only an accomplished linguist, but a most versatile liar into the bargain.

They argued and expostulated with me for some time.

"My dear fellow," said the linguist, "it is not that we want to deprive you of the passport. Good Heavens! if it will aid you in getting out of the country, I wish you could have six just like it. But for our own protection you owe it to us to proceed on your journey as best you can without it, because as long as you have it in your possession you jeopardize our lives, too. Don't you think it is fairer that you should risk your own safety rather than place the lives of three innocent men in danger?"

"That may be as it is, my friends," I retorted, as I made my way to the door, "and I am glad you realise your danger. Keep it in mind, for in case any of you should happen to feel inclined to notify the German authorities that I am in this part of the country, think it over before you do so. Remember always that if the Germans get me, they get the passport, too, and if they get the passport, your lives won't be worth a damn! When I tell the history of that clever little piece of pasteboard I will implicate all three of you, and whomever else is working with you, and as I am an officer I rather think my word will be taken before yours. Goodnight!"

The bluff evidently worked, because I was able to get out of the city without molestation from the Germans.

I have never seen these men since. I hope I never shall, because I am afraid I might be tempted to do something for which I might afterward be sorry.

I do not mean to imply that all Belgians are like this. I had evidently fallen into the hands of a gang who were endeavouring to make capital out of the misfortunes of those who were referred to them for help. In all countries there are bad as well as good, and in a country which has suffered so much as poor Belgium it is no wonder if some of the survivors have lost their sense of moral perspective.

I know the average poor peasant in Belgium would divide his scanty rations with a needy fugitive sooner than a wealthy Belgian would dole out a morsel from his comparatively well-stocked larder. Perhaps the poor have less to lose than the rich if their generosity or charity is discovered by the Huns.

There have been many Belgians shot for helping escaped prisoners and other fugitives, and it is not to be wondered at that they are willing to take as few chances as possible. A man with a family, especially, does not feel justified in helping a stranger when he knows that he and his whole family may be shot or sent to prison for their pains.

Although I suffered much from the attitude of Huyliger and his associates, I suppose I ought to hold no grudge against them in view of the unenviable predicament which they are in themselves.

## Chapter 13

# Five Days in an Empty House

The five days I spent in that house seemed to me like five years. During all that time I had very little to eat—less, in fact, than I had been getting in the fields. I did not feel it so much, perhaps, because of the fact that I was no longer exposed to the other privations which had helped to make my condition so wretched. I now had a good place to sleep, at any rate, and I did not awake every half-hour or so as I had been accustomed to do in the fields and woods, and, of course, my hunger was not aggravated by the physical exertions which had been necessary before.

Nevertheless, perhaps because I had more time now to think of the hunger pains which were gnawing at me all the time, I don't believe I was ever so miserable as I was at that period of my adventure. I felt so mean toward the world I would have committed murder, I think, with very little provocation.

German soldiers were passing the house at all hours of the day. I watched them hour after hour from the keyhole of the door—to have shown myself at the window was out of the question because the house in which I was concealed was supposed to be untenanted.

Because of the fact that I was unable to speak either Flemish or German I could not go out and buy food, although I still had the money with which to do it. That was one of the things that galled me—the thought that I had the wherewithal in my jeans to buy all the food I needed, and yet no way of getting it without endangering my liberty and life.

At night, however, after It was dark, I would steal quietly out of the house to see what I could pick up in the way of food. By that time, of course, the stores were closed, but I scoured the streets, the alleys, and the byways for scraps of food, and occasionally got up courage enough to appeal to Belgian peasants whom I met on the streets, and in that way I managed to keep body and soul together.

It was quite apparent to me, however, that I was worse off in the city than I had been in the fields, and I decided to get out of that house just as soon as I knew definitely that Huyliger had made up his mind to do nothing further for me.

When I was not at the keyhole of the door I spent most of my day on the top floor in a room which looked out on the street. By keeping well away from the window I could see much of what was going on without being seen myself. In my restlessness I used to walk back and forth in that room, and I kept it up so constantly that I believe I must have worn a path on the floor. It was nine steps from one wall to the other, and as I had little else to amuse me I figured out one day, after I had been pacing up and down for several hours, just how much distance I would have covered on my way to Holland if my footsteps had been taking me in that direction instead of just up and down that old room. I was very much surprised that in three hours I crossed the room no less than five thousand times and the distance covered was between nine and ten miles. It was not very gratifying to realise that after walking all that distance I wasn't a step nearer my goal than when I started, but I had to do something while waiting for Huyliger to help me, and pacing up and down was a natural outlet for my restlessness.

While looking out of that top-floor window one day I noticed a cat on a window-ledge of the house across the street. I had a piece of a broken mirror which I had picked up in the house and I used to amuse myself for an hour at a time shining it in the cat's eyes across the street. At first the animal was annoyed by the reflection and would move away, only to come back a few moments later. By and by, however, it seemed to get used to the glare and wouldn't budge, no matter how strong the sunlight was. Playing with the cat in this way was the means of my getting food a day or two later—at a time when I was so famished that I was ready to do almost anything to appease my hunger.

It was about seven o'clock in the evening. I was expecting Huyliger at eight, but I hadn't the slightest hope that he would bring me food, as he had told me that he wouldn't take the risk of having food in his possession when calling on me. I was standing at the window in such a way that I could see what was going on in the street without being observed by those who passed by, when I noticed my friend the cat coming down the steps of the opposite house with something in his mouth. Without considering the risks I ran, I opened the front door, ran down the steps and across the street, and pounced on the cat before it could get away with its supper, for that, as I had imagined, was what I had seen in its mouth. It turned out to be a piece of stewed rabbit, which I confiscated eagerly and took back with me to the house.

Perhaps I felt a little sorry for the cat, but I certainly had no other qualms about eating the animal's dinner. I was much too hungry to dwell upon niceties, and a piece of stewed rabbit was certainly too good for a cat to eat when a man was starving. I ate it and enjoyed it, and the incident suggested to me a way in which I might possibly obtain food again when all other avenues failed.

From my place of concealment I frequently saw huge carts being pushed through the streets gathering potato peelings, refuse of cabbage, and similar food remnants which, in America, are considered garbage and destroyed. In Belgium they were using this "garbage" to make their bread out of, and while the idea may sound revolting to us, the fact is that the Germans have brought these things down to such a science that the bread they make in this way is really very good to eat. I know it would have been like cake to me when I was in need of food; indeed, I would have eaten the "garbage" direct, let alone the bread.

Although, as I have said, I suffered greatly from hunger while occupying this, house, there were one or two things I observed through the keyhole or from the windows which made me laugh, and some of the incidents that occurred during my voluntary imprisonment were really rather funny.

From the keyhole I could see, for instance, a shop window on the other side of the street, several houses down the block. All day long German soldiers would be passing in front of the house, and I noticed that practically every one of them would stop in front of this store window and look in. Occasionally a soldier on duty bent would hurry past, but I think nine out of ten of them were sufficiently interested to spend at least a minute, and some of them three or four minutes, gazing at whatever was being exhibited in that window, although I noticed that it failed to attract the Belgians.

I have a considerable streak of curiosity in me and I couldn't help wondering what it could be in that window which almost without exception seemed to interest German soldiers, but failed to hold the Belgians, and after conjuring my brains for a while on the problem I came to the conclusion that the shop must have been a book-shop and the window contained German magazines, which, naturally enough, would be of the greatest interest to the Germans, but of none to the Belgians.

At any rate, I resolved that as soon as night came I would go out and investigate the window. When I got the answer I laughed so loud that I was afraid for the moment I must have attracted the attention of the neighbours, but I couldn't help it. The window was filled with huge quantities of sausage. The store was a butcher-shop, and one of the principal things they sold, apparently, was sausage. The display they made, although it consisted merely of quantities of sausage piled in the windows, certainly had plenty of "pulling" power. It "pulled" nine Germans out of ten out of their course and indirectly it "pulled" me right across the street. The idea of those Germans being so interested in that window display as to stand in front of the window for two, three, or four minutes at a time, however, certainly seemed funny to me, and when I got back to the house I sat at the keyhole again and found just as much interest as before in watching the Germans stop in their tracks when they reached the window, even though I was now aware what the attraction was.

One of my chief occupations during those days was catching flies. I would catch a fly, put him in a spider's web—there were plenty of them in the old house—and sit down to wait for the spider to come and get him. But always I pictured myself in the same predicament and rescued the fly just as the spider was about to grab him. Several times when things were dull I was tempted to see the tragedy through, but perhaps the same Providence that guided me safely through all perils was guarding, too, the destiny of those flies, for I always weakened and the flies never did suffer from my lust for amusement.

The house was well supplied with books—in fact, one of the choicest libraries I think I ever saw—but they were all written either in Flemish or in French. I could read no Flemish and very little French. I might have made a little headway with the latter, but the books all seemed too deep for me and I gave it up. There was one thing, though, that I did read and re-read from beginning to end—that was a New York *Herald* which must have arrived just about the time war was declared. Several things in there interested me, and particularly the baseball scores, which I studied with as much care as a real fan possibly would an up-to-date score. I couldn't refrain from laughing when I came to an account of Zimmerman (of the Cubs) being benched for some spat with the umpire, and it afforded me just as much interest three years after it had happened—perhaps more—than some current item of worldwide interest had at the time.

I rummaged the house many times from cellar to garret in my search for something to eat, but the harvest of three years of war had made any success along that line impossible. I was like the man out on the ocean in a boat and thirsty, with water everywhere, but not a drop to drink.

I was tempted while in this city to go to church one Sunday, but my better judgment told me it would be a useless risk. Of course someone would surely say something to me, and I didn't know how many Germans would be there, or what might happen, so I gave up that idea.

During all the time I was concealed in this house I saw but one automobile, and that was a German staff officer's. That same afternoon I had one of the frights of my young life.

I had been gazing out of the keyhole as usual when I heard coming down the street the measured tread of German soldiers. It didn't sound like very many, but there was no doubt in my mind that German soldiers were marching down the street. I went upstairs and peeked through the window, and sure enough a squad of German infantry was coming down the street, accompanying a military truck. I hadn't the slightest idea that they were coming after me, but still the possibilities of the situation gave me more or less alarm, and I considered how I could make my escape if by any chance I was the man they were after. The idea of hiding in the wine-cellar appealed to me as the most practical; there must have been plenty of places among the wine kegs and cases where a man could conceal himself, but, as a matter of fact, I did not believe that any such contingency would arise.

The marching soldiers came nearer. I could hear them at the next house. In a moment I would see them pass the keyhole through which I was looking.

"*Halt!*"

At the word of command shouted by a junior officer the squad came to attention right in front of the house.

I waited no longer. Running down the stairs, I flew down into the wine-cellar, and although it was almost pitch dark—the only light coming from a grating which led to the backyard—I soon found a satisfactory hiding-place in the extreme rear of the cellar. I had the presence of mind to leave the door of the wine-cellar ajar, figuring that if the soldiers found a closed door they would be more apt to search for a fugitive behind it than if the door were open.

My decision to get away from the front door had been made and carried out none too soon, for I had only just located myself between two big wine-cases when I heard the tramp of soldiers' feet marching up the front steps, a crash at the front door, a few hasty words of command which I did not understand, and then the noise of scurrying feet from room to room and such a banging and hammering and smashing and crashing that I could not make out what was going on.

If Huyliger had revealed my hiding-place to the Huns, as I was now confident he had, I felt that there was little prospect of their overlooking me. They would search the house from top to bottom and, if necessary, raze it to the ground before they would give up the search. To escape from the house through the backyard through the iron grating, which I had no doubt I could force, seemed to be a logical thing to do, but the chances were that the Huns had thrown a cordon around the entire block before the squad was sent to the house. The Germans do these things in an efficient manner always. They take nothing for granted.

My one chance seemed to be to stand pat in the hope that the officer in charge might possibly come to the conclusion that he had arrived at the house too late—that the bird had flown.

My position in that wine-cellar was anything but a comfortable one. Rats and mice were scurrying across the floor, and the smashing and crashing going on overhead was anything but promising. Evidently those soldiers imagined that I might be hiding in the walls, for it sounded as though they were tearing off the wainscoting, the picture-moulding, and, in fact, everything that they could tear or pull apart.

Before very long they would finish their search upstairs and would come down to the basement. What they would do when they discovered the wine I had no idea. Perhaps they would let themselves loose on it and give me my chance. With a bottle of wine in each hand I figured I could put up a good fight in the dark, especially as I was becoming more and more accustomed to it and could begin to distinguish things here and there, whereas they would be as blind as bats in the sun when they entered the pitchy darkness of the cellar.

Perhaps it was twenty minutes before I heard what sounded like my death-knell to me; the soldiers were coming down the cellar steps. I clutched a wine bottle in each hand and waited with bated breath.

*Tramp! Tramp! Tramp!* In a moment they would be in the cellar proper. I could almost hear my heart beating. The mice scurried across the floor by the scores, frightened, no doubt, by the vibration and noise made by the descending soldiers. Some of the creatures ran across me where I stood between the two wine-cases, but I was too much interested in bigger game to pay attention to mice.

*Tramp! Tramp!* "Halt!" Again an order was given in German, and although I did not understand it, I am willing to bless every word of it, because it resulted in the soldiers turning right about face, marching up the stairs again, through the hall, and out of the front door and away!

I could hardly believe my ears. It seemed almost too good to be true that they could have given up the search just as they were about to come on their quarry, but unless my ears deceived me that was what they had done.

The possibility that the whole thing might be a German ruse did not escape me, and I remained in the cellar for nearly an hour after they had apparently departed before I ventured to move, listening intently in the mean while for the slightest sound which would reveal the presence of a sentry upstairs.

Not hearing a sound, I began to feel that they had indeed given up the hunt, for I did not believe that a German officer would be so considerate of his men as to try to trap me rather than carry the cellar by force if they had the slightest idea that I was there.

I took off my shoes and crept softly and slowly to the cellar steps, and then step by step, placing my weight down gradually so as to prevent the steps from creaking, I climbed to the top. The sight that met my eyes as I glanced into the kitchen told me the whole story. The water faucets had been ripped from the sinks, the water pipes having been torn from the walls. Everything of brass or copper had been torn off, and gas fixtures, cooking utensils, and everything else which contain even only a small proportion of the metals the Germans so badly needed had been taken from the kitchen. I walked upstairs now with more confidence, feeling tolerably assured that the soldiers hadn't been after me at all, but had been merely collecting metals and other materials which they expected an elaborate dwelling-house like the one in which I was concealed to yield.

Later I heard that the Germans have taken practically every ounce of brass, copper, and wool they could lay their hands on in Belgium. Even the brass out of pianos has been ruthlessly removed, the serious damage done to valuable property by the removal of only an insignificant proportion of metal never being taken into consideration. I learned, too, that all dogs over fourteen inches high had been seized by the Germans. This furnished lots of speculation among the Belgians as to what use the Germans were putting the animals to, the general impression apparently being that they were being used for food.

This, however, seemed much less likely to me than that they were being employed as despatch dogs in the trenches, the same as we use them on our side of the line. They might possibly kill the dogs and use their skins for leather and their carcasses for tallow, but I feel quite sure that the Huns are by no means so short of food that they have to eat dogs yet awhile.

Indeed, I want to repeat here what I have mentioned before: if any one has the idea that this war can be won by *starving* the Huns, he hasn't the slightest idea how well provided the Germans are in that respect. They have considered their food needs in connection with their resources for several years to come, and they have gone at it in such a methodical, systematic way, taking into consideration every possible contingency, that, provided there is not an absolute crop failure, there isn't the slightest doubt in my mind that they can last for years, and the worst of it is they are quite cocksure about it.

It is true that the German soldiers want peace. As I watched them through the keyhole in the door I thought how unfavourably they compared with our men. They marched along the street without laughter, without joking, without singing. It was quite apparent that the war is telling on them. I don't believe I saw a single German soldier who didn't look as if he had lost his best friend—and he probably had.

At the same time, there is a big difference—certainly a difference of several years—between wishing the war was over and giving up, and I don't believe the German rank and file any more than their leaders have the slightest idea at this time of giving up at all.

But to return to my experiences while concealed in the house. After the visit of the soldiers, which left the house in a wretched condition, I decided that I would continue my journey toward the frontier, particularly as I had got all I could out of Huyliger, or rather he had got all he was going to get out of me.

During my concealment in the house I made various sorties into the city at night, and I was beginning to feel more comfortable, even when German soldiers were about. Through the keyhole I had studied very closely the gait of the Belgians, the slovenly droop that characterized most of them, and their general appearance, and I felt that in my own dirty and unshaven condition I must have looked as much like the average poor Belgian as a man could. The only thing that was against me was my height. I was several inches taller than even the tallest Belgians. I had often thought that red hair would have gone well with my name, but now, of course, I was mighty glad that I was not so endowed, for red-haired Belgians are about as rare as German charity.

There are many, no doubt, who will wonder why I did not get more help than I did at this time. It is easily answered. When a man is in hourly fear of his life and the country is full of spies, as Belgium certainly was, he is not going to help just anyone that comes along seeking aid.

One of the Germans' most successful ways of trapping the Belgians has been to pose as an English or French prisoner who has escaped; appeal to them for aid; implicate as many as possible, and then turn the whole German police force loose on them.

As I look back now on those days I think it remarkable that I received as much help as I did, but when people are starving under the conditions now forced upon those unfortunate people it is a great temptation to surrender these escaped prisoners to German authorities and receive the handsome rewards offered for them—or for alien spies, as I was classed at that time.

The passport which I had described me as a Spanish sailor, but I was very dubious about its value. If I could have spoken Spanish fluently it might have been worth something to me, but the few words I knew of the language would not have carried me very far if I had been confronted with a Spanish interpreter. I decided to use the passport only as a last resort, preferring to act the part of a deaf and dumb Belgian peasant as far as it would carry me.

Before I finally left the house I had a remarkable experience which I shall remember as long as I live.

CHAPTER 14

# A Night of Dissipation

During the first two days I spent with Huyliger after I had first arrived in the big city he had told me, among other things, of a moving-picture show in town which he said I might have a chance to see while there.

"It is free every night in the week except Saturdays and Sundays," he said, "and once you are inside you would not be apt to be bothered by anyone except when they come to take your order for something to drink. While there is no admission, patrons are expected to eat or drink while enjoying the pictures."

A day or two later, while walking the streets at night in search of food, I had passed this place, and was very much tempted to go in and spend a few hours, particularly as it would perhaps give me an opportunity to buy something to eat, although I was at a loss to know how I was going to ask for what I wanted.

While trying to make up my mind whether it was safe for me to go in, I walked half a block past the place, and when I turned back again and reached the entrance with my mind made up that I would take the chance I ran full tilt into a German officer who was just coming out!

That settled all my hankerings for moving pictures that night. "Where you came from, my friend," I figured, "there must be more like you! I guess it is a good night for walking."

The next day, however, in recalling the incident of the evening before, it seemed to me that I had been rather foolish. What I needed more than anything at that time was confidence. Before I could get to the frontier I would have to confront German soldiers many times, because there were more of them between this city and Holland than in any section of the country through which I had so far travelled.

Safety in these contingencies would depend largely upon the calmness I displayed. It wouldn't do to get all excited at the mere sight of a spiked helmet. The Belgians, I had noticed, while careful to obey the orders of the Huns, showed no particular fear of them, and it seemed to me the sooner I cultivated the same feeling of indifference the better I would be able to carry off the part I was playing.

For this reason, I made up my mind then and there that, officers or no officers, I would go to that show that night and sit it through, no matter what happened. While people may think that I had decided unwisely because of the unnecessary risk involved in the adventure, it occurred to me that perhaps, after all, that theatre was about one of the safest places I could attend, because that was about the last place Germans would expect to find a fugitive English officer in, even if they were searching for one.

As soon as evening came, therefore, I decided to go to the theatre. I fixed myself up as well as possible. I had on a fairly decent pair of trousers which Huyliger had given me and I used a clean handkerchief as a collar.

With my hair brushed up and my beard trimmed as neatly as possible with a pair of rusty scissors which I had found in the house, while my appearance was not exactly that of a Beau Brummel, I don't think I looked much worse than the average Belgian. In these days, the average Belgian is very poorly dressed at best.

I can't say I had no misgivings as I made my way to the theatre; certainly I was going there more for discipline than pleasure, but I had made up my mind and I was going to see it through.

The entrance to the theatre or beer-garden—for it was as much one as the other—was on the side of the building, and was reached by way of an alley which ran along the side. Near the door was a ticket-seller's booth, but as this was one of the free nights there was no one in the booth.

I marched slowly down the alley, imitating as best I could the indifferent gait of the Belgians, and when I entered the theatre I endeavoured to act as though I had been there many times before. A hasty survey of the layout of the place was sufficient to enable me to select my seat. It was early and there were not more than half a dozen people in the place at that time, so that I had my choice.

There was a raised platform, perhaps two feet high, all round the walls of the place, except at the end where the stage was located. On this platform tables were arranged, and there were tables on the floor proper as well.

I decided promptly that the safest place for me was as far back as possible where I would not be in the line of vision of others in back of me. Accordingly, I slouched over to a table on the platform directly opposite the stage and I took the seat against the wall. The whole place was now in front of me. I could see everything that was going on and everyone who came in, but no one, except those who sat at my own table, would notice me unless they deliberately turned around to look.

The place began to fill up rapidly. Every second person who came in the door seemed to me to be a German soldier, but when they were seated at the tables and I got a chance later on to make a rough count, I found that in all there were not more than a hundred soldiers in the place and there must have been several hundred civilians.

The first people to sit at my table were a Belgian and his wife. The Belgian sat next to me and his wife next to him. I was hoping that other civilians would occupy the remaining two seats at my table because I did not relish the idea of having to sit through the show with German soldiers within a few feet of me. That would certainly have spoiled my pleasure for the evening.

Every uniform that came in the door gave me cause to worry until I was sure it was not coming in my direction. I don't suppose there was a single soldier who came in the door whom I didn't follow to his seat—with my eyes.

Just before they lowered the lights two German officers came in the door. They stood there for a moment looking the place over. Then they made a bee-line in my direction, and I must confess my heart started to beat a little faster. I hoped that they would find another seat before they came to my vicinity, but they were getting nearer and nearer, and I realised with a sickening sensation that they were headed directly for the two seats at my table, and that was indeed the case.

These two seats were in front of the table, facing the stage, and except when they would be eating or drinking their backs were toward me, and there was considerable consolation in that. From my seat I could have reached right over and touched one of them on his bald head. It would have been more than a touch, I am afraid, if I could have got away with it safely.

As the officers seated themselves a waiter came to us with a printed bill of fare and a program. Fortunately, he waited on the others first, and I listened intently to their orders. The officers ordered some light wine, but my Belgian neighbour ordered "Bock" for himself and his wife, which was what I had decided to order, anyway, as that was the only thing I could say. Heaven knows I would far rather have ordered something to eat, but the bill of fare meant nothing to me, and I was afraid to take a chance at the pronunciation of the dishes it set forth.

There were a number of drinks listed which I suppose I might safely enough have ordered. For instance, I noticed "Lemon Squash, 1.50," "Ginger Beer, 1.," "Sparkling Dry Ginger Ale, 1.," "Apollinaris, 1.,'" and "Schweppes Soda, 0.80," but it occurred to me that the mere fact that I selected something that was listed in English might attract attention to me and something in my pronunciation might give further cause for suspicion.

It seemed better to parrot the Belgian and order "Bock," and that was what I decided to do.

One item on the bill of fare tantalised me considerably. Although it was listed among the "*Prizzen der dranken*," which I took to mean "Prices of drinks," it sounded very much to me like something to eat, and Heaven knows I would rather have had one honest mouthful of food than all the drinks in the world. The item I refer to was "*Dubbel Gersten de Flesch (Michaux)*." A *double* portion of anything would have been mighty welcome to me, but I would have been quite contented with a *single* "*Gersten*"—whatever that might happen to be—if I had only had the courage to ask for it.

To keep myself as composed as possible, I devoted a lot of attention to that bill of fare, and I think by the time the waiter came around I almost knew it by heart. One drink that almost made me laugh out loud was listed as "*Lemonades Gazeuses*," but I might just as well have introduced myself to the German officers by my right name and rank as to have attempted to pronounce it.

When the waiter came to me, therefore, I said "Bock" as casually as I could, and felt somewhat relieved that I got through this part of the ordeal so easily.

While the waiter was away I had a chance to examine the bill of fare, and I observed that a glass of beer cost eighty *centimes*. The smallest change I had was a two-mark paper bill.

Apparently the German officers were similarly fixed, and when they offered their bill to the waiter he handed it back to them with a remark which I took to mean that he couldn't make change.

Right there I was in a quandary. To offer him my bill after he had just told the officers he didn't have change would have seemed strange, and yet I couldn't explain to him that I was in the same boat and he would have to come to me again later. The only thing to do, therefore, was to offer him the bill as though I hadn't heard or noticed what had happened with the Germans, and I did so. He said the same thing to me as he had said to the officers, perhaps a little more sharply, and gave me back the bill. Later on he returned to the table with a handful of change and we closed the transaction. I gave him twenty-five *centimes* as a tip—I had never yet been in a place where it was necessary to talk to do that.

During my first half-hour in that theatre, to say I was on pins and needles is to express my feelings mildly. The truth of the matter is I was never so uneasy in my life. Every minute seemed like an hour, and I was on the point of getting up and leaving a dozen times. There were altogether too many soldiers in the place to suit me, and when the German officers seated themselves right at my table I thought that was about all I could stand. As it was, however, the lights went out shortly afterward and in the dark I felt considerably easier.

After the first picture, when the lights went up again, I had regained my composure considerably and I took advantage of the opportunity to study the various types of people in the place.

From my seat I had a splendid chance to see them all. At one table there was a German medical corps officer with three Red Cross nurses. That was the only time I had ever seen a German nurse, for when I was in the hospital I had seen only men orderlies. Nurses don't work so near the first-line trenches.

The German soldiers at the different tables were very quiet and orderly. They drank Bock beer and conversed among themselves, but there was no hilarity or rough-housing of any kind.

As I sat there, within an arm's reach of those German officers and realised what they would have given to know what a chance they had to capture an escaped British officer, I could hardly help smiling to myself, but when I thought of the big risk I was taking, more or less unnecessarily, I began to wonder whether I had not acted foolishly in undertaking it.

Nevertheless, the evening passed off uneventfully, and when the show was over I mixed with the crowd and disappeared, feeling very proud of myself and with a good deal more confidence than I had enjoyed at the start.

I had passed a night which will live in my life as long as I live. The bill of fare, program, and a "throw-away" bill advertising the name of the attraction which was to be presented the following week, which was handed to me as I came out, I still have and they are among the most valued souvenirs of my adventure.

CHAPTER 15

# Observations in a Belgian City

One night, shortly before I left this city, our airmen raided the place. I didn't venture out of the house at the time, but the next night I thought I would go out and see what damage had been done. When it became dark I left the house, accordingly, and, mixing with the crowd, which consisted largely of Germans, I went from one place to another to see what our "strafing" had accomplished. Naturally I avoided speaking to any one. If a man or woman appeared about to speak to me, I just turned my head and looked or walked away in some other direction. I must have been taken for an unsociable sort of individual a good many times, and if I had encountered the same person twice I suppose my conduct might have aroused suspicion.

I had a first-class observation of the damage that was really done by our bombs. One bomb had landed very near the main railroad station, and if it had been only thirty yards nearer would have completely demolished it. As the station was undoubtedly our airman's objective, I was very much impressed with the accuracy of his aim. It is by no means an easy thing to hit a building from the air when you are going at anywhere from fifty to one hundred miles an hour and are being shot at from beneath from a dozen different angles—unless, of course, you are taking one of those desperate chances and flying so low that you cannot very well miss your mark, and the Huns can't very well miss you, either!

I walked by the station and mingled with the crowds which stood in the entrances. They paid no more attention to me than they did to real Belgians, and the fact that the lights were all out in this city at night made it impossible, anyway, for anyone to get as good a look at me as if it had been light.

During the time that I was in this city I suppose I wandered from one end of it to the other. In one place, where the German staff had its headquarters, a huge German flag hung from the window, and I think I would have given ten years of my life to have stolen it. Even if I could have pulled it down, however, it would have been impossible for me to have concealed it, and to have carried it away with me as a souvenir would have been out of the question.

As I went along the street one night a lady standing on the corner stopped me and spoke to me. My first impulse, of course, was to answer her, explaining that I could not understand, but I stopped myself in time, pointed to my ears and mouth, and shook my head, indicating that I was deaf and dumb, and she nodded understanding, and walked on. Incidents of this kind were not unusual, and I was always in fear that the time would come when some inquisitive and suspicious German would encounter me and not be so easily satisfied.

There are many things that I saw in this city which, for various reasons, it is impossible for me to relate until after the war is over. Some of them, I think, will create more surprise than the incidents I am free to reveal now.

It used to amuse me, as I went along the streets of this town, looking in the shop windows, with German soldiers at my side looking at the same things, to think how close I was to them and they had no way of knowing. I was quite convinced that if I were discovered my fate would have been death, because I not only had the forged passport on me, but I had been so many days behind the German lines after I had escaped that they couldn't safely let me live with the information I possessed. One night I walked boldly across a park. I heard footsteps behind me and, turning around, saw two German soldiers. I slowed up a trifle to let them get ahead of me. It was rather dark and I got a chance to see what a wonderful uniform the German military authorities have picked out.

The soldiers had not gone more than a few feet ahead of me when they disappeared in the darkness like one of those melting pictures on the moving-picture screen. As I wandered through the streets I frequently glanced in the *café* windows as I passed. German officers were usually dining there, but they didn't conduct themselves with anything like the light-heartedness which characterizes the Allied officers in London and Paris. I was rather surprised at this, because in this part of Belgium they were much freer than they would have been in Berlin, where, I understand, food is comparatively scarce and the restrictions are very rigid.

As I have said, my own condition in this city was in some respects worse than it had been when I was making my way through the open country. While I had a place to sleep and my clothes were no longer constantly soaking, my opportunities for getting food were considerably less than they had been. Nearly all the time I was half famished, and I decided that I would get out of there at once, since I was entirely through with Huyliger.

My physical condition was greatly improved. While the lack of food showed itself on me, I had regained some of my strength, my wounds were healed, my ankle was stronger, and, although my knees were still considerably enlarged, I felt that I was in better shape than I had been at any time since my leap from the train, and I was ready to go through whatever was in store for me.

Chapter 16

# I Approach the Frontier

To get out of the city it would be necessary to pass two guards. This I had learned in the course of my walks at night, having frequently travelled to the city limits with the idea of finding out just what conditions I would have to meet when the time came for me to leave.

A German soldier's uniform, however, no longer worried me as it had at first. I had mingled with the Huns so much in the city that I began to feel that I was really a Belgian, and I assumed the indifference that the latter seemed to feel.

I decided, therefore, to walk out of the city in the daytime when the sentries would be less apt to be on the watch. It worked splendidly. I was not held up a moment, the sentries evidently taking me for a Belgian peasant on his way to work.

Travelling faster than I had ever done before since my escape, I was soon out in the open country, and the first Belgian I came to I approached for food. He gave me half his lunch and we sat down on the side of the road to eat it. Of course, he tried to talk to me, but I used the old ruse of pretending I was deaf and dumb and he was quite convinced that it was so. He made various efforts to talk to me in pantomime, but I could not make out what he was getting at, and I think he must have concluded that I was not only half-starved, deaf, and dumb, but "loony" into the bargain.

When night came I looked around for a place to rest. I had decided to travel in the daytime as well as night, because I understood that I was only a few miles from the frontier, and I was naturally anxious to get there at the earliest possible moment, although I realised that there I would encounter the most hazardous part of my whole adventure. To get through that heavily guarded barbed and electrically charged barrier was a problem that I hated to think of, even, although the hours I spent endeavouring to devise some way of outwitting the Huns were many.

It had occurred to me, for instance, that it would not be such a difficult matter to vault over the electric fence, which was only nine feet high. In college, I know, a ten-foot vault is considered a high-school boy's accomplishment, but there were two great difficulties in the way of this solution. In the first place, it would be no easy matter to get a pole of the right length, weight, and strength to serve the purpose. More particularly, however, the pole-vault idea seemed to be out of the question because of the fact that on either side of the electric fence, six feet from it, was a six-foot barbed-wire barrier. To vault safely over a nine-foot electrically charged fence was one thing, but to combine with it a twelve-foot broad vault was a feat which even a college athlete in the pink of condition would be apt to flunk. Indeed, I don't believe it is possible.

Another plan that seemed halfway reasonable was to build a pair of stilts about twelve or fourteen feet high and walk over the barriers one by one. As a youngster I had acquired considerable skill in stilt-walking, and I have no doubt that with the proper equipment it would have been quite feasible to have walked out of Belgium as easily as possible in that way, but whether or not I was going to have a chance to construct the necessary stilts remained to be seen.

There were a good many bicycles in use by the German soldiers in Belgium, and it had often occurred to me that if I could have stolen one, the tires would have made excellent gloves and insulated coverings for my feet in case it was necessary for me to attempt to climb over the electric fence bodily. But as I had never been able to steal a bicycle, this avenue of escape was closed to me.

I decided to wait until I arrived at the barrier and then make up my mind how to proceed.

To find a decent place to sleep that night I crawled under a barbed-wire fence, thinking it led into some field.

As I passed under, one of the barbs caught in my coat, and in trying to pull myself free I shook the fence for several yards.

Instantly there came out of the night the nerve-racking command, "*Halt!*"

Again I feared I was done for. I crouched close down on the ground in the darkness, not knowing whether to take to my legs and trust to the Hun's missing me in the darkness if he fired, or stay right where I was. It was foggy as well as dark, and although I knew the sentry was only a few feet away from me I decided to stand, or rather lie still. I think my heart made almost as much noise as the rattling of the wire in the first place, but it was a tense few moments for me.

I heard the German say a few words to himself, but didn't understand them, of course, and then he made a sound as if to call a dog, and I realised that his theory of the noise he had heard was that a dog had made its way through the fence.

For perhaps five minutes I didn't stir, and then, figuring that the German had probably continued on his beat, I crept quietly under the wire again, this time being mighty careful to hug the ground so close that I wouldn't touch the wire, and made off in a different direction. Evidently the barbed-wire fence had been thrown around an ammunition-depot or something of the kind and it was not a field at all that I had tried to get into.

I figured that other sentries were probably in the neighbourhood and I proceeded very gingerly.

After I had got about a mile away from this spot I came to a humble Belgian house, and I knocked at the door and applied for food in my usual way, pointing to my mouth to indicate I was hungry and to my ears and mouth to imply that I was deaf and dumb. The Belgian woman who lived in the house brought me a piece of bread and two cold potatoes, and as I sat there eating them she eyed me very keenly.

I haven't the slightest doubt that she realised I was a fugitive. She lived so near the border that it was more than likely that other fugitives had come to her before, and for that reason I appreciated more fully the extent of the risk she ran, for no doubt the Germans were constantly watching the conduct of these Belgians who lived near the line.

My theory that she realised that I was not a Belgian at all, but probably some English fugitive, was confirmed a moment later when, as I made ready to go, she touched me on the arm and indicated that I was to wait a moment. She went to a bureau and brought out two pieces of fancy Belgian lace, which she insisted upon my taking away, although at that particular moment I had as much use for Belgian lace as an elephant has for a safety-razor, but I was touched with her thoughtfulness and pressed her hand to show my gratitude. She would not accept the money I offered her.

I carried that lace through my subsequent experiences, feeling that it would be a fine souvenir for my mother, although, as a matter of fact, if she had known that it was going to delay my final escape for even a single moment, as it did, I am quite sure she would rather I had never seen it.

On one piece of lace was the Flemish word "*Charité*" and on the other the word "*Espérance.*" At the time, I took these words to mean "Charity" and "Experience," and all I hoped was that I would get as much of the one as I was getting of the other before I finally got through. I learned subsequently that what the words really stood for was "Charity" and "Hope," and then I was sure that my kind Belgian friend had indeed realised my plight and that her thoughtful souvenir was intended to encourage me in the trials she must have known were before me.

I didn't let the old Belgian lady know, because I did not want to alarm her unnecessarily, but that night I slept in her backyard, leaving early in the morning before it became light.

Later in the day I applied at another house for food. It was occupied by a father and mother and ten children. I hesitated to ask them for food without offering to pay for it, as I realised what a task it must have been for them to support themselves without having to feed a hungry man. Accordingly, I gave the man a *mark* and then indicated that I wanted something to eat. They were just about to eat, themselves, apparently, and they let me partake of their meal, which consisted of a huge bowl of some kind of soup which I was unable to identify and which they served in ordinary wash-basins! I don't know that they ever used the basins to wash in as well, but whether they did or not did not worry me very much. The soup was good and I enjoyed it very much.

All the time I was there I could see the father and the eldest son, a boy about seventeen, were extremely nervous. I had indicated to them that I was deaf and dumb, but if they believed me it didn't seem to make them any more comfortable.

I lingered at the house for about an hour after the meal, and during that time a young man came to call on the eldest daughter, a young woman of perhaps eighteen. The caller eyed me very suspiciously, although I must have resembled anything but a British officer. They spoke in Flemish and I did not understand a word they said, but I think they were discussing my probable identity. During their conversation, I had a chance to look around the rooms. There were three altogether, two fairly large and one somewhat smaller, about fourteen feet long and six deep. In this smaller room there were two double-decked beds, which were apparently intended to house the whole family, although how the whole twelve of them could sleep in that one room will ever remain a mystery to me.

From the kitchen you could walk directly into the cow-barn, where two cows were kept, and this, as I have pointed out before, is the usual construction of the poorer Belgian houses.

I could not make out why the caller seemed to be so antagonistic to me, and yet I am sure he was arguing with the family against me. Perhaps the fact that I wasn't wearing wooden shoes—I doubt whether I could have obtained a pair big enough for me—had convinced him that I was not really a Belgian, because there was nothing about me otherwise which could have given him that idea.

At that time—and I suppose it is true today—about ninety *per cent*, of the people in Belgium were wearing wooden shoes. Among the peasants I don't believe I ever saw any other kind of footwear, and they are more common there than they are in Holland. The Dutch wear them more as a matter of custom. In Belgium they are a dire necessity because of the lack of leather. I was told that during the coming year practically all the peasants and poorer people in Germany, too, will adopt wooden shoes for farm-work, as that is one direction in which wood can be substituted for leather without much loss.

When the young man left I left shortly afterward, as I was not at all comfortable about what his intentions were regarding me. For all I knew, he might have gone to notify the German authorities that there was a strange man in the vicinity—more, perhaps, to protect his friends from suspicion of having aided me than to injure me.

At any rate, I was not going to take any chances and I got out of that neighbourhood as rapidly as I could.

That night found me right on the frontier of Holland.

CHAPTER 17

# Getting Through the Lines

Waiting until it was quite dark, I made my way carefully through a field and eventually came to the much-dreaded barrier.

It was all that I had heard about it. Every foot of the borderline between Belgium and Holland is protected in precisely the same manner. It is there to serve three purposes: first, to keep the Belgians from escaping into Holland; second, to keep enemies, like myself, from making their way to freedom; and, third, to prevent desertions on the part of Germans themselves. One look at it was enough to convince anyone that it probably accomplished all three objects about as well as any contrivance could, and one look was all I got of it that night, for while I lay on my stomach gazing at the forbidding structure I heard the measured stride of a German sentry advancing toward me, and I crawled away as fast as I possibly could, determined to spend the night somewhere in the fields and make another and more careful survey the following night.

The view I had obtained, however, was sufficient to convince me that the pole-vault idea was out of the question even if I had a pole and were a proficient pole-vaulter. The three fences covered a span of at least twelve feet, and to clear the last barbed-wire fence it would be necessary to vault not only at least ten feet high, but at least fourteen feet wide, with certain knowledge that to touch the electrically charged fence meant instant death. There would be no second chance if you came a cropper the first time.

The stilt idea was also impracticable because of the lack of suitable timber and tools with which to construct the stilts.

It seemed to me that the best thing to do was to travel up and down the line a bit in the hope that some spot might be discovered where conditions were more favourable, although I don't know just what I expected along those lines.

It was mighty disheartening to realise that only a few feet away lay certain liberty and that the only thing that prevented me from reaching it were three confounded fences. I thought of my machine and wished that some kind fairy would set it in front of me for just one minute.

I spent the night in a clump of bushes and kept in hiding most of the next day, only going abroad for an hour or two in the middle of the day to intercept some Belgian peasant and beg for food. The Belgians in this section were naturally very much afraid of the Germans, and I fared badly. In nearly every house German soldiers were quartered, and it was out of the question for me to apply for food in that direction. The proximity of the border made everyone eye one another with more or less suspicion, and I soon came to the conclusion that the safest thing I could do was to live on raw vegetables, which I could steal from the fields at night as I had previously done.

That night I made another survey of the barrier in that vicinity, but it looked just as hopeless as it had the night before, and I concluded that I only wasted time there.

I spent the night wandering west, guided by the North Star, which had served me so faithfully in all my travelling. Every mile or two I would make my way carefully to the barrier to see if conditions were any better, but it seemed to be the same all along. I felt like a wild animal in a cage, with about as much chance of getting out.

The section of the country in which I was now wandering was very heavily wooded and there was really no very great difficulty in keeping myself concealed, which I did all day long, striving all the time to think of some way in which I could circumvent that cursed barrier.

The idea of a huge stepladder occurred to me, but I searched hour after hour in vain for lumber or fallen trees out of which I could construct one. If I could only obtain something which would enable me to reach a point about nine feet in the air, it would be a comparatively simple matter to jump from that point over the electric fence.

Then I thought that perhaps I could construct a simple ladder and lean it against one of the posts upon which the electric wires were strung, climb to the and leap over, getting over the barbed-wire fences in the same way.

This seemed to be the most likely plan, and all night long I sat constructing a ladder for this purpose.

I was fortunate enough to find a number of fallen pine-trees from ten to twenty feet long. I selected two of them which seemed sufficiently strong and broke off all the branches, which I used as rungs, tying them to the poles with grass and strips from my handkerchief and shirt as best I could.

It was not a very workmanlike-looking ladder when I finally got through with it. I leaned it against a tree to test it and it wobbled considerably. It was more like a rope ladder than a wooden one, but I strengthened it here and there and decided that it would probably serve the purpose.

I kept the ladder in the woods all day and could hardly wait until dark to make the supreme test. If it proved successful, my troubles were over; within a few hours I would be in a neutral country out of all danger. If it failed—I dismissed the idea summarily. There was no use worrying about failure; the thing to do was to succeed.

The few hours that were to pass before: night came on seemed endless, but I utilised them to reinforce my ladder, tying the rungs more securely with long grass which I plucked in the woods.

At last night came, and with my ladder in hand I made for the barrier. In front of it there was a cleared space of about one hundred yards, which had been prepared to make the work of the guards easier in watching it.

I waited in the neighbourhood until I heard the sentry pass the spot where I was in hiding, and then I hurried across the clearing, shoved my ladder under the barbed wire, and endeavoured to follow it. My clothing caught in the wire, but I wrenched myself clear and crawled to the electric barrier.

My plan was to place the ladder against one of the posts, climb up to the top, and then jump. There would be a fall of nine or ten feet, and I might possibly sprain my ankle or break my leg, but if that was all that stood between me and freedom I wasn't going to stop to consider it.

I put my ear to the ground to listen for the coming of the sentry. There was not a sound. Eagerly but carefully I placed the ladder against the post and started up. Only a few feet separated me from liberty, and my heart beat fast.

I had climbed perhaps three rungs of my ladder when I became aware of an unlooked-for difficulty.

The ladder was slipping!

Just as I took the next rung the ladder slipped, came in contact with the live wire, and the current passed through the wet sticks and into my body. There was a blue flash, my hold on the ladder relaxed, and I fell heavily to the ground unconscious!

Of course, I had not received the full force of the current or I would not now be here. I must have remained unconscious for a few moments, but I came to just in time to hear the German guard coming, and, the thought came to me that if I didn't get that ladder concealed at once, he would see it even though, fortunately for me, it was an unusually dark night.

I pulled the ladder out of his path and lay down flat on the ground, not seven feet away from his beat. He passed so close that I could have pushed the ladder out and tripped him up.

It occurred to me that I could have climbed back under the barbed-wire fence and waited for the sentry to return and then felled him with a blow on the head, as he had no idea, of course, that there was anyone in the vicinity. I wouldn't have hesitated to take life, because my only thought now was to get into Holland, but I thought that as long as he didn't bother me perhaps the safest thing to do was not to bother him, but to continue my efforts during his periodic absences.

His beat at this point was apparently fairly long and allowed me more time to work than I had hoped for.

My mishap with the ladder had convinced me that escape in that way was not feasible. The shock that I had received had unnerved me and I was afraid to risk it again, particularly as I realised that I had fared more fortunately than I could hope to again if I met with a similar mishap. There was no way of making that ladder hold, and I gave up the idea of using it.

I was now right in front of this electric barrier, and as I studied it I saw another way of getting by. If I couldn't get over it, what was the matter with getting under it?

The bottom wire was only two inches from the ground, and, of course, I couldn't touch it, but my plan was to dig underneath it and then crawl through the hole in the ground.

I had only my hands to dig with, but I went at it with a will, and fortunately the ground was not very hard.

When I had dug about six inches, making a distance in all of eight inches from the lowest electric wire, I came to an underground wire. I knew enough about electricity to realise that this wire could not be charged, as it was in contact with the ground, but still there was not room between the live wire and this underground wire for me to crawl through, and I either had to go on digging deep enough under this wire to crawl under it or else pull it up.

This underground wire was about as big around as a lead-pencil and there was no chance of breaking it. The jack-knife I had had at the start of my travels I had long since lost, and even if I had had something to hammer with, the noise would have made that method impracticable.

I went on digging. When the total distance between the live wire and the bottom of the hole I had dug was thirty-inches I took hold of the ground wire and pulled on it with all my strength.

It wouldn't budge. It was stretched taut across the narrow ditch I had dug—about fourteen inches wide—and all my tugging didn't serve to loosen it.

I was just about to give it up in despair when a staple gave way in the nearest post. This enabled me to pull the wire through the ground a little, and I renewed my efforts. After a moment or two of pulling as I had never pulled in my life before a staple on the next post gave way, and my work became easier. I had more leeway now and pulled and pulled again until in all eight staples had given way.

Every time a staple gave way it sounded in my ears like the report of a gun, although I suppose it didn't really make very much noise. Nevertheless, each time I would put my ear to the ground to listen for the guard, and, not hearing him, went on with my work.

By pulling on the wire I was now able to drag it through the ground enough to place it back from the fence and go on digging.

The deeper I went the harder became the work, because by this time my finger-nails were broken and I was nervous—afraid every moment that I would touch the charged wire.

I kept at it, however, with my mind constantly on the hole I was digging and the liberty which was almost within my reach.

Finally I figured that I had enough space to crawl through and still leave a couple of inches between my back and the live wire.

Before I went under that wire I noticed that the lace which the Belgian woman had given me as a souvenir made my pocket bulge, and lest it might be the innocent means of electrocuting me by touching the live wire, I took it out, rolled it up, and threw it over the barrier.

Then I lay down on my stomach and crawled or rather writhed under the wire like a snake, with my feet first, and there wasn't any question of my hugging Mother Earth as closely as possible, because

I realised that even to touch the wire above me with my back meant instant death.

Anxious as I was to get on the other side, I didn't hurry this operation. I feared that there might be some little detail that I had overlooked, and I exercised the greatest possible care in going under, taking nothing for granted.

When I finally got through and straightened up there were still several feet of Belgium between me and liberty, represented by the six feet which separated the electric barrier from the last barbed-wire fence, but before I went another step I went down on my knees and thanked God for my long series of escapes and especially for this last achievement, which seemed to me to be about all that was necessary to bring me freedom.

Then I crawled under the barbed-wire fence and breathed the free air of Holland! I had no clear idea just where I was, and I didn't much care. I was out of the power of the Germans, and that was enough. I had walked perhaps a hundred yards when I remembered the lace I had thrown over the barrier, and, dangerous as I realised the undertaking to be, I determined to walk back and get it. This necessitated my going back on to Belgian soil again, but it seemed a shame to leave the lace there, and by exercising a little care I figured I could get it easily enough.

When I came to the spot at which I had made my way under the barbed wire I put my ear to the ground and listened for the sentry. I heard him coming and lay prone on the ground till he had passed. The fact that he might observe the hole in the ground or the ladder occurred to me as I lay there, and it seemed like an age before he finally marched out of earshot. Then I went under the barbed wire again, retrieved the lace, and once again made my way to Dutch territory.

It does not take long to describe the events just referred to, but the incidents themselves consumed several hours in all. To dig the hole must have taken me more than two hours, and I had to stop frequently to hide while the sentry passed. Many times, indeed, I thought I heard him coming and stopped my work, and then discovered that it was only my imagination. I certainly suffered enough that night to last me a lifetime. With a German guard on one side, death from electrocution on the other, and starvation staring me in the face, my plight was anything but a comfortable one.

It was the 19th of November, 1917, when I got through the wires. I had made my leap from the train on September 9th. Altogether, therefore, just seventy-two days had elapsed since I escaped from the Huns. If I live to be as old as Methuselah, I never expect to live through another seventy-two days so crammed full of incident and hazard and lucky escapes.

## Chapter 18

# Experiences in Holland

But I was not yet quite out of the woods.

I now knew that I was in Holland, but just where I had no idea. I walked for about thirty minutes and came to a path leading to the right, and I had proceeded along it but a few hundred yards when I saw in front of me a fence exactly like the one I had crossed.

"This is funny," I said to myself. "I didn't know the Dutch had a fence, too." I advanced to the fence and examined it closely, and judge of my astonishment when I saw beyond it a nine-foot fence apparently holding live wires exactly like the one which had nearly been the death of me!

I had very little time to conjecture what it all meant, for just then I heard a guard coming. He was walking so fast that I was sure it was a Dutch sentry, as the Huns walk much more slowly.

I was so bewildered, however, that I decided to take no chances, and as the road was fairly good I wandered down it and away from that mysterious fence. About half a mile down I could see the light of a sentry station, and I thought I would go there and tell my story to the sentries, realising that as I was unarmed it was perfectly safe for me to announce myself to the Dutch authorities. I could be interned only if I entered Holland under arms.

As I approached the sentry box I noticed three men in gray uniforms, the regulation Dutch colour. I was on the verge of shouting to them when the thought struck me that there was just a chance I might be mistaken, as the German uniforms were the same colour, and I had suffered too many privations and too many narrow escapes to lose all at this time.

I had just turned off the road to go back into some bushes when out of the darkness I heard that dread German command:

"*Halt! Halt!*"

He didn't need to holler twice. I heard and heeded the first time. Then I heard another man come running up, and there was considerable talking, but whether they were Germans or Hollanders I was still uncertain. Evidently, however, he thought the noise must be a dog or the wind.

Finally I heard one of them laugh and heard him walk back to the sentry station where the guard was billeted, and I crawled a little nearer to try to make out just what it all meant. I had begun to think it was all a nightmare.

Between myself and the light in the sentry station I then noticed the stooping figure of a man bending over as if to conceal himself, and on his head was the spiked helmet of a German soldier!

I knew then what another narrow escape I had had, for I am quite sure he would have shot me without ceremony if I had foolishly made myself known. I would have been buried at once and no one would have been any the wiser, even though, technically speaking, I was on neutral territory and immune from capture or attack.

This new shock only served to bewilder me the more. I was completely lost. There seemed to be frontier behind me and frontier in front of me. Evidently, however, what had happened was that I had lost my sense of direction and had wandered in the arc of a circle, returning to the same fence that I had been so long in getting through. This solution of the mystery came to me suddenly, and I at once searched the landscape for something in the way of a landmark to guide me. For once my faithful friend, the North Star, had failed me. The sky was pitch black and there wasn't a star in the heavens.

In the distance, at what appeared to be about three miles away, but which turned out to be six, I could discern the lights of a village, and I knew that it must be a Dutch village, as lights are not allowed in Belgium in that indiscriminate way.

My course was now clear. I would make a bee-line for that village. Before I had gone very far I found myself in a marsh or swamp, and I turned back a little, hoping to find a better path. Finding none, I retraced my steps and kept straight ahead, determined to reach that village at all costs and to swerve neither to the right nor to the left until I got there.

One moment I would be in water up to my knees and the next I would sink in clear up to my waist. I paid no attention to my condition. It was merely a repetition of what I had gone through many times before, but this time I had a definite goal, and, once I reached it, I knew my troubles would be over.

It took me perhaps three hours to reach firm ground. The path I struck led to within half a mile of the village. I shall never forget that path; it was almost as welcome to my feet as the opposite bank of the Meuse had seemed.

The first habitation I came to was a little workshop with a bright light shining outside. It must have been after midnight, but the people inside were apparently just quitting work. There were three men and two boys engaged in making wooden shoes.

It wasn't necessary for me to explain to them that I was a refugee, even if I had been able to speak their language. I was caked with mud up to my shoulders, and I suppose my face must have recorded some of the experiences I had gone through that memorable night.

"I want the British consul," I told them.

Apparently they didn't understand, but one of them volunteered to conduct me to the village. They seemed to be only too anxious to do all they could for me; evidently they realised I was a British soldier.

It was very late when my companion finally escorted me into the village, but he aroused some people he knew from their beds and they dressed and came down to feed me.

The family consisted of an old lady and her husband and a son who was a soldier in the Dutch Army. The cold shivers ran down my back while he sat beside me, because every now and again I caught a glimpse of his gray uniform and it resembled very much that of the German soldiers.

Some of the neighbours, aroused by the commotion, got up to see what it was all about, and came in and watched while I ate the meal those good Dutch people prepared for me. Ordinarily, I suppose, I would have been embarrassed with so many people staring at me while I ate, as though I were some strange animal that had just been captured, but just then I was too famished to notice or care very much what other people did.

There will always be a warm place in my heart for the Dutch people. I had heard lots of persons say that they were not inclined to help refugees, but my experience did not bear these reports out. They certainly did much more for me than I ever expected.

I had a little German money left, but as the value of German money is only about half in Holland, I didn't have enough to pay the fare to Rotterdam, which was my next objective. It was due to the generosity of these people that I was able to reach the British consul as quickly as I did. Some day I hope to return to Holland and repay every single soul who played the part of Good Samaritan to me.

With the money that these people gave me I was able to get a third-class ticket to Rotterdam, and I am glad that I didn't have enough to travel first-class, for I would have looked as much out of place in a first-class carriage as a Hun would appear in heaven.

That night I slept in the house of my Dutch friends, where they fixed me up most comfortably. In the morning they gave me breakfast and then escorted me to the station.

While I was waiting in the station a crowd gathered round me, and soon it seemed as if the whole town had turned out to get a look at me. It was very embarrassing, particularly as I could give them no information regarding the cause of my condition, although, of course, they all knew that I was a refugee from Belgium.

As the train pulled out of the station the crowd gave a loud cheer, and the tears almost came to my eyes as I contrasted in my mind the conduct of this crowd and the one that had gathered at the station in Ghent when I had departed a prisoner *en route* for the reprisal camp. I breathed a sigh of relief as I thought of that reprisal camp and how fortunate I had really been, despite all my suffering, to have escaped it. Now, at any rate, I was a free man and I would soon be sending home the joyful news that I had made good my escape.

At Einhoffen two Dutch officers got into the compartment with me. They looked at me with very much disfavour, not knowing, of course, that I was a British officer. My clothes were still pretty much in the condition they were when I crossed the border, although I had been able to scrape off some of the mud I had collected the night before. I had not shaved nor trimmed my beard for many days, and I must have presented a sorry appearance. I could hardly blame them for edging away from me.

The trip from Einhoffen to Rotterdam passed without special incident. At various stations passengers would get into the compartment and, observing my unusual appearance, would endeavour to start a conversation with me. None of them spoke English, however, and they had to use their own imagination as to my identity.

When I arrived at Rotterdam I asked a policeman who stood in front of the station where I could find the British consul, but I could not make him understand. I next applied to a taxicab driver.

"English consul—British consul—American consul—French

consul," I said, hoping that if he didn't understand one he might recognise another.

He eyed me with suspicion and motioned me to get in and drove off. I had no idea where he was taking me, but after a quarter of an hour's ride he brought up in front of the British consulate. Never before was I so glad to see the Union Jack!

I beckoned to the chauffeur to go with me up to the office, as I had no money with which to pay him, and when we got to the consulate I told them that if they would pay the taxi fare I would tell them who I was and how I happened to be there.

They knew at once that I was an escaped prisoner and they readily paid the chauffeur and invited me to give some account of myself.

They treated me most cordially and were intensely interested in the brief account I gave them of my adventures. Word was sent to the consul-general, and he immediately sent for me. When I went in he shook hands with me, greeting me very heartily and offering me a chair.

He then sat down, screwed a monocle on his eye, and viewed me from top to toe. I could see that only good breeding kept him from laughing at the spectacle I presented. I could see he wanted to laugh in the worst way.

"Go ahead and laugh!" I said. "You can't offend me the way I feel this blessed day!" And he needed no second invitation. Incidentally, it gave me a chance to laugh at him, for I was about as much amused as he was.

After he had laughed himself about sick he got up and slapped me on the back and invited me to tell him my story,

"Lieutenant," he said, when I had concluded, "you can have anything you want. I think your experiences entitle you to it."

"Well, Consul," I replied, "I would like a bath, a shave, a hair-cut, and some civilized clothes about as badly as a man ever needed them, I suppose, but before that I would like to get a cable off to America to my mother, telling her that I am safe and on my way to England."

The consul gave the necessary instructions, and I had the satisfaction of knowing before I left the office that the cable, with its good tidings, was on its way to America.

Then he sent for one of the naval men who had been interned there since the beginning of the war and who was able to speak Dutch, and told him to take good care of me.

After I had been bathed and shaved and had a hair-cut, I bought some new clothes and had something to eat, and I felt like a new man.

As I walked through the streets of Rotterdam, breathing the air of freedom again and realising that there was no longer any danger of being captured and taken back to prison, it was a wonderful sensation.

I don't believe there will ever be a country that will appear in my eyes quite as good as Holland did then. I had to be somewhat careful, however, because Holland was full of German spies, and I knew they would be keen to learn all they possibly could about my escape and my adventures, so that the authorities in Belgium could mete out punishment to everyone who was in any respect to blame for it. As I was in Rotterdam only a day, they didn't have very much opportunity to learn anything from me.

The naval officer who accompanied me and acted as interpreter for me introduced me to many other soldiers and sailors who had escaped from Belgium when the Germans took Antwerp, and as they had arrived in Holland in uniform and under arms the laws of neutrality compelled their internment, and they had been there ever since.

The life of a man who is interned in a neutral country, I learned, is anything but satisfactory. He gets one month a year to visit his home. If he lives in England, that is not so bad, but if he happens to live farther away, the time he has to spend with his folks is very short, as the month's leave does not take into consideration the time consumed in travelling to and from Holland.

The possibility of escape from internment is always there, but the British authorities have an agreement with the Dutch Government to send refugees back immediately. In this respect, therefore, the position of a man who is interned is worse than that of a prisoner who, if he does succeed in making his escape, is naturally received with open arms in his native land. Apart from this restraint, however, internment, with all its drawbacks, is a thousand times—yes, a million times better than being a prisoner of war in Germany.

It seems to me that when the war is over and the men who have been imprisoned in Germany return home they should be given a bigger and greater reception than the most victorious army that ever marched into a city, for they will have suffered and gone through more than the world will ever be able to understand.

No doubt you will find in the German prison-camps one or two faint-hearted individuals with a pronounced yellow streak who voluntarily gave up the struggle and gave up their liberty rather than risk their lives or limbs. These sad cases, however, are, I am sure, extremely few. Nine hundred and ninety-nine out of a thousand of the men fighting in the Allied lines would rather be in the front-line trenches, fighting every day, with all the horrors and all the risks, than be a prisoner of war in Germany, for the men in France have a very keen realisation of what that means.

But to return to my day in Rotterdam.

After I was fixed up I returned to the consulate and arrangements were made for my transportation to England at once. Fortunately there was a boat leaving that very night, and I was allowed to take passage on it.

Just as we were leaving Rotterdam the boat I was on rammed our own convoy, one of the destroyers, and injured it so badly that it had to put back to port. It would have been a strange climax to my adventure if the disaster had resulted in the sinking of my boat and I had lost my life while on my way to England after having successfully outwitted the Huns. But my luck was with me to the last, and while the accident resulted in some delay, our boat was not seriously damaged and made the trip over in schedule time and without further incident, another destroyer having been assigned to escort us through the danger zone in place of the one which we had put out of commission.

When I arrived in London the reaction from the strain I had been under for nearly three months immediately became apparent. My nerves were in such a state that it was absolutely impossible for me to cross the street without being in deadly fear of being run over or trampled on. I stood at the curb, like an old woman from the country on her first visit to the city, and I would not venture across until some knowing policeman, recognising my condition, came to my assistance and convoyed me across.

Indeed, there are a great number of English officers at home at all times "getting back their nerve" after a long spell of active service at the front, so that my condition was anything but novel to the London bobbies.

It was not many days, however, before I regained control of myself and felt in first-class shape.

Although the British authorities in Holland had wired my mother from Holland that I was safe and on my way to England, the first thing I did when we landed was to send her a cable myself.

The cable read as follows:

Mrs. M. J. O'Brien, Momence, Ill., U. S. A.:

Just escaped from Germany. Letter follows.

Pat.

As I delivered it to the cable-despatcher I could just imagine the exultation with which my mother would receive it and the pride she would feel as she exhibited it among her neighbours and friends.

I could hear the volley of "I told you so's" that greeted her good tidings.

"It would take more than the *Kaiser* to keep Pat in Germany!" I could hear one of them saying.

"Knew he'd be back for Christmas, anyway," I could hear another remark.

"I had an idea that Pat and his comrades might spend Christmas in Berlin," I could hear another admitting, "but I didn't think any other part of Germany would appeal to him very much."

"Mrs. O'Brien, did Pat write you how many German prisoners he brought back with him?" I could hear still another credulous friend inquiring.

It was all very amusing and gratifying to me, and I must confess I felt quite cocky as I walked into the War Department to report.

For the next five days I was kept very busy answering questions put to me by the military authorities regarding what I had observed as to conditions in Germany and behind the lines.

What I reported was taken down by a stenographer and made part of the official records, but I did not give them my story in narrative form. The information I was able to give was naturally of interest to various branches of the service, and experts in every line of government work took it in turns to question me. One morning would be devoted, for instance, to answering questions of a military nature—German methods behind the frontline trenches, tactics, morale of troops, and similar matters. Then the aviation experts would take a whack at me and discuss with me all I had observed of German flying-corps methods and equipment. Then, again, the food experts would interrogate me as to what I had learned of food conditions in Germany, Luxembourg, and Belgium, and as I had lived pretty close to the ground for the best part of seventy-two days I was able to give them some fairly accurate reports as to actual agricultural conditions, many of the things I told them probably having more significance to them than they had to me.

There were many things I had observed which I have not referred to in these pages because their value to us might be diminished if the Germans knew we were aware of them, but they were all reported to the authorities, and it was very gratifying to me to hear that the experts considered some of them of the greatest value.

One of the most amusing incidents of my return occurred when I called at my banker's in London to get my personal effects.

The practice in the Royal Flying Corps when a pilot is reported missing is to have two of his comrades assigned to go through his belongings, check them over, destroy anything that it might not be to his interest to preserve, and send the whole business to his banker or his home, as the case may be. Every letter is read through, but its contents is never afterward discussed nor revealed in any way. If the pilot is finally reported dead, his effects are forwarded to his next of kin, but while he is officially only "missing" or is known to be a prisoner of war they are kept either at the squadron headquarters or sent to his banker's.

In my case, as soon as it was learned that I had fallen from the sky it was assumed that I had been killed, and my chum, Paul Raney, and another officer were detailed to check over my effects. The list they made and to which they affixed their signatures, as I have previously mentioned, is now in my possession and is one of the most treasured souvenirs of my adventure.

My trunk was sent to Cox & Co. in due course, and now that I was in London I thought I would go and claim it. When I arrived in the bank I applied at the proper window for my mail and trunk.

"Who are you?" I was asked, rather sharply.

"Well, I guess no one has any greater right to Pat O'Brien's effects than I have," I replied, "and I would be obliged to you if you would look them up for me."

"That may be all right, my friend," replied the clerk, "but according to our records Lieutenant O'Brien is a prisoner of war in Germany, and we can't very well turn over his effects to any one else unless either you present proof that he is dead and that you are his lawful representative, or else deliver to us a properly authenticated order from him to give them to you."

He was very positive about it all, but quite polite, and I thought I would kid him no more.

"Well," I said, "I can't very well present proofs to you that Pat O'Brien is dead, but I will do the best I can to prove to you that he is alive, and if you haven't quite forgotten his signature I guess I can

**POST OFFICE** ⚜ **TELEGRAPHS.**

Handed in at 1/33 pm   Office of Origin and Service Instructions: Om— 1   BUCKINGHAM PALACE   Words 52   Charges to pay

TO 2nd Lieut P. A. O'Brien Royal Flying Corps Regents Palace Hotel Lda

The King is very glad to hear of your escape from Germany and if you are to be in London on Friday next December 7th His Majesty will receive you at Buckingham Palace at 10.30 am please acknowledge = Cromer

COPY OF TELEGRAM INVITING LIEUTENANT O'BRIEN TO MEET KING GEORGE

TO Earl Cromer Buckingham Palace

will attend Buckingham Palace as directed Friday December ...

FROM

COPY OF TELEGRAM SENT BY LIEUTENANT O'BRIEN IN ANSWER TO AN INVITATION TO MEET KING GEORGE write you out an order that will answer all your requirements and enable you to give me Pat O'Brien's belongings without running any risks." And I scribbled my signature on a scrap of paper and handed it to him.

He looked at me carefully through the latticed window, then jumped down from his chair and came outside to clasp me by the hand.

"Good Heavens, Lieutenant!" he exclaimed as he pumped my hand up and down. "How did you ever get away?"

And I had to sit right down and tell him and half a dozen other people in the bank all about my experiences.

I had been in England about ten days when I received a telegram which, at first, occasioned me almost as much concern as the unexpected sight of a German spiked helmet had caused me in Belgium. It read as follows:

Lieut. P. A. O'Brien, Royal Flying Corps,
Regent's Palace Hotel, London:
The king is very glad to hear of your escape from Germany. If you are to be in London on Friday next, December 7th, His Majesty will receive you at Buckingham Palace at 10:30 a.m.
    Please acknowledge.                                 Cromer.

Of course, there was only one thing to do and that was to obey orders. I was an officer in the army and the king was my commander-in-chief. I had to go, and so I sat down and sent off the following answer:

Earl Cromer, Buckingham Palace, London:
I will attend Buckingham Palace as directed, Friday, December 7th, at 10:30.
                                Lieutenant Pat O'Brien.

In the interval that elapsed I must confess, the ordeal of calling on the King of England loomed up more dreadfully every day, and I really believe I would rather have spent another day in that empty house in the big city in Belgium, or, say, two days at Courtrai, than go through what I believed to be in store for me.

Orders were orders, however, and there was no way of getting out of it. As it turned out it wasn't half so bad as I had feared; on the contrary, it was one of the most agreeable experiences of my life.

## Chapter 19

# I am Presented to the King

When the dreaded 7th of December arrived I hailed a taxicab and in as matter-of-fact tone of voice as I could command directed the chauffeur to drive me to Buckingham Palace, as though I were paying my regular morning call on the king.

My friends' version of this incident, I have since heard, is that I seated myself in the taxi and, leaning through the window, said, "Buckingham Palace!" whereupon the taxi driver got down, opened the door, and exclaimed, threateningly:

"If you don't get out quietly and chuck your drunken talk, I'll jolly quick call a bobby, bli' me if I won't!"

But I can only give my word that nothing of the kind occurred.

When I arrived at the palace gate the sentry on guard asked me who I was, and then let me pass at once up to the front entrance of the palace.

There I was met by an elaborately uniformed and equally elaborately decorated personage, who, judging by the long row of medals he wore, must have seen long and distinguished service for the king.

I was relieved of my overcoat, hat, and stick and conducted up a long stairway, where I was turned over to another functionary, who led me to the reception-room of Earl Cromer, the king's secretary.

There I was introduced to another earl and a duke whose names I do not remember. I was becoming so bewildered, in fact, that it is a wonder that I remember as much as I do of this eventful day.

I had heard many times that before being presented to the king a man is coached carefully as to just how he is to act and what he is to say and do, and all this time I was wondering when this drilling would commence. I certainly had no idea that I was to be ushered into the august presence of the king without some preliminary instruction.

Earl Cromer and the other noblemen talked to me for a while and got me to relate in brief the story of my experiences, and they appeared to be very much interested. Perhaps they did it only to give me confidence and as a sort of rehearsal for the main performance, which was scheduled to take place much sooner than I expected.

I had barely completed my story when the door opened and an attendant entered and announced:

"The king will receive Lieutenant O'Brien!"

If he had announced that the *Kaiser* was outside with a squad of German guards to take me back to Courtrai my heart could not have sunk deeper.

Earl Cromer beckoned me to follow him, and we went into a large room, where I supposed I was at last to receive my coaching, but I observed the earl bow to a man standing there and realised that I was standing in the presence of the King of England.

"Your Majesty, Lieutenant O'Brien!" the earl announced, and then immediately backed from the room. I believed I would have followed right behind him, but by that time the king had me by the hand and was congratulating me, and he spoke so very cordially and democratically that he put me at my ease at once.

He then asked me how I felt and whether I was in a condition to converse, and when I told him I was he said he would be very much pleased to hear my story in detail.

"Were you treated any worse by the Germans, lieutenant," he asked, "on account of being an American? I've heard that the Germans had threatened to shoot Americans serving in the British Army if they captured them, classing them as murderers because America was a neutral country and Americans had no right to mix in the war. Did you find that to be the case?"

I told him that I had heard similar reports, but that I did not notice any appreciable difference in my treatment from that accorded Britishers.

The king declared that he believed my escape was due to my pluck and willpower, and that it was one of the most remarkable escapes he had ever heard of, which I thought was quite a compliment, coming as it did from the King of England.

"I hope that all the Americans will give as good an account of themselves as you have, lieutenant," he said, "and I feel quite sure they will. I fully appreciate all the service rendered us by Americans before the States entered the war."

At this point I asked him if I was taking too much time.

"Not at all, lieutenant, not at all!" he replied, most cordially. "I was extremely interested in the brief report that came to me of your wonderful escape, and I sent for you because I wanted to hear the whole story first-hand, and I am very glad you were able to come."

I had not expected to remain more than a few minutes, as I understood that four minutes is considered a long audience with the king. Fifty-two minutes elapsed before I finally left there!

During all this time I had done most of the talking, in response to the king's request to tell my story. Occasionally he interrupted to ask a question about a point he wanted me to make clear, but for the most part he was content to play the part of listener.

He seemed to be very keen on everything, and when I described some of the tight holes I got into during my escape he evinced his sympathy. Occasionally I introduced some of the few humorous incidents of my adventure, and in every instance he laughed heartily.

Altogether the impression I got of him was that he is a very genial, gracious, and alert sovereign. I know I have felt more ill at ease when talking to a major than when speaking to the king—but perhaps I had more cause to.

During the whole interview we were left entirely alone, which impressed me as significant of the democratic manner of the present King of England, and I certainly came away with the utmost respect for him.

In all of my conversation, I recalled afterward, I never addressed the king as "Your Majesty," but used the military "sir." As I was a British officer and he was the head of the army, he probably appreciated this manner of address more than if I had used the usual "Your Majesty." Perhaps he attributed it to the fact that I was an American. At any rate, he didn't evince any displeasure at my departure from what I understand is the usual form of address.

Before I left he asked me what my plans for the future were.

"Why, sir, I hope to rejoin my squadron at the earliest possible moment!" I replied.

"No, lieutenant," he rejoined, "that is out of the question. We can't risk losing you for good by sending you back to a part of the front opposed by Germany, because if you were unfortunate enough to be captured again they would undoubtedly shoot you."

"Well, if I can't serve in France, sir," I suggested, "wouldn't it be feasible for me to fly in Italy or Salonica?"

"No," he replied; "that would be almost as bad. The only thing that I can suggest for you to do is either to take up instruction—a very valuable form of service—or perhaps it might be safe enough for you to serve in Egypt; but, just at present, lieutenant, I think you have done enough, anyway."

Then he rose and shook hands with me and wished me the best of luck, and we both said, "Goodbye."

In the adjoining room I met Earl Cromer again, and as he accompanied me to the door he seemed to be surprised at the length of my visit.

"'His Majesty must have been very much interested in your story,'" he said.

As I left the palace a policeman and a sentry outside came smartly to attention. Perhaps they figured I had been made a general.

As I was riding back to the hotel in a taxi I reflected on the remarkable course of events which in the short space of nine months had taken me through so much and ended up, like the finish of a book, with my being received by His Majesty the King! When I first joined the Royal Flying Corps I never expected to see the inside of Buckingham Palace, much less to be received by the king.

CHAPTER 20

# Home Again!

That same day, in the evening, I was tendered a banquet at the Hotel Savoy by a fellow-officer who had bet three other friends of mine that I would be home by Christmas. This wager had been made at the time he heard that I was a prisoner of war, and the dinner was the stake.

The first intimation he had of my safe return from Germany and the fact that he had won his bet was a telegram I sent him reading as follows:

Lieutenant Louis Grant:
    War-bread bad, so I came home.
Pat.

He said he would not part with that message for a thousand dollars.

Other banquets followed in fast succession. After I had survived nine of them I figured that I was now in as much danger of succumbing to a surfeit of rich food as I had previously been of dying from starvation, and for my own protection I decided to leave London. Moreover, my thoughts and my heart were turning back to the land of my birth, where I knew there was a loving old mother who was longing for more substantial evidence of my safe escape than the cables and letters she had received.

Strangely enough, on the boat which carried me across the Atlantic I saw an R. F. C. man—Lieutenant Lascelles.

I walked over to him, held out my hand, and said, "Hello!"

He looked at me steadily for at least a minute.

"My friend, you certainly look like Pat O'Brien," he declared, "but I can't believe my eyes. Who are you?"

I quickly convinced him that his eyes were still to be relied upon, and then he stared at me for another minute or two, shaking his head dubiously.

His mystification was quite explicable.

The last time he had seen me I was going down to earth with a bullet in my face and my machine doing a spinning nose dive. He was one of my comrades in the flying corps and was in the fight which resulted in my capture. He said he had read the report that I was a prisoner of war, but he had never believed it, as he did not think it possible for me to survive that fall.

He was one of the few men living out of eighteen who were originally in my squadron—I do not mean the eighteen with whom I sailed from Canada last May, but the squadron I joined in France. He rehearsed for me the fate of all my old friends in the squadron, and it was a mighty sad story. All of them had been killed except one or two who were in dry-dock for repairs. He himself was on his way to Australia to recuperate and get his nerves back into shape again. He had been in many desperate combats.

As we sat on the deck exchanging experiences I would frequently notice him gazing intently in my face as if he were not quite sure that the whole proposition was not a hoax and that I was not an impostor.

Outside of this unexpected meeting, my trip across was uneventful.

I arrived in St. John, New Brunswick, and eventually the little town of Momence, Illinois, on the Kankakee River.

I have said that I was never so happy to arrive in a country as I was when I first set foot on Dutch soil. Now I'm afraid I shall have to take that statement back. Not until I finally landed in Momence and realised that I was again in the town of my childhood days did I enjoy that feeling of absolute security which one never really appreciates until after a visit to foreign parts.

Now that I am back, the whole adventure constantly recurs to me as a dream, and I'm never quite sure that I won't wake up and find it so.

# ALSO FROM LEONAUR
## AVAILABLE IN SOFTCOVER OR HARDCOVER WITH DUST JACKET

**WINGED WARFARE** *by William A. Bishop*—The Experiences of a Canadian 'Ace' of the R.F.C. During the First World War.

**THE STORY OF THE LAFAYETTE ESCADRILLE** *by George Thenault*—A famous fighter squadron in the First World War by its commander..

**R.F.C.H.Q.** *by Maurice Baring*—The command & organisation of the British Air Force during the First World War in Europe.

**SIXTY SQUADRON R.A.F.** *by A. J. L. Scott*—On the Western Front During the First World War.

**THE STRUGGLE IN THE AIR** *by Charles C. Turner*—The Air War Over Europe During the First World War.

**WITH THE FLYING SQUADRON** *by H. Rosher*—Letters of a Pilot of the Royal Naval Air Service During the First World War.

**OVER THE WEST FRONT** *by "Spin" & "Contact"* —Two Accounts of British Pilots During the First World War in Europe, Short Flights With the Cloud Cavalry by "Spin" and Cavalry of the Clouds by "Contact".

**SKYFIGHTERS OF FRANCE** *by Henry Farré*—An account of the French War in the Air during the First World War.

**THE HIGH ACES** *by Laurence la Tourette Driggs*—French, American, British, Italian & Belgian pilots of the First World War 1914-18.

**PLANE TALES OF THE SKIES** *by Wilfred Theodore Blake*—The experiences of pilots over the Western Front during the Great War.

**IN THE CLOUDS ABOVE BAGHDAD** *by J. E. Tennant*—Recollections of the R. F. C. in Mesopotamia during the First World War against the Turks.

**THE SPIDER WEB** *by P. I. X. (Theodore Douglas Hallam)*—Royal Navy Air Service Flying Boat Operations During the First World War by a Flight Commander

**EAGLES OVER THE TRENCHES**  *by James R. McConnell & William B. Perry*—Two First Hand Accounts of the American Escadrille at War in the Air During World War 1-Flying For France: With the American Escadrille at Verdun and Our Pilots in the Air

**KNIGHTS OF THE AIR** *by Bennett A. Molter*—An American Pilot's View of the Aerial War of the French Squadrons During the First World War.

AVAILABLE ONLINE AT **www.leonaur.com**
AND FROM ALL GOOD BOOK STORES

## ALSO FROM LEONAUR
### AVAILABLE IN SOFTCOVER OR HARDCOVER WITH DUST JACKET

**FARAWAY CAMPAIGN** *by F. James*—Experiences of an Indian Army Cavalry Officer in Persia & Russia During the Great War.

**REVOLT IN THE DESERT** *by T. E. Lawrence*—An account of the experiences of one remarkable British officer's war from his own perspective.

**MACHINE-GUN SQUADRON** *by A. M. G.*—The 20th Machine Gunners from British Yeomanry Regiments in the Middle East Campaign of the First World War.

**A GUNNER'S CRUSADE** *by Antony Bluett*—The Campaign in the Desert, Palestine & Syria as Experienced by the Honourable Artillery Company During the Great War.

**DESPATCH RIDER** *by W. H. L. Watson*—The Experiences of a British Army Motorcycle Despatch Rider During the Opening Battles of the Great War in Europe.

**TIGERS ALONG THE TIGRIS** *by E. J. Thompson*—The Leicestershire Regiment in Mesopotamia During the First World War.

**HEARTS & DRAGONS** *by Charles R. M. F. Crutwell*—The 4th Royal Berkshire Regiment in France and Italy During the Great War, 1914-1918.

**INFANTRY BRIGADE: 1914** *by John Ward*—The Diary of a Commander of the 15th Infantry Brigade, 5th Division, British Army, During the Retreat from Mons.

**DOING OUR 'BIT'** *by Ian Hay*—Two Classic Accounts of the Men of Kitchener's 'New Army' During the Great War including *The First 100,000* & *All In It*.

**AN EYE IN THE STORM** *by Arthur Ruhl*—An American War Correspondent's Experiences of the First World War from the Western Front to Gallipoli-and Beyond.

**STAND & FALL** *by Joe Cassells*—With the Middlesex Regiment Against the Bolsheviks 1918-19.

**RIFLEMAN MACGILL'S WAR** *by Patrick MacGill*—A Soldier of the London Irish During the Great War in Europe including *The Amateur Army*, *The Red Horizon* & *The Great Push*.

**WITH THE GUNS** *by C. A. Rose & Hugh Dalton*—Two First Hand Accounts of British Gunners at War in Europe During World War 1- Three Years in France with the Guns and With the British Guns in Italy.

**THE BUSH WAR DOCTOR** *by Robert V. Dolbey*—The Experiences of a British Army Doctor During the East African Campaign of the First World War.

AVAILABLE ONLINE AT **www.leonaur.com**
AND FROM ALL GOOD BOOK STORES

www.ingramcontent.com/pod-product-compliance
Lightning Source LLC
Chambersburg PA
CBHW031621160426
43196CB00006B/227